TRANSLATION
THEORIES
TECHNIQUES
PRACTICES

翻译
理论、技巧与实践

刘重霄 ◎ 主　编
李双燕 ◎ 副主编
宁心铭　刘思涵　丁艳平　程宇佳 ◎ 编　者

首都经济贸易大学出版社
Capital University of Economics and Business Press
·北京·

图书在版编目(CIP)数据

翻译理论、技巧与实践 / 刘重霄主编. -- 北京：首都经济贸易大学出版社，2021.9

ISBN 978-7-5638-3269-9

Ⅰ. ①翻… Ⅱ. ①刘… Ⅲ. ①翻译理论—研究—西方国家 Ⅳ. ①H059

中国版本图书馆 CIP 数据核字(2021)第 171514 号

翻译理论、技巧与实践
刘重霄　主　编
李双燕　副主编
宁心铭　刘思涵　丁艳平　程宇佳　编　者
FANYI LILUN JIQIAO YU SHIJIAN

责任编辑	佟周红　胡　兰
封面设计	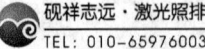
出版发行	首都经济贸易大学出版社
地　　址	北京市朝阳区红庙(邮编 100026)
电　　话	(010)65976483　65065761　65071505(传真)
网　　址	http://www.sjmcb.com
E - mail	publish@cueb.edu.cn
经　　销	全国新华书店
照　　排	北京砚祥志远激光照排技术有限公司
印　　刷	北京九州迅驰传媒文化有限公司
成品尺寸	170 毫米×240 毫米　1/16
字　　数	283 千字
印　　张	18.5
版　　次	2021 年 9 月第 1 版　2023 年 8 月第 2 次印刷
书　　号	ISBN 978-7-5638-3269-9
定　　价	46.00 元

目录

理论篇

第一章　翻译的基本概念 …………………………………………… 2
第二章　翻译发展概述及中西主要翻译理论 …………………… 25
第三章　英汉思维对比与英汉句式特点 ………………………… 52
第四章　英汉互译语言转换中的辩证思维 ……………………… 65

技巧篇

第五章　　择词 …………………………………………………… 88
第六章　　增词 …………………………………………………… 106
第七章　　减词 …………………………………………………… 123
第八章　　词类转换 ……………………………………………… 132
第九章　　附属成分的翻译 ……………………………………… 149
第十章　　肯定句与否定句转译 ………………………………… 168
第十一章　被动语态翻译 ………………………………………… 178
第十二章　语序调整 ……………………………………………… 187
第十三章　长句翻译 ……………………………………………… 197

实践篇

第十四章　再现与审美 ················· 216
第十五章　翻译错误分析 ··············· 230
第十六章　经典翻译赏析 ··············· 247
参考文献 ································· 276
参考答案 ································· 278
后记 ····································· 289

理论篇

第一章 翻译的基本概念

一、翻译的本质

(一)翻译的界定

1. 翻译的理解

什么是翻译?一般来讲,存在以下几种理解:

(1) Translation is a science (on rule or regulation).

翻译是科学(强调规则性)。

(2) Translation is an art (on creation or innovation).

翻译是艺术(强调创造性)。

(3) Translation is a craft (on intelligence).

翻译是技艺(强调智慧性)。

(4) Translation is a skill (on practice).

翻译是技巧(强调实践性)。

(5) Translation is an operation (on motion, action, and process).

翻译是操作和运行(强调行动、动作和过程)。

(6) Translation is a language activity (on exchange of signals and forms).

翻译是语言活动(关注符号的转换)。

(7) Translation is communicating (on information, contents).

翻译是交流(关注信息和内容)。

本质上讲,可以将以上理解归纳为(1)和(2),即翻译是一门科学和翻译是一种艺术两大类别。前者认为翻译应该通过语言对等转换,再现原文信息,它注重对翻译过程的描述、语言结构和形式等方面的研究,揭示翻译的客观规律。后者认为翻译是用另一种语言对原作品进行重新表达与创作,它强调翻译效果及影响。

翻译到底是一门科学,还是一种艺术,或者说是以科学性为主导还是艺术性为主导,历来受到国内外学者的广泛关注。董秋斯是力主科学论的突出代表。他强烈反对"神而明之""不受任何理论约束"的艺术论,也反对"油漆匠"式的技术论,主张"翻译是一种科学",率先设想建立"中国翻译学"(黄振定,1999)。董秋斯对翻译的科学性解释如下:"早就有人说过,翻译是一种科学。这是什么意思呢?这是说,从一种文字译成另一种文字,在工作过程中,有一定的客观规律可以遵循,并不完全靠天才和灵感,如某些人所说的。这规律是客观存在的,不是某些人凭空想出来的。要发现它和通晓它,就得向与此有关的客观事物作一番调查研究的工作。那就是说,我们首先考察各种语文的构造、特点和发展法则,各学科的内容和表现方式,各时代和各国家的翻译经验。然后把这三样东西的调查研究所得结合起来,构成一个完整的理论体系。翻译界有了这样一种东西,就等于有了一套度量衡,初学的人不再要浪费很多时力去摸索门径,也不至不自觉地蹈了前人的覆辙。从事翻译批评的人也有一个可靠的标准。"(董秋斯,1951)林语堂则坚持翻译的艺术性。他在《论翻译》中说,翻译是一门艺术,它的成功取决于一个人的艺术才能和足够的训练(转引自:陈荣东,1997)。他将译者的责任归为三种:对原著者的责任、对中国读者的责任以及对艺术的责任。张经浩先生一向主张翻译不是科学,是艺术。"由于艺术贵在创造,艺术上的成功,无论是狭义的还是广义的艺术,都极大程度上取决于个人的能耐,甚至完全取决于个人的能耐。"(张经浩,1993)当然,也有一种观点认为可以将两种理论综合起来,即翻译具有双重性,既包含科学层次的规则和规律,也包含艺术层面的创作和改造。正如尤金·奈达(Eugene A. Nida)在他的著作 *Language and Culture: Contexts in Translation* 中谈到"one of the most crucial activities in our present world, namely, interlingual communication, traditionally divided into translating and interpreting and studied as both a skill and a science. Effective translating and interpreting from one language to another is a highly developed skill and must be learned primarily as a skill by imitating the experience of proven experts. But the experience and resulting texts produced by translators and interpreters can and should be studied as a science, in the same way that any human activity can be analyzed scientifically..."杨司贵(2019)将奈达的思想解读为"翻译过程应该进行科学的描述,而翻译活动本身则是艺术性的"。奈达(1969)在《翻译理论与实践》(The Theory and Practice of Translation)一书的序言中,对翻译性质的归属再次进行了阐述,翻译活动(translating)不仅仅是一门科学,它还是一种技巧,但归根结底,令人十分满意的译作(translation)总是一种艺术品。翻译是一门有独特规律和方法的科学,也是一门与多种因素相关的艺术。长期以来的翻译实践证明:只讲科学性而缺乏艺术性的译作没有感染力,因而丧失了文学的价值;只讲艺术性而缺乏科学性的译作,则不是对原作再现的艺术,而是对原作的歪曲和背叛。翻译(特别是文学翻译)工作者应该坚持辩证法,树立正确的翻译观,不应把翻译的科学性与艺术性作为水火不容的对立面,而将它们视为翻译活动中互相依存、相辅相成的两个方面,集科学和艺术于一体,做到统筹兼顾(孙致礼,1999)。

2. 翻译的内涵

翻译是用一种语言的创造性方式再现另一种语言反映的原作特质。翻译是跨语言(cross-linguistic)/跨文化(cross-cultural)的交际活动①。翻译的过程,不仅是语言转换过程,而且是反映不同社会特征的文化转换过程。

根据索绪尔(1980)提出的结构语言学理论,翻译的媒介存在于不同规则的符号系统之间,语言是人类最重要的符号系统(semiotic system)。交际是信息的传导,语言是传导工具,该工具具有层次性特征,由语音、词汇、语法、句法等组成;此外,还具有线条性特征,在同一线条上,词与词的组合聚合是有规律的,不是随意说都行,每一种文化都有自己的语言规则,例如:汉语重语序和虚词;英

---

① 当然,翻译不仅包括语际层面的翻译,还包括语内层面的翻译,在不同行业、不同代际之间有时也需要翻译,年轻人经常使用的一些网络用语,如凉凉、吃鸡(当然,"吃鸡"本身就是翻译过来的,出自于 winner winner, chicken dinner)、佛系等,都需要翻译,或者至少需要在一定程度上进行释译。

语重形态变化。

翻译学是一门独立、开放、综合性的人文社会学科。翻译学是研究翻译的科学,是一门介于语言学、文艺学、社会学、国情学、文化学、心理学、信息论、计算机科学等学科之间的综合性科学,或称多边缘交叉性科学。

翻译与翻译学的界定、内涵及内容的多元性充分说明了翻译活动的复杂性,因此需要一定的科学方法论作为指导。

(二) 翻译的分类

翻译是按社会认知需要,在具有不同规则的符号系统之间传递信息的语言文化活动。翻译首先是满足社会认知需求(social demand),如中国古代佛经的翻译、明清的西学东渐、五四新思潮的翻译引入以及现代通过翻译对西方先进科学技术的借鉴和吸收等,都是顺应社会需求。根据翻译需要及目的的不同,可以对翻译进行不同的分类。

翻译活动范围广泛,内容丰富,从不同角度可以划分出不同的种类:

从译出语(source language)和译入语(target language)角度来看,翻译可分为本族语译为外语,外语译为本族语两大类。

从涉及的语言符号来看,翻译可分为语内翻译(intralingual translation)、语际翻译(interlingual translation)和符际翻译(intersemiotic translation)(Jakobon, 1959)。所谓语内翻译,是指在同一语言内用一些语言符号去解释另一些语言符号,即通常的"改变说法(rewording)"。所谓语际翻译,是指在两种语言之间,即用一种语言符号去解释另一种语言符号,即严格意义上的翻译。所谓符际翻译,是指用非语言符号解释语言符号,或用语言符号解释非语言符号,比如把旗语或手势变成语言文字表达。

从翻译的手段来看,翻译可分为口译、笔译和机器翻译。

从翻译的题材或客体来看,翻译可分为文学翻译和非文学翻译(亦即实用翻译,pragmatic translation)。非文学翻译又可分为专业性翻译(specialized-subject translation,如法律翻译、商务翻译、旅游翻译、科技翻译等)和一般性翻译(general translation,如各类应用文和新闻报道等)。

从翻译方式上来看,翻译可分为全译(absolute translation)、摘译(selective

translation)和编译(translation with reconstruction)。全译是最基本的翻译方法，一直是翻译的主流。摘译适用于对自然科学和社会科学文献的翻译，但不太适用于文学作品的翻译，如政府文件、新闻报道、操作指南、书刊目录等。编译即译者根据不同要求，如特定读者对象、版面设计要求等，用简练的语言，短时间内将原来篇幅较长、文字繁杂的材料进行压缩翻译，但译文信息不走样。编译主要适用于注重实效性信息传播的新闻中。

(三) 翻译的矛盾

翻译作为一项思维活动，其最大的特点就是"矛盾丛生"，常见的矛盾有以下几种。

1. 理解-表达

由于对源语掌握的程度不够，不能深入把握源语信息的真实含义；或者表达能力不足，言不由衷。如对于"No reproduction is granted by implication or otherwise of this information."这句英文表达，首先要辨别出句子的主体结构 No reproduction is granted，还要明确介词 of 引出的是 reproduction 的宾语；此外，还要明晰 otherwise 的具体所指，才能够呈现以下译文："本资料不得私下或公开翻印。"再例如，"The grey-haired old man laughed toothlessly."，一般都能理解该句话的意思，大概是"头发灰白的老人很开心，咧开嘴大笑"。但 toothlessly 这一状态是咧开嘴大笑之后才表现出来的。这个状态副词置于何处才符合汉语的表达习惯，成为地道顺畅的汉语表达呢？这就要取决于译者的中文表达能力。后面有专门章节讲解理解与表达的问题。

2 直译-意译

将《流浪地球》译作 wandering earth，还是 Exodus(出埃及)？同样，将 eye for an eye 译为"以眼还眼"，还是"以牙还牙"？ shed crocodile's tear 应该翻译成"鳄鱼的眼泪"，还是"猫哭耗子假慈悲"？这便是直译与意译层面的问题。

3. 归化-异化

对于"不入虎穴，焉得虎子"这句俗语，有几种不同的英语表达，如："How can you catch tiger cubs without entering the tiger's lair？""Nothing venture, nothing win.""He who should search pearl must dive deep.""三个臭皮匠赛过

诸葛亮",同样具有不同的英语表达,"Three cobblers with theirs wits combined equal Zhuge Liang the master mind.""Two heads are better than one."。对以上两句中文的几种不同英文表达进行分析,涉及文化因素的处理也涉及原语句型结构的转换,这些都是归化和异化翻译需要注意的问题。

4. 译意-译味

这类矛盾主要关注翻译过程中是想强调传达信息还是意在体现韵味,如许渊冲先生曾用 power the face 和 face the power 来翻译"不爱红妆爱武装",旨在译出原文的味道,当然同时也巧妙地传达了原文的信息。

5. 保持"洋味"与避免"洋腔"①

"翻译语言"是一种边缘语言,或叫第三种语言,它是译者的创作语言。它不再以原文语言的面貌出现,但也不是纯粹的译文语言,它独具特色,读者通常一读便知这是译文,而非原创。"翻译语言"多种多样,自成一体,深入研究"翻译文体"的翻译状况将有助于研究译者的创作行为。也许可以从以下几个方面入手对此问题进行分析:句式的异化、外来词的引进、异样的语感等。这里还有一个问题,即有的"翻译腔"令人无法接受,有的则经过反复使用而得到了承认。

比如英语中的"when"句式,汉译文中经常会出现这样的表达:"1. 当他自己的妻子都劝不动他的时候,你怎么能劝得动呢? 2. 弥尔顿正在意大利游历,当国内传来内战的消息。3. 当他洗完了头发的时候,叫他来找我。4. 当你在罗马的时候,像罗马人那样做。"(余光中,2002)

这样的译文显然受到原文句式的影响,读起来不似地道的汉语那般顺畅。其实,此处应该做一些变通,摆脱原文句式的束缚,使译文更具可接受性。另一方面,汉语创作受欧化句式的影响,亦使用主语后置,独立使用伴随状语,用多重定语修饰中心词等,它们在某种程度上丰富了汉语的表达方式。总之,翻译语言的存在颇值得研究,其状况复杂,并非简单的好或不好就能概括得了。

什么是"翻译腔(体)"? 正如陈德彰(2004)所言,所谓的"翻译腔(体)",并没有什么不自然的语言表达,只是类似"离骚体""琼瑶体"等的一种文体表

---

① 翻译腔(翻译体:陈德彰)

达方式(style, pattern)。

当然，这里有个问题，两者之间的界限在哪里？将 Telephone 翻译成"德律风"是洋腔还是洋味？翻译成"电话"呢？"If winter comes, can spring be far away?"的译文，"冬天来了,春天还会远吗？""如果冬天来了,春天还会远吗？"哪个是洋腔？哪个又是洋味呢？

6. 神似-形似

如果将"What flower does everybody have? Tulips."这句英语翻译成"什么花是人人都有的？郁金香。"仅实现了形似的功能;若将其翻译成"人人都有的花是什么花？泪花。"便达到了神似的效果。

7. 忠实性-创造性

如将 winner winner, chicken dinner 翻译成"赢了赢了！今晚吃鸡肉饭！"，在语言形式上忠实于原文;若将其翻译成"大吉大利,晚上吃鸡",便具有了创作的特征。

此外，对于"忠实性-创造性"这一组矛盾，还应注意原文风格的问题，如：

【原文】

You say that you love rain,

But you open your umbrella when it rains...

You say that you love the sun,

but you find a shadow spot when the sun shines...

You say that you love the wind,

But you close your windows when wind blows...

This is why I am afraid;

You say that you love me too...

不同风格的译文：

【普通版】

你说你喜欢雨,但是下雨的时候你却撑开了伞；

你说你喜欢阳光,但当阳光播撒的时候,你却躲在阴凉之地；

你说你喜欢风,但清风扑面的时候,你却关上了窗户。

我害怕你对我也是如此之爱。

【诗经版】

子言慕雨,启伞避之。

子言好阳,寻荫拒之。

子言喜风,阖户离之。

子言偕老,吾所畏之。

【离骚版】

君乐雨兮启伞枝,

君乐昼兮林蔽日,

君乐风兮栏帐起,

君乐吾兮吾心噬。

【五言诗版】

恋雨偏打伞,爱阳却遮凉。

风来掩窗扉,叶公惊龙王。

片言只语短,相思缱绻长。

郎君说爱我,不敢细思量。

【七言绝句版】

微茫烟雨伞轻移,喜日偏来树底栖。

一任风吹窗紧掩,付君心事总犹疑。

【七律压轴版】

江南三月雨微茫,罗伞轻撑细细香。

日送微醺如梦寐,身依浓翠趁荫凉。

忽闻风籁传朱阁,轻蹙蛾眉锁碧窗。

一片相思君莫解,锦池只恐散鸳鸯。

在翻译过程中,是忠于作者,还是忠于读者,也是译者需要面对的问题。如:

◀ **原文** ▶

雨村先整了衣冠，带了小童，拿着"宗侄"的名帖至荣府的门前投了。

杨宪益的译文

Yu-tsun spruced himself up and went with his pages to the gate of the Jung Mansion, where he handed in his visiting-card on which he had styled himself Chia Cheng's "nephew".

霍克斯的译文

Yu-cun, dressed his best and with the two servant boy at his heels, betook himself to the gate of Rong Mansion and handed in his visiting-card, on which he had been careful to prefix the word "kinsman" to his own name.

"宗侄"在中国文化中是指同宗族中同辈亲友的儿子，而在西方文化里没有一个对等的词来表示此意。因为，不同的称谓反映在语言上，就是相关词汇的丰富度，概念切分很细，需要不同的概念使用不同的词汇，而在英语国家里相关的概念切分与之不对应，所以原文中某些所指对象无对等物。在这种情况下，霍克斯的译文借助所指的相近对象以取得等价效果，因此将"宗侄"译为kinsman，将"宗侄的名帖"译为"on which he had been careful to prefix the word 'kinsman' to his own name"，很好地发挥了译文的优势，容易为读者所接受和理解。而杨宪益的译文将"宗侄"译成 Chia Cheng's nephew，试图忠于原文，保留原文的文化信息，而"宗侄"一词与"老祖宗"等词汇相比，其民族文化特征略显不足，而且英语读者也有类似的文化背景知识，只不过不如汉语细致。

除了以上几组主要的矛盾外，在翻译中还存在"整体与细节""得与失（得意忘形）"等矛盾。

解决这些矛盾，需要站在辩证翻译观（Dialectical point of view）的视角，对于矛盾的双方，不可顾此失彼，或重此轻彼，而应统筹兼顾、统一权衡。译者所要选择的，并不是一成不变的"居中点"，而是矛盾双方都可接受的最佳"融会点"。

学会从多角度分析，综合全面地看问题，避免孤立片面思考、对翻译理论和技巧断章取义的理解。既要学习微观的技能，又要注意从宏观角度理解翻译过程的复杂性及其相互联系、相互转化的对立统一关系，从而把握好采用不同方法时的"度"，灵活运用。

唯物辩证法是科学的方法论，只有坚持将唯物辩证法作为指导思想，才能把本学科的理论与技巧紧密地结合起来，才能客观地、恰当地解决翻译中的不同矛盾。

（三）翻译的过程

翻译是对原文有较好的理解，并将原文适当地转换成另一种语言的过程。它通常由以下三个阶段组成。

1. 理解

通过上下文线索理解原文，是翻译的首要环节。在进行翻译之前，译者有必要仔细分析相关语境下原文的语法关系和逻辑布局。为了达到忠实地理解原文的目的，译者应注意以下两个问题：

首先，正确理解词汇的确切含义。词无定义，确定一个单词的意思，不能简单地通过查找字典或一成不变地从课本上摘抄下来。语境和搭配对词义的影响很大。同一个单词，在不同的情况下使用，也可能会产生不同的意思。例如：

Then we fed them four unidentified samples of cola one at a time, regular colas for the one group, diet version for the other.

unidentified 这个单词在这里不能被理解为 that can't be identified，而是指 not marked, not indicated。实际上原文是指他们没有被告知这种可乐的牌子，这样来看，这个单词应该被翻译成"没有标记的"或者"没有贴标签的"，而不是"未被鉴别的"或"没有被确认的"。

此外，译者还应该注意到该词相邻的其他词或短语，以及可以提供意义线索的一些关键表达，以此来确定该词的确切意义。version 一词可以是"对某一事件的描述"、"某事物的特殊或变体形式"、"某一本书、某一音乐作品的特殊改编"或"翻译成另一种语言"，但这里显然是指"某事物的特殊或变体形式"。再如：The medicine helps a cold. 根据《英汉大词典》的解释，help 作及物动词使用时应有七种最基本的词义,而不能简单地将 help 理解为常用的"帮助",应该联系上下文将其翻译为"对……有疗效"或"缓解"。

其次,我们必须仔细分析句子的语法结构和逻辑布局,以及它与其他部分的关系。通过分析,掌握原文的确切含义。例如:

The average man, says Shaw, can advance not a single reason for thinking that the earth is round.

有人将该句翻译为"萧伯纳说普通人可以举出不止一个理由来说明为什么相信地球是圆的",存在理解上的偏误。首先,译者没有理解句子结构。为了行文需要,作者对原文句子结构进行了调整,将 not 置于 advance 之后,正常的语序应该是"…can't advance a single reason for thinking that…"。其次,没有准确把握 not 的否定范围,而误将 not 和 single 合在一起,结果就译成了"拿出不止一个理由……"。正确的译文为"萧伯纳说普通人举不出一条理由来说明为什么相信地球是圆的"。再如:

My point is that the frequent complaint of one generation about the one immediately following it is inevitable.

首先我们需要理清其中的句法结构,整句话为复合结构,其中表语从句的主语为 complaint,该核心词被前置修饰语 the frequent、后置修饰语 one generation 和 about the one immediately following it 所修饰;而其中 about the one immediately following it 部分,the one 作为介词 about 的逻辑主语,又被现在分词结构 immediately following it 修饰。明晰这些逻辑关系之后,该句就可较为容易地译为"我的观点是一代人经常抱怨下一代人是不可避免的"。

还有,具有一定的文化背景知识,也是有助于正确理解原文的一个前提和重要因素。例如:

Governor Franklin D. Roosevelt stated in June of 1930.

如果我们没有美国历史背景知识,对于罗斯福的履历没有了解,或者仅从字面上看的话,很容易将原文译为"富兰克林·D. 罗斯福总统于 1930 年 6 月作了如下声明",或"统治者富兰克林·D. 罗斯福在 1930 年 6 月的讲话中谈道"。这两种理解和翻译都是不准确的,因为 1930 年时罗斯福尚未当选总统,而是纽约州的州长。所以,正确的理解和翻译应该是"富兰克林·D. 罗斯福州长在 1930 年 6 月作出声明"。

2. 表达或再现

在正确理解原文的基础上,译者应该对原文信息进行忠实、通顺的表达。但因英汉语言的差异,"忠实的表达"并不指单纯在语言形式上与原文保持词性、句法和语序的完全一致,而是要根据实际情况进行必要的调整和改变。比如:

But for many, the fact that poor people are able to support themselves almost as well without government aid as they did with it is in itself a huge victory.

这句话中的核心词 fact 具有一个很长的定语从句,这完全符合英语的表达规律,但汉语的特点是短小简洁。如果完全按照该句的表层结构进行翻译,译文将难以被汉语读者所接受。因此要进行必要的语序调整,可将原文译为"但是穷人在没有政府救济的情况下,生活得照样很好。对很多人来说,这本身就是一个巨大的胜利"。

除了语序的调整,出于表达顺畅的需要,在不改变原文含义的情况下,译者也可以在内容上进行一些必要的删减或添加,例如:

Long after the 1998 World Cup was won, disappointed fans were still cursing the disputed refereeing discussion that denied victory to their team.

若将其译为"1998 年世界杯足球赛早已尘埃落定,但失望的球迷们仍在责骂那些颇有争议的判罚,声称正是那些判罚使他们的球队没能获胜",显然,译文添加了转折连词"但"和动词"声称"。这种添加不但没有破坏原文含义,反而能够使汉语读者更好地理解和接受原文的意义。

这种情况不仅发生在语言层面,文化层面也存在类似的现象,例如:

I was not a Pygmalion, I was Frankenstein.

如果简单地将其译为"我不是皮格马利翁,我是弗兰肯斯坦",一般的汉语读者会感到莫名其妙,不知所云,到底原文想表达什么意思呢?这是其中存在的文化理解障碍,影响了我们的表达。皮格马利翁(Pygmalion)是希腊神话中的塞浦路斯国王,热恋自己所雕刻的少女。阿芙洛狄特(Aphrodite,希腊神话中的爱神)见其感情笃挚,便赋予雕像生命,使两人结为夫妻,成全了国王的爱情。弗兰肯斯坦(Frankenstein, M. W. Shelley 小说中的一个人物)是个年轻的医科大学生,他发明了一个怪物,结果最后被那个怪物吃掉了。由此可见,原语中前半部分暗含的意义是"享受自己所创造的美",而后半部分意指"作茧自缚,自作自受"。所以,可以将译文改为"我不是皮格马利翁一样的人,自己能享受自己创造的美;我是和弗兰肯斯坦一样,作茧自缚,自作自受"。这样的翻译表达才是既忠实又通顺。

3. 检查或校对

检查或校对的目的在于审查译文是否存在误译或遗漏,以确保译文质量。这是翻译的最后一个环节,但也是非常重要的一个环节。翻译检查或校对的主体可以是译者本人,还可以是编辑或出版方。

二、翻译的层次

翻译层次对应翻译单位,翻译单位较为微观,翻译层次较为宏观。但从另外一种视角来看,在某种程度上,亦可将翻译的层次视为翻译的单位;或者说,翻译层次之中包含翻译单位的要素。

所谓翻译单位,就是在译文中能找到的对应物的原文单位,但它的组成部分在译文中并没有对应物。换言之,翻译单位就是原语在译语中具备对应词的最小(最低限度)的语言单位。选择翻译单位在某种程度上就是选择翻译方法。一般来讲,以词为单位是直译,以语段为翻译单位是意译,以语篇为翻译单位就是述译。

不同文体的翻译对要达到的翻译层次有不同的要求。如,哲学、社会学、自然科学的专门读物(非科普读物)类的翻译,涉及思维、语义、专业三个层次,翻译大都以句子为单位;对于文学作品的翻译,涉及文化与美学层次,一般以语段为翻译单位;至于诗歌和广告的翻译,一般以语篇为翻译单位。具体可以从四个层次进行探讨。

(一)文化层次

语言只有在具体的文化语境中才能存在。任何一种文化,其核心都体现为

一种自然的语言结构。语言是文化的一部分,语言中的文化痕迹无所不在。这些特征必然体现在翻译过程中。如:

而且乱世衰草中间,仿佛应该有着妲己、褒姒的窈窕身影,若隐若现,迷离扑朔。(宗璞,"废墟的召唤")

译文A

I feel as if fluttering among the jumbled mass of ruins could be seen the graceful figures of Daji, imperial concubine of King Zhou, last ruler of the Shang Dynasty, and of Baosi, queen-consort of King You, last ruler of the Western Zhou Dynasty.

译文B

It would have been fitting too if the lissome figures of the fabled concubines of ill-fated ancient Chinese emperors could have been glimpsed flitting like phantoms among the litter of stones and jungle of grass.

以上两个译文的主要区别在于对文化元素的处理上。译文 A 采用具体化翻译策略,译文 B 采用抽象化翻译策略;前者倾向于异化,后者倾向于归化;前者翻译具有浓厚的文化情结,后者是站在目的语读者立场的翻译。

(二) 专业层次

该层次是从事文、理、工、医等不同学科和专业所进行翻译时需要考虑的重要层次。同一个词语,在不同学科、不同专业层次上有时会体现不同的意义,也会呈现出不同的表达。

例(1) Remove the parts from quench salt and cool in *still* air to room temperature.

把零件从淬火盐槽中取出,放在自然流动(或"非强制流动")的空气中冷却至室温。

如把 *still* air 译成"静止"的空气,在文学作品中或许可以,但从科学意义上来说,空气是不会静止的。因此,将其翻译成"自然流动"或"非强制流动"更符合专业表达。

例(2) Aluminum remained unknown until the nineteenth century, because nowhere in nature is it found free, owing to its always being combined with other elements, most commonly with oxygen, for which it has strong affinity.

铝总是和其他元素结合在一起,最普遍的是和氧结合在一起,因为铝对氧有很强的亲和力,由于这个原因,在自然界中任何地方都找不到游离状态的铝;所以直到19世纪人们才发现铝的存在。

如把 free 译成"自由的",不符合客观事实或专业表达,在物理学科中,我们经常将 free 译为"游离的"或者"纯粹的"。

(三)情境层次

情境是符号互动理论的术语,指在一定时间内各种情况相对的或结合的境况,是人们对外界刺激的内部解释过程。符合情境是衡量译文和原文是否具有同一性的标准,以情境为翻译层次,可以保证译文和原文具有同一性。

例(1) "老师傅,你的画眉逃出了笼子!"

"是的,让它散散步。"

"不怕它飞走了吗?"我说。

老人望望我,又冷冷一笑:"飞走,往哪飞! 它舍不得那个食罐。"

"Hello. Your bird has got out."

"Yeah. Let it go for a stroll."

"Aren't you afraid it might fly away?"

The old man cast a glance at me and gave an uncaring smile.

"Fly away? But why should it? It can't leave the food bowl."

原文中的"往哪飞!"表明说话者不相信鸟会飞走的不屑态度,若翻译成"Where to?"就脱离了具体的情境。

例(2) 当邮件来到的时候他站起来,他念着,将它们拣出来,然后小心扎成一堆。

When letters came, he would stand up, and sorted them out while murmuring the addresses on the envelopes, and then put them into a bundle.

若将原文中的"念着,将它们拣出来"翻译成 read and sorted them out,那原文所体现的情境就被曲解了(容易让读者产生"邮差怎么能去看别人的信呢?"的误解)。

例(3) 毛主席问陈妻:"你们俩感情好不好?"陈妻答"好。"主席听了很高兴。

在中国文化背景下,长辈或上司询问年龄、婚姻、家庭生活等个人问题,往往是一种关爱的表示,但在西方属于隐私,外人不好过问。上文若直译出 marriage , connubial love, mutual affection 等字眼,西方读者难以接受,不符合实际交际情境。

Chairman Mao talked with Chen's wife. He was pleased to know that they had a happy home life.

(四)语言层次

语言层面的翻译又可细分为以下七种情况。

1. 音位层翻译(phonological translation/ translation on phonemic level)

音位层翻译指原语音位可以由译语等值的音位来替换。如初学英语的人用汉字来标注英语发音一样,有人认为只有在翻译同源词、拟声词和专有名词时,此类翻译才会取得良好的效果。该层次的翻译在翻译人名时也会有所体现,类似"谐音"译法,如李梅的英文名字对应为 May Li,张雷的英文名字对应为 Ray Zhang,刘凯文的英文名字对应为 Kevin Liu,吴大伟的英文名字对应为 David Wu。

2. 词素层翻译(translation on sememe level)

词素层翻译指构成原文词的每一个词素在译入语对应词中都有与其相匹配的词素。如 macro-econom-ics 对应"宏观—经济—学",syn-chron-ize 对应"同—时—化",di-atom-ic 对应"两—原子—的"。

词素翻译对于新词,特别是科技新术语的翻译有重要意义,因为大量科技新词都是通过词素的结合而形成的。如:high-tech(high technology)——高科技;comsat(communication satellite)——通信卫星。

3. 词层翻译(translation of lexemic level)

词层翻译包含两方面的内容,词义的选择和词的对应。如将小说 *The French Lieutenant's Woman* 翻译成《法国中尉的女人》,有失偏颇。根据这部小说介绍的内容,故事情节与航海紧密联系。若将 Lieutenant 翻译成"中尉",则此军衔仅限于陆军,但故事与陆军没有关系,所以应该根据内容将此处的 Lieutenant 理解为 a naval office next in rank below captain 这一意思,即翻译成"大副",当代英语多用 first mate。所以,应将小说 *The French Lieutenant's Woman* 翻译成《法国大副的女人》。

此外,词层翻译还指逐词翻译,以词为翻译单位。在句子结构简单、双语结构形式类同的情况下得以运用。如:

We are going to visit the museum.
我们 要 去 参观 博物馆。

Twenty years later Kao Yu-pao returned to his home village.
二十年 后 高玉宝 回到 他的 家乡。

当然,词层翻译也并非绝对、完全地一一对应。are 与"要"并不对应,home village 是两个词,而"家乡"是一个词。将 his 翻译成"他的"也很牵强,译成"自己的"则更符合汉语表达习惯。又如:

她的 大女儿 是一个纺织 工人。
Her eldest daughter is a textile worker.

其中大与 eldest 并不等义,只是在一个特殊的组合中才对应。

4. 词组层翻译(translation of phrase level)

现代英语语法把词组作为句子结构的核心单位。词往往通过词组在句子结构中发挥作用。许多词组,其意义并不等于各个词义简单地叠加在一起。词组翻译有两种情况。

(1)习语(作为词组具有整体意义)比如:

This time he missed the boat.

这回他坐失良机。

(2)自由词组:两个或两个以上单词自由搭配组成。比如:

This receiver is indeed cheap and fine.

这台收音机真是物美价廉。

Note, therefore, that when we calibrate the scale to read in ohms, these calibrations go backward.

因此,要注意,当我们把刻度刻成欧姆读数时,这种刻度由大至小。

5. 句层翻译(translation of sentence level)

句层翻译是指以句子为单位进行翻译,寻求句子层次间的对等与一致。但鉴于英汉语言之间的差异,很难完全实现句层的对等。出于特殊表达的需要,译者有时也会刻意追求句层的翻译。

下面一段表述包含了中文戏剧性的句式、主观性句式、观察与感知等判断句式,引导读者进入人物内心。而三种不同翻译层次的处理,形成了三种不同的译文(特别体现在斜体词的应用上)。

◀ 原文 ▶

①大汽车和小汽车。②无轨电车和自行车。③鸣笛声和说笑声。④大城市的夜晚才最有大城市的活力和特点。⑤开始有了稀稀落落的,然而是引人注目的霓虹灯和理发馆门前的旋转花浪。⑥有烫了的头发和留了的长发。⑦高跟鞋和半高跟鞋,无袖套头的裙衫。⑧花露水和雪花膏的气味。⑨城市和女人刚刚开始略略打扮一下自己,已经有人坐不住了。⑩这很有趣。

译文A

① *Everywhere*, there were heavy vehicles, cars, trolley-buses, bicycles, and the hooting, voices and laughter typical of a big city at night-*full of life*. ② *He saw* occasional neon lights and barber's poles. ③ *Also*, permed hair, long hair, high-heeled shoes and frocks. ④ *In the air hung* the fragrance of toilet water and face cream. ⑤Though the city and women had just begun to pay a little attention to their appearance, they had already outraged certain people. ⑥ This was interesting.

译文B

① *He saw* trucks and cars, trolley buses, and bicycles. ② *He heard* the shriek of whistles and high-pitches din of voices talking and laughing. ③ *To ChenGao*, the city truly showed its peculiarities and vitality at night. ④ *He noticed* people with permanent-waved hair and naturally straight hair, women wearing sleeveless dress and shoes with spiked heels or pumps. ⑤ *He smelled* the strong scents of perfume and face powder. ⑥ *Chen gao was interested in* everything and everyone he saw.

译文C

① Vans and cars. ② Buses and bikes. ③ Hooting, chatting, laughing. ④ A big city reveals the most of its vigor and character only in the night. ⑤ There have appeared some neon lights and barber's poles, sparse but striking. ⑥ Permed hair and long hair. ⑦ High heels and semi-high heels, sleeveless dress. Smells of toilet water and face creams. ⑧ The city and women are just beginning to dress themselves up a little bit, and some people have already been upset. ⑨ That's interesting.

6. 语段层翻译(translation on sentence group level)

语段相当于句群或句子组合,是大于句子的语言片断,一般是由两个或个以上句子构成的语义整体,小于或等于段落。

以语段为翻译层次,在翻译思维中需要以语段为逻辑单元,确立译文与原文之间的对等关系,避免孤立、逐句地进行翻译,其中词、词组或句子的转换应服从于整个语段的等值转换需要。如:

As the manager of the performance sits before the curtain on the boards, and looks into the Fair, a feeling of melancholy comes over him in his survey of the bustling place. There is a great quantity of eating and drinking...(Vanity Fair)

领班的坐在戏台上幔子前面,对着地下闹哄哄的市场,瞧了半晌,心中不觉悲惨起来。市场上有的人在吃喝……

第二句there is 与第一句place进行衔接。翻译过程中,第一句句序发生了改变,第二句增加了"市场"。

7. 语篇层翻译(translation of discourse level)

语篇包括两个方面:语篇结构和语篇特点。结构指格式和构建方案;特点是衔接和连贯。翻译过程中,结构可复制;语篇特征衔接指将词语和单句连接在一起的可见的词汇和语法手段。衔接和连贯可体现在单句、复合句、语篇层次上。比如:

① Furthermore, says Mr. Evans, ② it would increase costs significantly for small to medium-sized business, ③ which would have to conduct regular searches to protect their own registered rights, ④ hitherto done by the Patent Office.

译文A

①埃文斯先生进而指出,③这么一来,中小企业为了保护自己已经注册的专利权,不得不自己进行定期检索,④而这种检索一向是由专利局负责的,②从而大大增加了中小企业的成本。

译文B

①埃文斯先生进而指出,③这么一来,中小企业为了保护自己已经注册的专利权,不得不自己进行④本来由专利局负责的定期检索,②从而大大增加了中小企业的成本。

译文A受原语结构的干扰而造成不连贯现象,对原语中的信息单元只是换了一下顺序,几乎原封不动地出现在译文;而译文B将④嵌入③,保证了信息流畅。

翻译小贴士

2019年7月31日的外交部记者会上,有记者提问,美国总统特朗普称,中方经常出尔反尔。如果要等到明年大选他连任之后才签订协议,那一定会是一个更差的协议。中方对此有何评论?

华春莹表示,我看到了有关报道。我只想"呵呵"两声。(On your third question, I have seen relevant reports and twitter. Hmm. How interesting.)

翻译将"呵呵"译成了"Hmm. How interesting!"。除此之外,这次记者会上,其实还有不少"呵呵"内容。

比如华春莹表示:事实上,(美国)自己生病,却让别人吃药,也是没有任何用的。这句话翻译成英语是:"In fact, it's useless to ask others to take pills when the US is ill itself."

再比如,2018年8月,华春莹曾在记者会上表示:对于美方各种花式"甩锅",对不起,我们不想接,也不能接。官方翻译为:"The US wants to make China a scapegoat. But so sorry, we don't want to be one. And don't even think of making us one."

还有,发言人耿爽曾表示"中国不是吓大的",官方翻译为:"Threats and intimidation will never work on China."(威胁及恐吓永远对中国起不了作用)

2018年7月3日,耿爽火力全开,曾连用了10个成语硬杠英国外交大臣亨特的涉港言论。这些成语是这样翻译的:

不思悔改、信口雌黄:keeps lying without remorse

自作多情、痴心妄想:nothing more than self-entertaining

厚颜无耻:how brazen is that

不自量力:overreach

附:7月31日记者会双语实录

问:第一个问题,中国文化和旅游部刚刚发布消息称,鉴于当前两岸关系,决定自8月1日起暂停47个城市大陆居民赴台个人游试点。台湾方面评论称,大陆的决定与蔡英文前不久"过境"美国并高调评价香港"反送中"问题有关。你对此有何评论?第二个问题,你昨天评论朝鲜《劳动新闻》涉港文章,称其发出了正义的声音,但同时却批评蓬佩奥涉港言论。香港有评论称,这是互相矛盾、双重标准。你对此有何回应?第三个问题,刚刚媒体报道称,在上海举行的中美经贸磋商结束得很快,是否表明此轮谈判不欢而散?此外,美国总统特朗普称,中方经常出尔反尔。如果要等到明年大选他连任之后才签订协议,那一定会是一个更差的协议。中方对此有何评论?

Q: First question, China's Ministry of Culture and Tourism just released this information. In view of the current cross-strait relations, it decided to suspend the individual travel of residents of 47 mainland cities to Taiwan from August 1. Taiwan media say this is related to Tsai Ing-wen's recent transit in the US and her blatant remarks on the recent protests in Hong Kong. What is your comment on that? Second question, yesterday you said the Hong Kong-related article in Rodong Sinmun is a voice of justice while criticizing US Secretary of State Mike Pompeo's comments on Hong Kong. Some in Hong Kong say this is double standards. Do you have any response to that? Third question, the media just reported that the trade talks in Shanghai were very short. Does that signal an unsuccessful meeting? Besides, President Trump twittered that China has been flip-flopping, and that if China wants to wait until he gets re-elected next year, the deal they get will be much tougher than what we are negotiating now. What's your comment?

答：关于第一个问题，台湾是中国的一部分，两岸事务不属于外交问题。请你向国台办询问。

On your first question, Taiwan is part of China, and cross-strait affairs are not diplomatic matters. I'd refer you to the Taiwan Affairs Office of the State Council.

关于第二个问题，我不知道你提到的是香港哪些人认为我昨天的表态有双重标准。我说的都是客观的，是根据事情本身的是非曲直作出判断和评价的。

On your second question, I don't know which people in Hong Kong think my comments yesterday are double standards. What I said is objective. I make judgments and comments based on facts.

关于第三个问题，我看到了有关报道。我只想"呵呵"两声。

On your third question, I have seen relevant reports and twitter. Hmm. How interesting.

因为你知道，中美经贸磋商一年多来，是谁出尔反尔、言而无信、反复无常，大家都有目共睹。而中方对于经贸磋商的立场始终如一。双方经贸团队目前正在上海磋商,你刚才说到的最新情况,我还不掌握。在这个时候,美方放话试图极限施压是没有意义的。事实上,自己生病,却让别人吃药,也是没有任何用的。我认为,在经贸磋商问题上,美方应该更多地展现诚意和诚信。

We all know who has been flip-flopping in the trade talks over the past year or so. In contrast, China's position remains consistent. The Chinese and American negotiating teams are now in Shanghai for trade talks. I'm not aware of the latest information you mentioned. It just doesn't make any sense if the US tries to exert maximum pressure at this particular time. In fact, it's useless to ask others to take pills when the US is ill itself. I believe the US needs to show more sincerity and good faith on this issue.

习题一

一、简答题

1. 简单陈述翻译的概念。

2. 翻译有哪些层次?

3. 一般来讲,翻译有几个步骤?

二、翻译词组与句子

1. copycat product

2. eco-village

3. 逍遥游

4. 在你们身上,寄托着中国和全人类的希望。

5. 肩负神圣使命,忠实履行职责

6. When she's angry, she is a dragon.

7. 狗嘴里吐不出象牙。

8. Some solid bodies have a tendency to maintain their shape, and when deformed by an external force, they return to their original shape as soon as the force is removed. This property is known as elasticity.

第二章

翻译发展概述及中西主要翻译理论

一、中西翻译发展史

(一) 中国翻译发展史

中国的翻译始于两千多年前汉代的佛经翻译,至今主要经历了四次高潮。

第一次翻译高潮是东汉至唐宋时期的佛经翻译。自从佛教于西汉末年传入中国以后,佛经翻译活动也随之展开。佛教初入中国时与儒学格格不入,为了迎合我国的儒道文化,佛教的译本中则采用"佛道"一词。并且在佛经翻译的全盛时期也产生了"四大译师",即鸠摩罗什、真谛、玄奘以及不空。东汉至三国时期人称"三支"的支娄迦谶、支亮、支谦,隋朝的彦琮等是佛经翻译的代表人物。这一全盛时期还成就了鸠摩罗什(梵语 Kumarajiva)、真谛、玄奘等三位堪称古代翻译界泰斗的翻译家。玄奘不仅翻译了七十五部佛经,还把老子的一部分著作译成梵文,成为第一个把汉文著作向国外译介的中国人,他提出的"既须求真,又须喻俗"的翻译标准,至今仍有一定的指导意义。

在长达一千多年的佛经翻译过程中,翻译家们留下了不少有关佛经翻译的经验,这些都是构建中国翻译理论的宝贵资源。在此阶段,佛经翻译大师支谦[①]是我国第一位在翻译理论方面颇有建树的重要人物。公元 224 年,佛经翻译界

[①] 支谦在《法句经序》中写道:"维祇难曰:'其传经者,当令易晓,勿失厥义,是则为善。'座中咸曰:'老氏称美言不信,信言不美。……今传胡义,实宜径达。'是以偈受译人口,因循本旨,不加文饰。"(支谦,224:22)——参谭载喜《翻译学》书目。

围绕《法句经》的翻译引发"文丽"与"质朴"的争论,并形成了两个学术流派。随后,支谦写了《法句经序》,提出了"因循本旨,不加文饰",就佛经在汉译过程中存在的一些问题阐述了他的思想和观点。此外,翻译家道安和玄奘也就佛经翻译理论提出了独到的见解。道安提出了佛经翻译中的"五失本"、"三不易"①和"案本而传"等直译的主张。鸠摩罗什则提出了"详其意旨,审其文中,然后书之"。这种意译的方法既充分照顾汉语的语言文字习惯,又力求不失梵文原意。玄奘提出了佛经翻译中的"五不翻"②原则。而彦琮则提出翻译要具备八个条件,即"八备"说。这一千多年的佛经翻译活动,基本上把印度的梵文佛经都译成了中文和藏文。这些经文有许多在印度本土都已经失传,但我国的中文和藏文译本却保存完好,流传至今,可以说我国的佛经翻译也为保存佛经这一世界文化遗产做出了贡献。

第二次翻译高潮是明末至清季的科技翻译,主要的代表人物是徐光启、林纾、严复等翻译家,他们在译介西欧各国的科学、哲学名著以及文学作品等方面做出了突出贡献,其中影响较大的译作包括严复③翻译的《天演论》(赫胥黎著)、《原富》(亚当·斯密著)、《法意》(孟德斯鸠著)和《社会通诠》(甄克思著)等。这些译著不仅推动了"新学"的发展,还在思想上起到了启蒙的作用。严复在其所译《天演论》(1898年出版)卷首的《译例言》中提出的译事三难中的"信、达、雅",成为我国译界所长期尊崇的翻译标准。

第三次翻译高潮是鸦片战争至"五四"时期的文学翻译。我国真正意义上的文学翻译始于19世纪六七十年代。在此之前,中国的一些文化典籍由传教

---

① "五失本""三不易",言翻译梵经,有五种失原本之义并三种之不容易者。晋道安曰:译胡为秦,有五失本也:一者,胡语尽倒,而使从秦,一失本也。二者,胡经尚质,秦人好文,传可众心,非文不合,斯二失本也。三者,胡经委悉,至于咏叹,丁宁反覆,或三或四,不嫌其烦,而今裁斥,三失本也。四者,胡有义说,正似乱辞,寻说向语,文无以异,或千五百,刈而不存,四失本也。五者,事已全成,将更傍及,反腾前辞,已乃后说,而悉除此,五失本也。然般若经,三达其心,覆面所演,圣必因时,时俗有易,而删雅古以适今时,一不易也。愚智天隔,圣人叵阶,乃欲以千岁之上微言,传使合百王之下末俗,二不易也。阿难出经,去佛未远,尊者大迦叶令五百六通,迭察迭书,今离千年,而以近意量裁,彼阿罗汉乃兢兢若此,此生死人而平平若此,岂将不知法者勇平,斯三不易也。

② 玄奘在总结多年翻译佛经的经验后,建立了"五不翻"原则,即:1. 秘密不翻(如咒语,要音译);2. 含义多不翻(即一词多义的);3. 我们没有的不翻;4. 已经有翻的不翻;5. 意义只可意会的不翻(要音译)。他说的"不翻"并不是不翻译,而是"不意译",主要"音译"。

③ 清末新兴资产阶级的启蒙思想家。

士译介到了欧洲,带动了欧洲的汉学热;与此同时,也有极少数的欧洲文学作品因传教士的译介而进入中国。洋务运动时期,被清政府派遣出国的中国留学生在西方社会生活、学习了一段时间后,逐渐感悟到,西方国家之所以强盛,并不全在于船坚炮利和发达的自然科学,主要还是由于它们先进的社会制度和文化,于是便对西方的政治、法律、教育、历史等知识萌生兴趣,并着手翻译,掀起了我国近代社会科学与文学翻译的高潮。这一时期以西学翻译为主要特征,涌现出鲁迅、瞿秋白、林语堂等中国近代翻译史上著名的翻译家。与前两次翻译高潮相比,此阶段的翻译在内容和形式上都有了很大的变化,内容上开始译介马列主义经典著作和东西方优秀的文学作品,特别是俄国及苏联的文学作品居多,对中国新思潮的形成以及中国社会发展起到了巨大的推动作用。从形式来说,白话文代替了文言文,白话文在译本中占了统治地位。这一时期对翻译标准亦有较为广泛和深入的讨论。在翻译理论方面,不论是"信顺"之争,还是傅雷的"神似"说、钱钟书的"化境"说的提出,近代以来的中国翻译理论一直在围绕着严复所提出的"信、达、雅"标准而展开。这些翻译理论是我国文学翻译理论的集中体现,也是我国翻译理论建设的重要资源。

第四次翻译高潮起源于 20 世纪 70 年代末,以实用翻译为主要特征。自 1978 年实行改革开放以来,我国的社会转型急剧而深刻,迎来了经济、科技、文化、教育等各领域迅速的发展。随着经济全球化和世界一体化进程的加快,我国的对外交流日益频繁,作为跨文化交流的重要工具,翻译事业进入了蓬勃发展时期,特别是实用文献翻译,成为推动我国外向型经济发展的助推器。20 世纪 80 年代对西方思潮的大讨论在国内引发了"文化热",原因主要有两方面:一是我国自身社会的经济和政治条件的变化引发了文化观念的变革;二是翻译为"文化热"打开了新思路。到了 20 世纪 90 年代初,经过十多年的改革开放探索,我国的市场经济得以真正确立。市场经济时代下的翻译服务于经济建设并得到前所未有的发展,翻译作品不论在数量上还是质量上都有飞跃发展,翻译理论日臻完善。这一阶段,我国的翻译工作者不仅译介了大量的外国科技文献、经济和管理专著以及其他领域的优秀作品,也了解和学习了更多的西方翻译理论。同时,越来越多的翻译工作者开始将中国几千年的典籍作品和当代文学译介到国外，传播了中华文化，推动了世界文化的发展。

至此，我们对中国翻译理论的发展历史做概括的梳理与归纳：

传统上讲，中国的翻译理论起始于严复《天演论·译例言》中提出的"信、达、雅"原则；至新中国成立之前，中国绝大多数翻译理论与实践都围绕着这一话题进行讨论或开展工作。

新中国成立以后，董秋斯①最早提出了翻译理论建设的问题。他认为，中国的翻译理论建设主要存在两个问题：一是没有完备的翻译体系，二是没有公认的客观标准。董秋斯详尽地阐述了他的翻译思想和翻译学术观点，具体描述了翻译理论领域需要做的工作，这标志着我国翻译理论建设和翻译研究开始进入了新的历史发展阶段。

20世纪50年初，翻译家傅雷②在前人研究基础之上，提出了"重神似不重形似"的翻译理论观。傅雷的"神似说"超越了严复"信、达、雅"的翻译原则，不再拘泥于字句表面的翻译，将翻译带入了美学的范畴，推动了翻译理论的发展。60年代中期，钱钟书先生提出了"化境说"，认为文学翻译的最高标准是"化"。把作品从一国文字转变成另一国文字，既能不因语文习惯的差异而露出生硬牵强的痕迹，又能完全保存原有语言的风味，那就算得入"化境"。17世纪有人赞美这种造诣的翻译，比为原作的"投胎转世"(the transmigration of souls)，躯壳换了一个，而精神资质依然故我。"化境说"比"神似说"更深化了一层。20世纪70年代末期，大量的西方翻译理论较为系统地传入中国，对中国的翻译理论和实践产生了较大的影响。

自20世纪80年代以来，随着不同文体翻译的快速发展，中国的翻译理论进入了反思期，对引进的西方翻译理论能否本土化进行了深刻的思考，以陈冬冬和吴道平的《论奈达深层理论在翻译中的应用》为主要标志。从90年代末期到21世纪初期，中国的翻译理论界从反思期进入批判期，对西方翻译理论特别

---

① 原名绍明，文学翻译家。主要译作有狄更斯的《大卫·科波菲尔》、列夫·托尔斯泰的《战争与和平》等。董秋斯是我国著名的翻译思想家，对中国传统译学思想在20世纪中期的创新发展做出了重要贡献，在我国乃至世界范围内率先构建了一个现代翻译学科的理论框架。

② 傅雷的观点是对鲁迅、茅盾、林语堂等人的"艺术翻译必须传神"观点的继承和发展。

是对奈达翻译理论从茫然接受到批判性采用。自此以后,中国翻译领域的学者开始将关注点转移到我国自身的翻译研究及翻译学科建设上,翻译研究也进入多元化发展时期。

总体来说,中国的翻译理论经历了从经验式、感悟式到系统性和科学性,从介绍引进西方翻译理论到中西结合,再到创造自己的翻译理论的发展阶段,中国的翻译研究将会开拓更广阔的发展空间,为世界翻译理论的发展贡献独特的方略。

(二) 西方翻译发展史

由于西方翻译活动历史悠久,时间跨度大,且所涉及的地域辽阔,要做客观的切分是比较困难的。西方译学界对翻译史有着不同划分,从严格意义上说,西方的第一部译作是在约公元前250年安德罗尼柯用拉丁语翻译的希腊荷马史诗《奥德赛》。而对这两千多年的西方翻译史的分期,因人们的视角不同,划分标准亦不同,观点颇不一致,所以,并无统一的结论。

西方翻译历史大致可分为传统、现代和当代三个大的阶段。传统阶段是从公元前4世纪开始到公元16世纪的文艺复兴时期;现代阶段是从公元17世纪到19世纪末期;当代阶段是从20世纪初至今。古罗马时期大规模地翻译古希腊文学艺术作品,是翻译历史上的第一次高潮。14世纪至16世纪席卷整个欧洲的文艺复兴运动,掀起了另一场规模空前的翻译浪潮。在这一时期,古希腊、古罗马作品以及各个新兴民族国家作品得以大量翻译。17世纪至18世纪对古典作品的翻译蓬勃发展,到19世纪翻译重心开始转移到近代或同时代的作品上来。第二次世界大战以后,各种政治、经济、科技、文学、文化方面的翻译达到了"前不见古人"的高潮。

西方的翻译理论发展及研究主要经历了五次高潮。

第一次翻译高潮起始于公元前3世纪中期。这一时期的主要翻译成就包括:从希伯来语译为希腊语的《希腊文旧约圣经》、荷马史诗《奥德赛》(*Odyssey*)和大批希腊戏剧作品译为拉丁语或用拉丁语改编为戏剧。这一时期的翻译工作打开了欧洲翻译的局面,传播和继承了古希腊文学。

第二次翻译高潮发生在公元4世纪至6世纪。这一时期的主要特征是对

《圣经》的翻译热潮,各种语言的《圣经》译本相继问世。为了广泛传播《圣经》这部基督教的经典,希伯来语和希腊语的《圣经》被翻译成拉丁语版本的《圣经》,以便于罗马人阅读。其中杰罗姆(Jerome)所翻译的《圣经通用本》(*Vulgate*),因其译文自然流畅、易于为读者接受的优点,而最具有影响力和权威性。

第三次翻译高潮是在公元 11 至 12 世纪之间。由于不同文化之间的影响与融通,不同宗教(特别是基督徒与穆斯林)间彼此交流与探究,大批的宗教和文学作品由阿拉伯语译成拉丁语,希腊语译成古叙利亚语。翻译领域的学术研究在欧洲兴起。此时期西方翻译家们多集中在西班牙的托莱多,形成了以托莱多为中心的欧洲学术中心,类似于巴格达的"翻译院"。

第四次翻译高潮发生在公元 14 至 16 世纪的文艺复兴时期。这一时期的翻译思想活跃,翻译活动深入而广泛,是一场思想和文学革新的大运动,也是西方翻译史上的大发展,翻译活动涉及宗教、思想、文化、政治、哲学和文学等众多领域,翻译作品的类别、数量和质量都达到了历史巅峰。其中主要的翻译作品有《钦定圣经译本》(*King James Version of the Bible*)、《伊利亚特》(*The Iliad*)和《奥德赛》(*Odyssey*)等,推动和促进了文艺复兴的发展和欧洲社会变革。尤其是 1611 年《钦定圣经译本》的出版,以其地道的英语风格和通俗优美的艺术风格赢得了"英语中最伟大的译著"的盛誉,这也标志着英国翻译史的一次大发展,对现代英语的发展产生了深刻的影响。

第二次世界大战结束以后迎来了第五次翻译高潮。战争的结束、世界的和平、文化交流的加强、经济与科技的飞速发展,为翻译事业的繁荣提供了良好的契机和优越的物质及社会基础。翻译涉及的领域进一步扩展,深入宗教、文学、文化、科技、教育、艺术、商业、旅游、军事、外交等各方面,使翻译得以发展成为一种专门的职业。随着现代科技进入翻译领域,人类开发了机器翻译。随之,传统意义上的翻译理论和翻译研究也呈现出不同层面的深化。

至此,我们对西方翻译理论的发展历史做一概括的梳理与归纳:

人类在圣经翻译之前的翻译活动,还处在翻译的摸索阶段,严格上来讲,这个阶段还谈不上理论认识,最多也仅是对翻译有些基本了解。从公元前 250 年左右《七十子希腊文本》(《希伯来圣经》最早的希腊文译本)的翻译活动开始,直到16世纪的圣经翻译,这段时期我们把它称作宗教典籍翻译阶段,这一阶段对翻译活动的探讨确立了人类关于翻译的基本理念,包括最基本的翻译方法论,如直译、意译、可译、不可译等问题。

随着民族语言与民族文学的确立,尤其是西方文艺复兴运动兴起之后,文学翻译开始成为翻译的主流,从而开启了以文学名著、社科经典为主要翻译对象的文学翻译阶段。在这一阶段,对于翻译理论的探讨更加丰富和深入,并且产生了针对各种类型、体裁作品的翻译理论,如著名的泰特勒"翻译三原则"、以德国为代表的异化翻译原则等。

第二次世界大战以后,实用性质的非文学翻译(即实用文献的翻译)成为翻译活动的主流,翻译也逐渐发展为一个专门的职业。在此阶段翻译理论意识空前高涨,翻译学科发展迅猛,自此拉开了人类翻译发展史的第三阶段——实用文献翻译。当然,有必要说明的是,我们对人类翻译发展史的这种三阶段划分,依据的是每一阶段的主流翻译对象,但它们之间是相互交叉的,而并不是说一个阶段只有一种翻译对象。同理,对翻译的观念也是相互交叉的,即使在目前的实用文献翻译阶段,文学翻译或宗教翻译阶段所形成的译学理念和理论仍然在发挥作用和影响,只是与实用文献的翻译相比,它们在整个翻译活动和翻译产业中所占的比例比之前要小,正在边缘化,其影响也日渐式微。

二、中西主要翻译理论及代表人物

(一) 中国主要的翻译理论家及其理论

除了著名翻译家严复和傅雷对翻译做出的贡献之外,在国内主要的翻译家及其翻译理论还包括:鲁迅的"硬译"、林语堂的美学、郭沫若的创作论、钱钟书的化境、许渊冲的优化论和三美论以及谭载喜的翻译综合论。这里主要介绍鲁迅、许渊冲和谭载喜三位翻译家。

1. 鲁迅先生的"硬译"

鲁迅先生的翻译理论主要体现在他关于"硬译"的翻译主张和实践,特别是他同梁实秋先生关于直译与意译的辩论(《"硬译"与"文学的阶级性"》,后收入

《二心集》)。在当时的背景下，文学有无阶级性，这是个意识形态色彩较强的理论问题，而翻译可以采取哪些方法则是一个技术层面上的问题，当时往往被扯在一起讨论甚至引发笔战。其实鲁迅先生并非一味坚持"硬译"，相反，在某些场合，他很强调意译，强调译文应当流畅易读。

鲁迅先生在当时指出，希望通过翻译从外文中吸取营养，让汉语更加丰富起来。他指出，既然"硬译"带有某种实验的性质，由此带来的西化性质的文法、句法、词法，有些可能会被接受，慢慢就成为汉语的新传统；另一些实在无法接受的，那就被淘汰。由于事前不能保证引进的东西全是好的，只好先引进来再说，一切留给历史来决定。虽然当时鲁迅先生所提出来的"硬译"尝试遭到多方的批评、指责，人们也未对鲁迅翻译理论关注重视，但是随着西方翻译研究的文化发展和解构主义理论的发展，人们开始注意到鲁迅翻译理论的价值。

鲁迅先生的翻译理论主要包括以下三个方面：翻译应为本民族的事业服务，异化的翻译策略有助于民族文化的重建；作为翻译主体的译者有一个文化定位的问题；通顺的译文有可能导致"知识"的虚伪，符合本土最容易被接受的保守思维定式。

鲁迅先生提出了文学创作和文学作品的"三美"，即文学有"意美、音美、形美"，后来许渊冲先生将其观点结合翻译实践，形成了翻译上的"三美论"。

2. 许渊冲的优化论和三美论

理论来自实践，又要受到实践的检验。实践是检验真理的唯一标准。这是许渊冲提出"创中国学派文学翻译理论"的哲学基础。许渊冲先生在继承前人理论学说的基础上，集毕生翻译之经验加以发展，提出了自成一派的翻译理论"优化论"。该理论用"美化之艺术，创优似竞赛"这十个字加以概括，并且在《翻译的艺术》(1984)、《文学翻译谈》(1998)、《文学与翻译》(2003)等著作中，对形似与神似、求真与求美、翻译与创作、"翻译腔"和"四字成语"、中西文化的差异、两种文化的竞赛等问题进行了具体的论述。

许渊冲最早在1981年《翻译的标准》一文中，提出要发挥译文语言优势。他说："翻译首先要忠实准确，主要是忠实于原文的内容，在可能的情况下也要忠实于原文的形式；其次是要求通顺流畅，符合译文语言的习惯用法；最后还要注重修辞,发挥译文语言的优势。"发挥语言优势,可以说是他的核心译论,即要达到"三美"必须发挥优势。

许渊冲的优化论可以简单地概括为"信、达、优"。"信"可以同等于忠实,要做到"三确":正确、准确、明确。"达"可以同等于通顺,就是要做到"三用":通用、连用、惯用,即"译文应该是全民族目前通用的语言,用词能和上下文连用,合乎汉语的惯用"。"优"就是要"扬长避短,发挥译语的语言优势"。许渊冲优化论中"优"的提出,非常具有创新精神,非常具有现实意义。"优"在许多优秀的文学翻译作品中得到广泛的使用,也是文学翻译的最高要求。

3. 谭载喜的翻译综合论

谭载喜论证了翻译学的性质和基本特征,又进一步指出翻译学是一门综合性学科,因为它需要综合运用语言学、文艺学、社会学、符号学、心理学以及数控论(包括概率论)、计算机等多种学科的知识。但他同时指出翻译学并不是个大杂烩。

谭载喜认为从广义上理解,翻译学研究不仅仅局限于翻译活动本身,而应包括与翻译活动有关的一切领域。他把翻译学研究的对象进行归纳得出以下五条:①翻译的实质;②翻译的原则和标准;③翻译的方法和技巧;④翻译的操作过程和程序;⑤翻译过程中出现的各种矛盾,如目的和手段的矛盾,内容和形式的矛盾,作者与译文读者的矛盾等。他认为除此之外,还应该研究对比语义学、对比句法学、对比修辞学、对比社会符号学、对比文化学、对比民族语言学以及对比心理学等。总之,一切与翻译有关的课题,都应纳入翻译学的研究范围,使翻译学真正成为一个独立的实体。因为他们强调中外翻译理论是相通的,是有共性的。谭载喜从概念上澄清了一些研究者对"翻译"及"翻译学"的模糊认识,揭示了翻译学内部的客观规律,对翻译学的内容、任务和研究方法都进行了详细的阐述,为翻译学的进一步发展指出了方向,具有很高的学术价值和实际意义。

(二)西方主要的翻译理论家及相关理论

20世纪60年代末,美国著名翻译理论家尤金·奈达在与简·德·沃德合著的《从一种语言到另一种语言》(*From One Language to Another*,1969)一书中,将西方翻译理论大体上分为四个基本流派,即语文学理论、语言学理论、交际学理论和社会符号学理论,这四种理论流行于不同时期,先后承接,相辅相成。

翻译的语文学理论强调原文话语的主题结构和风格,着眼于原文的文学特征。该理论注重话语的源点,即原文的作者和背景,而不关注读者的感觉和反应。语文学理论研究的基本问题是,翻译的大方向是让信息适应人,还是人适应信息。杰罗姆、马丁·路德、施莱尔马赫以及当代的詹姆斯·霍姆斯等人的观点都属于语文学派。

翻译的语言学理论,顾名思义,是从语言学视角研究翻译的问题,主要围绕源语和译入语在语言结构上的差异、源语和译入语在语言形式上的对等及翻译原则等问题展开探讨。本质上讲,翻译的语言学理论探讨的是对等规则,这些对等规则对于翻译具有指导意义和价值。但是,这些建立在对比语言学基础上的对等规则,过分地强调语言中的语法功能和表层结构的对等,而忽略了文本底层的语义关系。还有,严格意义上的语言学翻译理论往往对话语的交际问题没有足够的重视。

正是为了弥补语言学翻译理论的缺陷,产生了翻译的交际学理论。该理论是一种基于交际理论的翻译体系,它把翻译纳入语言交际的范畴,从信息源点、信息、信息受体、信息反馈、信息噪声、信道和信息传播手段的角度研究翻译中出现的问题,并且特别关注在信息论中作为研究对象的信息传播效果和冗余信息的处理问题(方梦之,2004)。翻译理论家卡特福德(J. D. Catford, 1965)、奈达(Eugene A. Nida, 1964、1969)、纽伯特(A. Newbert, 1968)、威尔斯(Wolfram Wils, 1982)以及纽马克(Peter Newmark, 1988)等分别论述了交际翻译法。

然而,交际理论对语言与文化的关系并未进行深入探讨,而把这一问题留给了社会符号学。20世纪70年代,奈达等人从社会语言学、符号学的角度剖析了社会中的人及其行为与语言运用的关系。社会符号学翻译理论是从语言符号和代码角度研究语言转换和语际交际的一种理论,它与社会语言学理论(该理论强调人的社会行为与语言使用之间存在的关系)密切相关联。正确理解社会符号学理论,不仅有助于更好地理解词、句和话语结构的意义,同时也有助于更好地理解话语中的各种动作和物体的象征意义。

社会符号学翻译理论对于区分所指含义和联想含义具有重要意义。社会符号学理论强调,与信息有关的一切都具有意义,如果用错了字体和版式,都会严重地损害或歪曲话语的意义。

请看下边这个例子:

```
"Fury said to
    a mouse, That
        he met
           in the
              house,
         'Let us
             both go
                to law:
                 I will
                 Prosecute
you.
 Come, I'll
    take on
       denial
          We must
              have a
                 trial:
                    For
                    really
                  this
                 morning
                I've
              nothing
             to do.'
          …
           …"
```

```
        火儿狗在屋子
           里头遇着个
        耗子。狗说
               "你别充'忙',
          咱们去
   上公堂。
         我不承
            认你赖。
               谁不知
                  道你
                     坏?我
                  今儿早
               晨没事,
            咱们同
      上公堂。"
   ……
     ……
```

广义来说,信息不但包含内容与意义,而且包含形式与风格,对于后者的充分表达,有时也是很重要的。保留原文格式进行翻译,也是非常有必要的。

1. 社会符号学理论简介

社会符号学理论的代表人物是奈达、韩礼德,其主要论点包括:

(1)翻译的核心内容是翻译意义。

(2)翻译也是一种文化交流。

(3)语言本质上是一套独特的符号系统。在这个系统中,最重要的是语义系统(亦即信息),它体现语言最根本的作用和功能。

(4)文本(text)是具有功能和意义的语义单位,是在一定的语境中人们交际的过程和产物(衔接、连接、逻辑、转换)。

(5)语境(context situation)指文本得以存在的环境,该环境可指语言环境也可指非语言环境,即社会环境。("鸡不吃了"这种歧义句,属于同形同构异义:"鸡"既可以作"吃"的施事者,又可作"吃"的受事者。但是,当这个句子进入具体的语境时,歧义就自然排除了。如在酒宴吃饭的语境中说"鸡不吃了","鸡"当然是作为受事者,语义是"鸡不吃了,酒也不喝了"。如果这个句子出现在养鸡场或农家茅舍喂鸡这个情境中,"鸡"则是施事者,其语义是"鸡已经喂饱了,不再吃食了")孤立的一个词,本无意义,也无所谓好坏,一旦进入上下文的具体语境时,是黑是白、是好是坏,就清清楚楚、一目了然了。古代文人写诗作赋,对于选词练字非常讲究,主要的目的是切合语境。"柳絮飞来片片红"并非上乘诗句,因为"红"字用在这里不通,跟"白"的柳絮相矛盾,出现了语境不一致的问题。于是有人在原诗句的基础上增加了一句,变为"夕阳方照桃花坞,柳絮飞来片片红",这样便使得原本不通的"红"字,不仅通顺,而且精彩起来了。红彤彤的夕阳斜射,洒落在桃花坞,而白色的柳絮在夕阳中飞舞,顿时被染成了"红"色,呈现出一副极为美丽的图景。此处用词从不通而到精彩,其中语境是一个重要的因素。在韩愈的建议下,贾岛"鸟宿池边树,僧推月下门"改为"鸟宿池边树,僧敲月下门",由"推"至"敲",成为"推敲"佳话,实际上也是出于适切诗中语境的考虑。

(6)语域(register)指语言的语体,它取决于语言使用的场合。英国语言学家韩礼德(M. A. K. Halliday)认为,语言变体可以按照使用的情况划分为不同语域。语言使用的领域种类很多,例如:新闻广播、演说语言、广告语言、课堂用语、办公用语、家常谈话、与幼童谈话、与外国人谈话、口头自述等。

语域包括语场、语旨和语式。语场指交流的场合,如法庭、诊所和课堂,都是一种语场。不同的语场对词汇、话语结构和语态选择具有制约作用。语旨指由交际双方的社会地位和角色所确定的语言使用的正式程度和态度,分为刻板体、正式体、随便体、亲密体等。语旨主要用来表达感情。比如同样是祝酒语场,不宜将 bottom up 这一非正式的语言表达用于正式、盛大的场合。语式指话语方式,分为口头语或书面语等。人物角色应该与语式对应,如儿童读物宜用口头语,科技文章宜用书面语。

下面的例子可以说明这一问题。"禽流感没有把你吓到,鸡瘟也没有磨灭你为家族延续而努力的精神,见你又毅然决然走进产房,我默默地祝福你,生蛋(圣诞)快乐。"这是一则关于圣诞节祝福的短信,其中充满了诙谐幽默。但如果将其发给领导或上级,就显得不伦不类,有些尴尬。因为它忽略了上下级之间的身份差距和亲密程度,原本美好的祝愿,却给对方留下轻浮、随便、草率的不良印象,适得其反。

再如,一个学生在完成外教布置的任务之后,询问外教"I am desirous of exploring your feeling on the report.",外教听后面露尴尬之色。因为这种表达使用了书面用语,显得过于正式,不符合交际的语境。可以将其改为"I'd like to hear your view on the report.",比较恰当。

(7)社会结构(social structure)是个体之间的社会关系。社会符号学认为,社会结构界定了交际的各种社会情景并赋予它们真实的意义,如社会地位、角色、社会群体、群体内成员的亲密程度(平等、种族制度等)以及社会类型等。

(8)意义和功能是语言作为一种符号系统所具备的固有特征,也是任何文本的固有特征。它们是衡量译文质量不可缺少的两个方面。

根据社会符号学理论,翻译的标准之一便是意义相符、功能相似。其中的意义相符一般包括三个层面的相符:

A. 指称意义(reference)如:太阳 sun;蓝天 blue sky。

B. 言内意义(speech)如:接收竟成劫搜 taking-over turns out to be loot-taking。

C. 语用意义(pragmatics)如:年饭 family reunion meal on the eve of the Spring Festival(而不是简单的 the meal on the eve of the Spring Festival)。

指称意义是语言符号与它所描绘或叙述的主观世界或客观世界的实体和事件之间的关系,是词语、句子和篇章所反映的客观世界。

言内意义是语言符号之间的关系,它具体体现在语音、词汇、句法和语篇等层次。

语音层次主要包括各种音韵(如头韵、腹韵、元音叠韵、和声、尾韵)、格律及重读等方面,如:He described the claim in alliteration fashion as a composite of fantasy, fallacy and fiction. 他用押头韵的方式把这种要求描绘成"虚幻、虚妄和虚构"的混合物。(头韵)

词汇层次有谐音双关、一语双叙等。比如: The senator picked up his hat and courage. 参议员捡起了帽子,鼓起了勇气。(一语双叙)

春晓(孟浩然)

春眠不觉晓,

处处闻啼鸟。

夜来风雨声,

花落知多少?

The Spring Dawn (Meng Haoran)

Slumbering, / know not the spring dawn is peeping,

But everywhere the singing birds are cheeping.

Last night / heard the rain dripping and wind weeping,

How many petals are now on the ground sleeping. (尾韵)

句法层次有组合关系、排比、倒装等,如: of the people, by the people, for the people. (民有、民治、民享)。

篇章层次则有句式的变化、段落衔接、粘连等。

语用意义是语言符号与语言符号使用者之间的关系。它包括五方面意义。

表征意义(indexical meaning)指话语中揭示发讯人的身份、性别、年龄、阶级和教育背景以及在交际中的态度。

表达意义(expressive meaning)指语言符号表达说话人的感情。

社交意义(social meaning)指语言符号在交际过程中建立或保持人际关系的一种特殊功能。

祈使意义(imperative meaning)指发讯人企图改变收讯人的行为或心态的意向。

联想意义(associative meaning)指附加在指称意义上的意义,是语言符号唤起收讯人对其他事物的联想,如 woman 一词一般会让人联想到女性所特有性别特征类词汇,frail(脆弱的)、emotional(感性的)、gentle(温柔的)、compassionate

(有同情心的)等。

2. 社会符号学的代表人物

美国翻译理论家尤金·奈达是当代西方重要的翻译理论家、交际理论学派的代表人物,他所提出的"等效论"在翻译理论界具有广泛而深刻的影响,他的理论核心为"功能对等或动态对等",提倡翻译要努力实现原文和译文在语言交际功能上对等,而不是刻意追求在语言表层形式上的对应。该理论重点关注读者或目的语信息接受者的作用,强调如何将原文信息最大限度地传递给目的语读者,目的语读者被视为交际(翻译)的终极目标,译文与原文的等效程度和译文的可接受程度被视为翻译的最高标准。奈达的翻译思想发展经历了三个阶段:20 世纪 40 年代至 50 年代,是奈达翻译思想的初创期(第一阶段),亦即描写语言学阶段;20 世纪 50 年代末至 60 年代末,是奈达翻译思想的完善期(第二阶段),亦即交际理论阶段;从 20 世纪 70 年代开始,是奈达翻译思想的成熟期(第三阶段),奈达将其原理论中的有用成分纳入新的理论体系,最终形成了社会符号学理论体系,于 1986 年出版了该理论体系的代表著作《从一种语言到另一种语言》,系统地阐述了他的翻译学术思想。奈达在该著作中倡导翻译的"三性原则",即译文要追求可懂性、可读性和可接受性并重的原则,提出了"最切近的自然对等"观。该理论观念所包括的三层含义"最切近"、"自然"和"对等",本质上是要求译者和译文应该最大限度地贴近原文。译文要行文自然,便于读者阅读,不带翻译腔。

可以简单地将奈达"功能对等"理论的具体内容概括为以下几个部分:

(1)用词类(word classes)取代词性(parts of speech),以此重新描写词与词之间的语义关系;

(2)采用核心句(kernel sentence)和句子转换的概念,以此突破源语的句法对译者的所产生的束缚;

(3)采用同构体理论(isomorphism),以此克服社会文化差异对作者、译者和读者所造成的理解和交际障碍。

请看下边的例句:

Her ideal husband must be as handsome as Adonis and as rich

as Mammon.

首先要弄清楚两个词:Adonis 和 Mammon 的意思,才能更好地翻译。Adonis 是希腊、罗马神话中的阿多尼斯(爱与美的女神阿芙罗狄娜所爱恋的美少年),代指美少年。Mammon 在《新约圣经》中是财富的象征(Mammon in the New Testament of the Bible is commonly thought to mean money, material wealth, or any entity that promises wealth.)。

如果直接把 Adonis 和 Mammon 翻译成阿多尼斯和玛蒙,很多中文读者不知道他们所代表的意思,也就达不到原文作者所要表达的 ideal husband 的英俊和富有,但是运用同构体理论,我们可以结合中国文化环境,将其翻译为潘安和邓通这两个中国读者熟知的人物,便实现了原文信息再现,于是得出译文:她的理想夫君人选必须具备潘安之美,邓通之富。

同样,下面几个句子的翻译也是应用了奈达的核心句和同构理论。

(1) This is a though-provoking different explanation.

这个解释完全不同,但却很能给人启发/引人深思。(核心句)

(2) The area could be profitable rehabilitated.

重建这些地区是十分有利可图的。(核心句)

(3) Rural enterprises have been growing like mushrooms.

乡镇企业如雨后春笋般地发展起来。(同构理论)

奈达抛弃了传统的词性分类法,改用实体(object,指具体的人和物等,如 desk,man,ghost 等)、事件(event,事情发生的行动、过程等,如 come,love,discuss,plant 等)、抽象概念(abstract conception,指对实体和事件的质量和程度的描写,比如 white,deeply,always 等)和关系(relations,指用来将实体、事件、抽象概念连接起来的方式或手段,比如 conjunction, prepositions 等)等概念和术语,将词进行重新分类,确立词与事物间的关系。具体的分类如下:

(1) 实体类词(entities),如 woman,book,table 等;

(2) 活动类词(activities),如 talk,think,climb 等;

(3) 状态类词(states),如 dead,happy,angry 等;

(4) 过程类词(processes),如 grow,enlarge,complete 等;

(5) 特征类词(characteristics)，如：tall，small，handsome 等；

(6) 连接类词(links)，如 where，during，if 等；

(7) 指示类词(deictic)，如：that，here，there 等。

奈达提出的新的词汇分类观点和方法，对翻译有着重要的影响，如：

(1) I was reliably informed.

(2) There is certainly some historical possibility.

(3) The actor has a small circle of admirers.

如果按照传统的词性分类法，一般会将原文翻译成以下译文：

(1) 我被很可靠地告知。

(2) 确实有一些历史的可能性。

(3) 那个演员有一个较小的钦佩者的圈子。

根据奈达提出的理论，可以得到以下译文：

(1) 我得到的信息很可靠。

(2) 从历史上看，这种可能性确实存在(或者：历史上确有这种可能)。

(3) 那个演员没有那么叫座(或者：那个演员的人气不太旺)。

3. 交际翻译理论的代表人物

英国翻译教育家和理论家彼得·纽马克(Peter Newmark)认为，译者应根据文本的不同功能采取相应的翻译方法，而不能仅仅强调目的语读者的反应，这点不同于奈达提出的翻译"等效论"。纽马克认为不分原作语篇类型，一律采用等效翻译法不可取。他创立了一个多元的翻译模式，包括逐字翻译、直译、忠实翻译、语义翻译、改写、意译、交流翻译等多种翻译模式和方法，而最常用的两种翻译模式为语义翻译和交流翻译。语义翻译要求译文忠实于原文的语篇，最大限度地实现与原文在形式上的对等；交流翻译要求译者重组语言结构，翻译要忠实于目的语读者，译文追求通顺、地道、易于读者理解。

纽马克认为，语言是一套具有心理功能和社会功能的符号系统。纽马克对语言的功能进行了分类，将其划分为六类：信息功能(informative function)，主要功能是传达信息；表达功能(expressive function)，主要功能是表达感情；呼唤功能(vocative function)，让听者或读者做出期望的反应；美感功能(aesthetic function),能够带来感观上的愉悦;应酬功能(phatic function),有助于交际者保持接触,反映交际者之间的关系;元语言①功能(metalingual function),语言能够解释或命名自身特点的功能。比如:

信息功能:He is on vacation now. 他正在度假。(传递信息)

表达功能:How beautiful it is! 好漂亮哦!(表达赞叹的情绪)

呼唤功能:Come here. 过来。(表示召唤)

美感功能:Dawn breaking over the islands, very beautiful in a soft grey light with many clouds. 曙色中的海岛美极了,晨曦柔和,彩云片片。(阅读能带来感官上的愉悦和满足)

应酬功能:How are you doing? 你好!(应酬交际)

元语言功能:指语言解释、命名或批评自身特点的功能。

在不同的语境或上下文中,语言的3类符号意义(指称意义、言内意义和语用意义)以及6种语言功能(信息功能、表达功能、呼唤功能、美感功能、应酬功能和元语言功能)所占比重往往是不同的。有时指称意义、信息功能比较突出(如专业性表达),有时语用意义、言内意义及美感功能相对较为显著(如文学性表达)。在翻译时,译者应根据具体的情况,将原文所承载的全部意义和功能,完整地再现给目的语读者。但若受客观因素和主观能力的制约,不能传递出原

---

① 当我们讨论一件事物时,我们所使用的语言被称为对象语言,因为它是对象的表现。而当我们谈论一种语言时,我们所使用的语言被称为元语言(Metalanguage)。在任何语言研究中,都有一种作为研究对象的语言,还有一种由研究者用来谈论对象语言的元语言。对象语言与元语言是相对而言的。任何语言,无论它多么简单或者多么复杂,当它作为被谈论的对象的时候,它就是对象语言;当它用来讨论一种语言的时候,它就是元语言。因此,元语言是关于语言的一种语言,也就是针对文本或者言语行为而进行讨论、写作、思考的语言。在日常的语言使用中,由于被谈论的语言(对象语言)和用来谈论语言的语言(元语言)常常是用同一种语言(例如汉语或英语)来表述,人们往往意识不到语言层次的区分,而把两者混淆起来,这种混淆的结果直接导致了悖论的出现。说谎者悖论是最古老的语义悖论。公元前4世纪麦加拉学派的欧布里德(Eubulides)提出如下问题:如果某人说他正在说谎,那么他说的话是真还是假?欧布里德的问题经常被重述为:"我现在说的这句话是谎话。"这句话是否可赋真值?假设这句话为真,根据其语义,可得它为假;假设这句话为假,其语义又恰好"是其所是",可得它为真。这样,矛盾等价式便得以建构。"我现在说的这句话是谎话",通称为"说谎者语句",就是其中的典型一例。从这个意义上来说,两个语言层次的区分,很可能为最终消解语义悖论找到一条极有希望的途径。语言分层理论的意义不仅仅局限于语言研究的范围。譬如哲学,它不仅要研究世界,研究人生,而且要研究哲学自身。这种对哲学自身的研究,亦即对哲学概念、命题、理论等的研究,被称作"元哲学研究"。显然这种"元哲学研究"要借助于语言分层理论,以区别对象语言和元语言,否则"元哲学研究"便无从进行。近年来新崛起的所谓"元科学""元方法论"等理论,便包含着语言分层理论的具体应用。

文的所有意义和功能,应抓住原文话语的主要意义和功能进行翻译。如:"It's a lovely day, isn't it?"这句话在不同语境中,可以被解读为不同的语言功能,也便存在多种相对应的意义。假如是在一个晴天丽日,这句话可以用来描述天气,它实现的是信息功能。假如是两个陌生人在一起,说话者想打破沉默,开启交流模式,它实现的便是交际功能。假如朋友看到你整日闭门不出,想邀请你出去活动一下,那么这句话所实现的就是呼唤功能(意动功能)。

由此可见,话语所发挥的功能离不开它所在的具体语境,要正确理解和再现话语的功能及意义,必须结合语境来进行分析。再如,一位妇女对其丈夫说:"Don't just stand there. You've got exactly ten minutes to shave and dress. I've got your clothes laid out on the bed."这句话同时发挥着三种功能:

(1)信息功能:妻子向丈夫说明了有关的情况。

(2)表达功能:妻子表达了一种不耐烦和焦急情绪。

(3)祈使功能:妻子催促丈夫赶快刮脸穿衣。

该例句表明,一般来讲,语言功能并非单一地存在于话语之中,而往往是多种功能交叉并存于话语之中。在几种功能并存的情况下,并非所有功能都具有同等重要的地位,可能其中某种功能显得更加重要。以上例句虽然具有三种功能,但最主要的,显然是妻子催促丈夫赶快做好出发的准备。因此,祈使是例句的主要功能。在翻译过程中,我们不仅要注意分析话语的全部功能,还要分析其主要功能,并尽量在译语中体现出来。

根据这一原则,上述例句可以被翻译为:"别光站在那里呀。你只有10分钟刮胡子穿衣服了。我已经把你的衣服放到床上去了。"这样翻译就把话语的祈使和信息功能都体现出来了,而且强调了祈使功能。

话语功能的实现效果,取决于话语所包含的信息、话语传达信息的方式和话语传达信息的对象这三方面的因素。首先,源语通过传达一定的信息对读者产生影响,以发挥其功能。因此,译者必须能够完整、准确、忠实地传递源语的信息,才能取得功能上的对等。其次,话语信息是通过一定的语言形式来传递的。同一话语信息,可以用不同的语言形式来传递,当然,也会产生不同的效果。例如,爸爸要儿子到地里拾马铃薯,可以采取直接命令的形式即"Tom, go and pick potatoes in the fields. ",也可以采取较为委婉的建议形式,即"Tom, you can go and pick potatoes in the fields if you want to. "。这两句话传达的信息相同,发挥的语言功能相同(祈使功能),但由于它们传达信息的形式不同,自然就会产生不同效果。

因此,为了再现原文话语的功能,译语不仅要传达源语的信息内容,还要重现传达源语信息内容的形式。语言形式具有其自身的独特性,一种语言的形式,有时承载着其他语言所无法传递的信息(王天明,1989)。当语言在表现形式方面具有突出特点时,它往往给人一种深刻的印象和强烈的美感,具有了某种审美的功能。但当一种语言的形式无法用另一种语言再现出来时,其自身的审美功能也就难以在译语中得到传播和体现。

现代英语名剧 *Singing in the Rain* 中有这样一句话,"Moses supposes his toes are roses. "。这句话所包含的信息内容十分简单,但在表现形式上,却使用了一系列的押韵和英诗中的扬抑抑格,读起来韵味十足,节奏感强,内含强烈的美感功能,但因为英汉两种语言表现形式的差异,这种审美效果难以在汉译中得到再现。如果将其译为"摩西以为他的脚趾是玫瑰花",那么译文仅是再现了原文的信息功能,传达了原文的信息内容,但毫无审美效果可言。如果将其译为"摩西自以为,脚趾是玫瑰",那么相比于前译而言,该译文具有了一定的节奏和押韵,部分地还原了原文的审美功能,但远远没有传达原文的音乐感信息。

语言要有交际的价值、履行交际的功能,必须具备三种功能,即概念功能、人际功能和语篇功能。相应地,这三种功能承载了人们使用语言所要表达的三种意义,即概念意义、人际意义和语篇意义。一般来讲,语言主要用来帮助人们表达概念意义和人际意义,但若实现这两种意义的表达,必须通过语篇功能的联结和组织,并以文本或语篇的形式呈现出来。相对于概念意义和人际意义而言,语篇意义仅发挥着组织意义,它是一种基于语言内部对语言信息的组织(Halliday,1994),其作用是辅助于前两种意义的实现,并不表示"内容"的意义(司显柱,2004)。但若要完整传达信息、完成有效交际,语篇功能及语篇意义是不可或缺的。

语言(langue)是抽象的,言语(parole)是具体的。彭宣维(2000)认为,语言是以语篇为代表的,语篇是语言使用的实际存在形式,而语篇以书面的形式表现出来,就是文本。语篇和文本是语言使用者从语言这一巨大系统词库中选择一些特定的词汇和语法结构进行交际的产物。

语言学家布勒在《语言理论》(1990)一书中创造了一个新的进行语言研究的方法模式,他将语言的语意功能分为三类:再现功能、表达功能和感染功能。再现功能主要针对事物而言,语言符号能够客观地再现事物,符号与事物之间是"暗指"(symbol)关系,语言指涉的是事物。表达功能主要针对发送者而言,语言符号能够主观地表达发送者的内心状态,符号与发送者之间是"暗含"(symptom)的关系,语言隐含着发送者的感情。感染功能主要针对接受者而言,语言符号感动、影响接受者的内心感受或外在行动,符号与接受者之间是"暗示"(signal)的关系,语言能够指示接受者的行动。

以布勒的三种语言功能为基础,赖斯划分出了三种不同的文本类型,即"重内容(content-focused)文本"、"重形式(form-focused)文本"和"重感染(appeal-focused)文本"。后来,她又将其分别凝练提升为"信息(informative)文本"、"表情(expressive)文本"和"感染(operative)文本"。

作为对语言系统的使用,任何一个文本必然同时表现出三种语言功能(概念、人际和语篇)和三种文本功能(再现、表达和感染),因此具有多种功能特征。但由于文本组成部分及组织上的不同情形,就某一具体文本来讲,功能之间有主次之分。针对不同的文本类型,在翻译过程中,语言功能和文本功能将会表现出不同的关系:对信息类文本而言,一般只需要在组成语篇的微观成分,如小句层面实现概念意义和人际意义等的对等转换即可;对于感染类文本而言,为追求原文和译文类似的表达效果,需要借助类似"文化过滤"等手段调整原文的篇章结构、表达方式等,这样译文就难以与原文保持概念意义上的一致,语言功能和文本功难以统一。因此,为了实现对原文主要功能的传递,译文不必刻意追求语言形式层面的概念意义和人际意义(或功能)对等。

翻译最重要的变量就是原文文本类型,它是译者进行翻译的参照,决定了译者后面的所有选择,因为翻译的标准之一就是要保证译文与原文的文本类型一致①。

如何在翻译中实现文本类型一致？就翻译策略而言,对于表情类和感染类文本,语篇(文本)翻译的关注点分别是"发送者"和"接受者",翻译要重形式、重感染,而非内容。所以,对于表情类和感染类文本的翻译,为了实现基于"形式的"和"感染的"文本主导功能的对等,可以在一定程度上忽略内容,在语言概念功能上稍有偏离。当然,这种忽略和偏离是有条件、有限度的,不能随意地偏离原文,造成因形损意。例如:

◀ 原文 ▶

I love my love with an E, because she is enticing;
I hate her with an E, because she is engaged.
I took her to the sign of exquisite, and treated her with an elopement,
Her name is Emily, and she lives in the East.

译文一

我爱我的爱人为了一个E,因为她是enticing(迷人的);
我恨我的爱人为了一个E,因为她是engaged(订了婚的)。
我用我的爱人象征exquisite(美妙),
我劝我的爱人从事elopement(私奔),
她的名字是Emily(爱弥丽),
她的住处在East(东方)。

译文二

我爱我的所爱,因为她长得实在招人爱。
我恨我的所爱,因为她不回报我的爱。
我带着她到挂着浮荡子招牌的一家,和她谈情说爱。
我请她看一出潜逃私奔,为的是我和她能长久你亲我爱。

---

① 当然,在实际翻译过程中,出于不同原因,译文的文本功能有时会与原文不同,比如《格列佛游记》属讽刺文学,原有感染(警世或劝世)功能,而在译文中通常当作表情文本对待。

她的名字叫爱弥丽,她的家住在爱仁里。

译文三

我爱我的爱人,因为她很迷人;

我恨我的爱人,因已许配他人;

她在我心中是美人,我带她私奔,以避开外人;

她名叫虞美人,是东方丽人。

译文四

吾爱吾爱,因伊可爱;

吾恨吾爱,因伊另有所爱;

吾视吾爱,神圣之爱;

吾携吾爱,私逃为爱;

吾爱名爱弥丽,吾东方之爱。

译文五

我爱我的那个"丽",可爱迷人有魅力;

我恨我的那个"丽",和他人结为伉俪;

她文雅大方又美丽,和我出逃去游历;

她芳名就叫爱弥丽,家住东方人俏丽。

原文是一首英文打油诗,全部运用嵌入句①,读起来朗朗上口。先从语言功能、意义及文本类型角度,对以上几个译文进行分析:译文一传递了原诗的文本信息(内容),但没有再现其艺术形式;译文二在一定程度上体现了原文的形式特征,但在内容方面与原诗存在出入;译文三在形式上更接近于原诗,所有的诗行都以同一个"人"字结尾,再现了原诗的艺术魅力,在信息内容上也较忠实原文,只是"虞美人"使用不当,存在文化偏差,容易给读者造成误解。译文四无论形式上还是内容上都基本传递了原诗信息,但在文体风格上与原诗反差较大。译文五不仅在形式上再现了原诗的特征,而且在"概念意义"的表达方面也比除

---

① 每一小句最后一个单词都是以同一字母 E 开头。

译文一之外的其他几个译本更忠实于原诗。

下面我们再看感染类文本——广告的翻译。广告语篇的意图明确,功能单一,主要通过宣传和推介,引起人们的消费欲望和购买行为,具有明显的指示功能。所以,这种类型的语篇一般以读者为中心,语篇在读者身上产生的效果和读者的反应是评判语篇功能实现与否的标准。基于此,翻译必须对原语篇进行适当调整,适应目的语语篇的要求和规范,以实现语篇的指示功能为宗旨。例如:

在四川西部,有一美妙去处。它背依岷山主峰雪宝顶,树木苍翠,花香袭人,鸟声婉转,流水潺潺。它就是松潘县的黄龙景区。

One of Sichuan's finest spots is Huanglong (Yellow Dragon), which lies in Songpan County, just beneath Xuebao, the main peak of the Minshan Mountain. Its lush green forest, filled with fragrant flowers, bubbling streams and songbirds, are rich in historical interest as well as natural beauty.

这段文字为旅游地介绍,主要目的自然是吸引游客。为实现译文与原文在指示功能的对应,译文按英语语篇的规范,对原文在语篇结构①上做了调整,但并没有改变原文的内容,保证了内容上基本忠实于原文。

翻译小贴士

1. 专业知识

翻译不仅仅是语言与文化的转换,还需要专业知识,如最新专业词汇、专业术语表达等,特别对于非文学翻译,更需要相关专业的知识储备。例如:

◀ 原文 ▶

蚂蚁科技集团上市暂缓

上交所11月3日晚间发布公告,暂缓金融科技巨头蚂蚁集团科创板上市。上交所在公告中称,蚂蚁集团报告所处的金融科技监管环境发生变化等重大事

---

① 原文反映了中国人的思维方式,先行描述,最后点明这一妙处究竟是哪里。而相应英语语篇往往开门见山,点明地点,再行描述。

项。该重大事项可能导致蚂蚁集团不符合发行上市条件或者信息披露要求。根据上交所有关规定,并征询保荐机构的意见,上交所决定蚂蚁集团暂缓上市。蚂蚁集团及保荐人应当依照规定作出公告。蚂蚁集团也曾申请在港交所上市。11月3日,蚂蚁集团宣布将暂缓港交所上市。蚂蚁集团原定于11月5日在上交所和港交所上市。

译文

Ant Group's IPO suspended

Fintech giant Ant Group's initial public offering on the STAR Market will be suspended, the Shanghai Stock Exchange announced on Tuesday night. The Shanghai bourse explained that Ant Group has reported major matters, such as the change in supervision environment concerning fintech, due to which Ant Group may not be able to meet listing requirements at the bourse or meet related information disclosure requirements. Based on the stock exchange's regulations and sponsors' opinions, Ant Group's IPO on the STAR Market will be postponed. The fintech company and its sponsors are required to make relevant announcements. Ant Group, which also filed for a dual listing on the Hong Kong Stock Exchange, announced on Tuesday it will suspend the listing on the Hong Kong bourse. Its debut on the two exchanges was scheduled for November 5.

作为一名从事经济管理或金融专业的译员,除了具备专业词汇储备,还应了解相关的专业知识。就该话题而言,还应了解股市指数(Stock Index)和证券交易所相关的知识。股市指数反映股价波动的整体走势,以供投资者参考。全球比较流行的指数有英国富时100指数、道琼斯工业平均指数、标准普尔(S&P)指数、纳斯达克指数、日经指数、摩根士丹利资本国际(MSCI)指数、恒生指数等。世界四大证券交易所是指东京证券交易所(Tokyo Stock Exchange)、伦敦证券交易所(London Stock Exchange)、纽约证券交易所(New York Stock Exchange, NYSE)、纳斯达克证券交易所(National Association of

Securities Dealers Automated Quotation,NASDAQ)。

2. 语言知识是进行翻译的最基本前提

(1)为什么美方将香港的所谓"港独"和黑色暴力分子美化为"英雄""斗士",而将美国国内抗议种族歧视的民众称为"暴徒"?

Why does the US refer to those "Hong Kong independence" and black-clad rioters as "heroes" and "fighters" but label its people protesting against racial discrimination as "thugs"?

汉译英时切忌望文生义,"黑色暴力分子"如果简单译为 black rioters,一定让人摸不着头脑,还会引起误会。这里的黑色暴力,是指暴力分子大多身着黑衣,所以译为 black-clad rioters。对比下面的表达:"扫黑除恶"(颜色的内涵意用法) crackdown on gang-related crimes。此外,还应注意 clad 的用法,如 leather-clad,身着皮衣的; snow-clad hills,白雪覆盖的山峦。

(2)为什么美方对香港警察克制文明执法横加指责,却对国内抗议者威胁开枪射击,甚至动用国民警卫队?

Why did the US have so many problems with the restrained and civilized way of law enforcement by the Hong Kong police but have no problem at all with threatening to shoot at and mobilizing the National Guard against its domestic protesters?

这句话的翻译运用了 have a problem with something 这一表达的两个变形,通过近似的形式,进一步突出了对比,简洁又有力。

have a problem with something

不喜欢某事或不赞同某事

have no problem with something

对某人来说不成问题,或同意某事

(3)美方的做法是最典型的"世界驰名双重标准"。这背后反映出的问题是值得人们深思和警惕的。

This double-standard way of behaving is so typical of the US. The reasons behind this are worth reflecting on and staying vigilant against.

第一句可以拆分为两层意思：美国的做法是典型的双重标准，美国的双重标准世界闻名。双重标准的形容词表达为 double-standard。译文对"典型的"和"世界闻名"进行了合译：so typical of the US。typical 最常见的意思是典型的、有代表性的。typical of somebody 常用来表达某人的行为是其一贯的作风。

If you say that something is typical of a person, situation, or thing, you are criticizing them or complaining about them and saying that they are just as bad or disappointing as you expected them to be.

如果将 typical of 用于人、情境或是事件，可以表达其恶劣程度、令人失望的程度不出所料。用 typical of 来表达"双重标准是美国的一贯作风，而且已众所周知"，是非常贴切的。"值得深思和警惕"可翻译为 worth reflecting on and staying vigilant against。

"值得做某事"可以表达为 worth doing something，需注意动词-ing 形式。

"深思"，即反思，可以译为 reflect on 或 reflect upon。保持警惕则可以译为 stay vigilant against，同时要注意介词搭配。

习题二

简答题

1. 简述中西翻译发展史。
2. 介绍西方的主要翻译理论及翻译理论家。

第三章 英汉思维对比与英汉句式特点

一、英汉思维方式差异

思维是人类大脑的一种功能。语言是展现思维的工具,思维依靠语言来进行表达。思维对语言起决定作用,语言是思维活动的一种结果。不同的思维方式决定了语言表达的不同形态。

(一)客体型思维与本体型思维

西方文化以物本为主体,以自然为本位,偏重于对自然客体的观察和研究,逐渐形成了客体型的思维方式,即把客观自然世界作为观察、分析、推理和研究的中心。与之相对,中国文化以人为主体,以人生为本位,富有人文意识和人文精神,本质上是一种人本文化。中国人本文化的长期积淀,形成了本体型的思维方式,即以人为中心来观察、分析、推理和研究事物的思维方式。

语言是思维表达的载体,不同的思维方式必然会体现在不同的语言上。客体型和本体型两种不同的思维方式反映在语言形态上,其标志之一就是在描述事物和阐述事理的过程中,特别是当涉及行为主体时,英语习惯于用表示非生物的名词(inanimate)作主语,而汉语则习惯于用表示人或生物的词(animate)作主语。请看下边的例子:

1. 英译汉

The past thirties saw much progress in China.

中国在过去三十年里取得了很大的进步。

That night sleep eluded him.

那天夜里他没睡好。

From the moment we stepped into the People's Republic of China, care and kindness surrounded us on every side.

一踏上中华人民共和国国土,我们就受到各方面的关怀和照顾。

Anger began to take entire possession of him at the sight of that boy.

他一看到那个孩子,气就不打一处来。

Later success favored me.

我后来就一帆风顺了。

The loss of her dog made Mary very dull for several days.

狗走丢以后,玛丽郁闷了好几天。

2. 汉译英

我一直头疼。

The headache attacked me on and on.

我从家到学校步行需要20分钟。

A twenty-minute walk brought me to the school.

钟表显示4点了。

The clock says it's 4 o'clock.

(二)分析型思维与综合型思维

1. 分析型思维和综合型思维的内涵

一般可以将人类的思维方式分为两种基本类型:分析型思维和综合型思维。分析型思维,顾名思义,是把事物的整体分解为许多部分,其优点是能比较深入地观察事物的本质,其缺点是过于关注细节,容易忽略整体。综合型思维是把事物的各部分关联起来,作为一个不可分割的整体去思考。综合型思维强调事物的普遍联系,既关注部分,更强调整体。分析型思维和综合型思维并不是完全分割的,是东西方民族共有的思维方式,但由于受到各自传统文化的长期影响,最终形成了"西方重分析,东方重综合"的思维习惯。

西方哲学的分析型思维表现为,将自然作为人类的认知对象,将认识宇宙、征服自然视为人类的根本任务;人和自然永远处于一种矛盾对立关系。当然,在近代科学的发展过程中,也有综合性思维和综合法的融入,但主体是分析法。医学上的解剖学、神经学、文化学中的个人主义等就是典型分析型思维和分析法的产物。

中国哲学的综合型思维表现为人与人、人与自然、世间万物的和谐统一,将"人与天地万物为一体""天人合一"作为最高境界,倾向于从总体上观察事物的特征,对事物从整体观点进行综合研究。传统中医的望、闻、问、切,文化学中的集体主义、和谐社会都是综合型思维和综合法的产物。

2. 分析型思维与综合型思维对语言形式的不同影响

分析型与综合型两种不同的思维方式,对英汉两种语言的结构形态造成了一定的影响:以分析型思维方式为典型代表语言的英语为例,具有明显的词形变化,多样的语法形式,灵活的语序结构;作为综合型思维方式的典型代表语言的汉语,并无词形的变化,语法形式主要依靠词汇手段表达,主要依据语义逻辑和动作发生的时间先后决定词语和分句的排列顺序。汉语以妙言为贵,讲究希言,强调知识真谛是非语言所能传达和交流的。

英汉两种语言在表达形式上具体体现为:焦点式与散点式,树型与线性句子结构。从马致远的诗歌《天净沙》的原文和译文,可以非常明显地看出上述差异。

枯藤,老树,昏鸦。

小桥,流水,人家。

古道,西风,瘦马。

夕阳西下,

断肠人在天涯。

Crows hovering over rugged old trees wreathed

With rotten vine —the day is about done.

Yonder is a tiny bridge over a sparkling stream,

And on the far bank, a pretty little village.

But the traveler has to go on down this ancient road, the west wind

Moaning, his bone horse groaning, trudging towards the sinking sun,

Farther and farther away from home.

请再看下边的例句：

(1) As soon as we set foot on Chinese soil, we thrilled with joy.

我们一踏上中国的土地,就觉得欢欣鼓舞。

(2) The technical characteristics of the commodity are such that it would be suited to action with a view, if judged appropriate, to sustaining or improving the terms of trade of developing countries.

这个商品的技术特点使它适于采取旨在维护或改进发展中国家贸易条件的行动。

(三) 汉英心理文化对比

首先,中国人的综合型思维表现为直觉性与具象性,语言上则表现为汉语的形象性;西方人的分析型思维表现为理性与逻辑性,语言上则表现为英语的功能性。

汉字具有象形性：人——man,山——mountain

汉字词语具有直观性：连衣裙——overall skirt,(哄小孩子的)橡皮奶头——comforter,回形针——paper clip

此外,汉语的直观性还表现在用具体比喻抽象,如：势如破竹——with irresistible force;如日中天——at the apex of one's power;失之交臂——just miss the opportunity (or person)。

汉语丰富的量词是形象化体现,如：一杆枪——a gun;一堵墙——a wall;一口井——a well。

其次,中国人重整体,西方人重个体,表现在语言上则形成了如下不同的特征。

第一,汉语词义一般比较笼统、模糊,英语词义一般比较具体、准确。[①]

车来了。

Here comes the bus /car/truck / taxi.

吃饭了吗?

Have you had you breakfast /lunch/supper/dinner?

第二,汉语词类的界定比较模糊,英语词类界定比较具体,如红色(red)、脸红了(flush);此外,汉语的句子成分的功能也不如英语明晰,如,星期天天气晴朗,英语则要表示为 Sunday is fine. /It is fine on Sunday.

第三,汉语强调篇章的整体结构,注重意合;英语强调句式结构的严谨,注重形合。

选自《声声慢》(李清照)

寻寻觅觅,

冷冷清清,

凄凄惨惨戚戚。

Tune: "Slow, Slow Tune"

I look for what I miss

I know not what it is

I felt so sad and so drear

So lonely without cheer.

(许渊冲 译)

第四,汉语中会频繁使用对仗修辞和四字词组,而英语则没有这些特征。

天涯海角

at the end of the earth

[①] 但是,任何事情都不是绝对的。因制度文化的影响,汉语中对亲戚的称呼细微之至,英语中的 cousin 一词便可对应汉语中的堂(兄、弟、姐、妹)、表(兄、弟、姐、妹);表示动作的英文词 carry 可对应汉语中的搬、运、送、提、拎、挑、担、抬、背、扛、抱、端、举、夹、捧等不同的词汇;表示粮食作物的英文词 rice,既可以指汉语中的稻子、谷子、稻种等粮食作物,还可以指食用的米。同样,英语中也有类似的情况,汉语中的"医生"一词可以对应英语中的 doctor(医生的统称)、physician(内科医生)、surgeon(外科医生)、medical man(医生)、intern(住院实习医生)、gynecologist(妇科医生)、pediatrician(儿科医生)等不同词汇。实质上,这仍然是文化差别的体现。

四通八达

extended in all directions

十拿九稳

practically certain

年富力强

in the prime of life

第五,英语一般先讲主题后说明细节,汉语一般先阐述细节后归纳主题。

Please turn off the light when you leave the room.

离开房间时请关灯。

The crops failed because the weather was dry.

因为气候干旱,作物歉收。

第六,英语多用带有动词性质的名词性短语,汉语则一般用简洁的句子。

In the absence of mathematics science would not exist.

如果没有数学,就不会有科学。

The mastery of English is not easy and requires painstaking efforts.

英语不是随便就可以学好的,非下苦功不可。

No violation of this principle can be tolerated.

绝不能违反这个原则。

二、英汉语言的主要特点

(一) 英汉两种语言属于不同语系

英语属于印欧语系(Indo-European Family),是拼音(alphabetic)文字,形态变化丰富,词形上的变化同时也表示意义的变化。它可以通过词的派生表示词性或词义的变化,可以通过名词的单复数形式表示数量及人称的变化,还可以通过动词的不同时态表示时间的变化,通过语态表示动作主体和客体的变化,以及不同的人称代词表示格的变化等。所以,英语是一种具有形合特征的语言。

汉语属汉藏语系(Sino-Tibetan Family),汉语文字是表意文字(ideographic),

用非语音化的词序手段表达意义,这是与形态变化相对立的另一种方式。汉语在表示动作和事物关系上完全依赖意念和感觉。所以,汉语是一种具有意合特征的语言。

英语是综合性①(synthetic)语言,汉语是黏着性(agglutinative)语言。综合性语言②的主要特征是名词、代词、形容词、冠词和动词有性、数、格的变化(此外,动词还有时态的变化);黏着性语言的特点是词的组合主要依靠词素的黏着。汉字虽然形态匮乏,但文字本身意义丰富,一字多意、同音异义,使用起来灵活方便,词的次序、位置稍有变化,就产生新的意义,包括语法意义。例如,胡子(beard)一词,通过黏着其他一些词汇,便可形成具有新意的一些词汇,"络腮胡子"(whisker)、"山羊胡"(chin tuft)、"八字胡"(moustache/handle bars)等。

(二)英汉两种语言在词法、句法结构上的主要区别

基本上来讲,英语是注重逻辑分析的一种形合(hypotaxis)语言(即英语以形态表意),而汉语则是注重综合整体的一种意合(parataxis)语言(即汉语以词汇表意)。两者之间的基本区别表现在词法和句法方面。

1. 词法区别

(1)名词的数

There is a sharp difference between the two twins.

这对双胞胎存在一种显著的差别。

There exist some differences between the two languages.

这两种语言之间有着许多显著的不同。

(2)名词(代词)的格

I don't need your car, and I just hope to take back mine.

我不需要你的车,我只想要回我自己的车。

That is the table's leg, don't throw it away.

那是桌子腿,别扔了它。

---

① 这里的综合性语言不同于综合型思维,是两个完全不同的概念。
② 综合性语言分为全综合性语言和部分综合性语言,与印欧语系中其他语言不同,英语为部分综合性语言,因为英语的名词、形容词、冠词和部分情态助动词没有性、数、格的变化。

(3) 动词的时态

a. 一般现在时(do/does；is/am/are)

He always helps others.

他总是帮助别人。

b. 现在进行时(am/is/are doing)

He is listening to the music now.

他正在听音乐。

c. 现在完成时(have/has done)

Great as Newton was, many of his ideas have been challenged today and are being modified by the work of scientists of our time.

虽然牛顿是个伟大的人物,但他的许多见解直到今天还在受到质疑,并且被现代科学家的研究所修正。

d. 现在完成进行时(have/has been doing)

We have been working on this project for over a month now.

到目前为止,我们一直在处理那个项目,已经花了一个多月时间了。

e. 一般过去时(did；was/were)

They were good friends and there is no friendship left between them any more.

他们过去是挚友,但是现在已经没有友情可言了。

f. 过去完成时(had done)

Until then, his family hadn't heard from him for six months.

到那时为止,他家里已经有六个月没得到他的消息了。

g. 过去将来时(would do)

I said on Thursday I should see my friend the next day.

我星期四说我将于第二天拜访我的朋友。

h. 过去进行时(was/were doing)

I was travelling in London last summer vacation.

去年暑假我在伦敦旅行。

i. 一般将来时

My mother is coming to visit me next week.

我妈妈下周将来看我。

j. 将来进行时(will/shall be doing)

After you take the medicine, you will be feeling much better.

服药之后,你会感觉好得多。

k. 将来完成时(will have done)

The conference will have lasted a full week by the time it ends.

会议从开始到结束将持续整整一个星期。

(4)动词的语态:

Anywhere he went to make a speech, he was welcomed by the audiences.

无论他到哪里去演讲,他都会受到热烈的欢迎。

In every game, they were bested by the visitors.

每场比赛他们都败在客队的手下。

2. 句法区别

英语句法结构重逻辑分析而轻感官意合,表达意义完整精确,属于高度形式化和逻辑化的语言。英语句法结构严谨,一般以动词为核心,句子之间、句中的各部分都需要用表示逻辑关系的词汇进行连接,强调句子成分之间的主次、从属、修饰、并列、对比等逻辑关系。

一般来讲,英语句子意义完整,形式齐全,各语法功能和组成部分很少省略,特别是类似主语等关键的部分。一些表面上的无主句也必须加上一个逻辑主语,在语法上构成一个完整的句子。这是形合语言所具有的特征。

(1) It is a fine day today.

(2) It is ten miles to school from my home.

(3) It cost ten dollars to get it.

与词法结构类似,汉语的句法结构也同样注重意合(即个人的主观感受和心领神会)。句中各成分之间很少用连接词来表示相互间的关系,而是更多地依靠语义的贯通和语境的映衬。因而汉语句子具有简洁灵活、充满隐喻的语言特征。

与英语整个句子以谓语动词为中心的句子结构不同,汉语句子虽然在结构上也多以主、谓、宾顺序排列,但它主要以词序或语义为中心,无论句子是否完备,不关注语言形式和语法功能上的完整性。因此,汉语中无主句和省略句较多,主动语态用得多,词句追求平衡与对称,连接词用得少。例如:"你不去,我去。"因为是一种意合法,所以这句话本身存在一些歧义。这句话可以理解为假设关系,意即"如果你不去,我去";也可以理解为因果关系,意即"因为你不去,所以我去";还可以理解为转折关系,意即"(虽然)你不去,(但是)我去";或者理解为让步关系,"(即使)你不去,我(也)去"。再例如,如果将"再跑,就毙了你。"这句话译为英语,只有进行必要的成分添加,才符合英语的表达习惯和要求,译为"I will shoot you if you try to escape again."，if 引导的从句即为根据原语意义和英语语法要求进行的必要成分添加。

鉴于英汉语言的差别,在翻译过程中,译者要处理好英汉两种语言在转换时所遇到的一些差异,还应注意处理好因英汉思维方式、文化传统和语言表达等方面的不同引起的矛盾和困难。这些问题均与思维方式和语言表达紧密相关,主要表现在描述角度和表达形式方面。句式翻译既涉及用词问题,又与句法的特征密切相关。

翻译小贴士

1. 英汉语言对比

英汉语言之间存在很大差异,必须对此有所认识,才能避免翻译过程中逐字翻译(word for word translation)。四字句是中文的主要特征之一,四字句对仗工整、简洁凝练、表意深刻、颇具美感。但英语中没有四字句这种语言表达,所以在中译英时,译者不必苛求四字句形式上的对等,而应关注意义和信息的传递和再现。如:

◀ 原文 ▶

我们要以更大的力度、更实的措施保障和改善民生,加强和创新社会治理,坚决打赢脱贫攻坚战，促进社会公平正义，在幼有所育、学有所教、劳有所得、病有所医、老有所养、住有所居、弱有所扶上不断取得新进展，让实现人民共同富裕的目标在广大人民现实生活中更加充分地展示出来。

译文

We will devote more energy and take more concrete measures in ensuring and improving people's living standards, strengthening and developing new approaches to social governance, resolutely winning the battle against poverty, promoting social fairness and justice, making steady progress in ensuring people's access to childcare, education, employment, medical services, elderly care, housing, and social assistance, so as to better demonstrate the realization of common prosperity for everyone in people's real life.

很显然，译文并没有在形式上对原文中的四字句进行完全的移植和等值的再现，但在信息传递上实现了等价效果。而且英文表达精炼到位，能够让英语读者感受到汉语四字句所表达原文内容的艺术效果。

2. 语言的特殊性以及双语转换的困境：歧义结构的翻译

歧义是人类语言的一个普遍现象。随着跨文化交际的不断发展和深入，这一现象正越来越强烈地引起人们的关注。人们从语音、语法和语义等方面进行了较为系统的研究。但由于语言歧义在不同的语言文化中的表现形式及其文化内涵不尽相同，因此在翻译过程中总会产生一些障碍。比如：

(1) I went to the bank.

(2) 老张有个女儿，很骄傲。

(3) — How is the bread made?

　　— Take some flour and…

　　— Where do I pick the flower? In the garden or in the hedges?

句(1)中的 bank 是个多义词。此句有两种理解："我去银行了。"和"我到大堤上去了。"句(2)是个复句，在理解上也有两种可能：一指老张骄傲，二指老张女儿骄傲。而句(3)中的 flour 和 flower 是同音异义。这样的歧义结构虽然较为简单,但在翻译中稍有不慎就会造成一些误解或误译。

再如:

(4) Seven days without water make one weak (week).

(5)生活的海里起过小小的波浪,如今似乎又平静下去。一切跟往常一样,一切似乎都是外甥打灯笼,照舅(旧)。

(6) Are you engaged? ("忙"和"订婚"两个意思)

(7)请他送两本书给图书馆。(递送和赠送)

(8) Flying planes can be dangerous. (Flying planes 既可是动宾结构,也可是限定性结构)

(9)我们不需要进口设备。("进口设备"可做动宾结构,也可做偏正结构)

(10) They saw her duck. (既可把 her duck 看作宾语,又可看作宾语补足语)

(11) He did not beat her wife because she cried. (否定词 not 的辖域不清,即不能确定否定的是主句的动词,还是后面的原因从句)

(12) I found her a secretary. ("给她找了个秘书"或者"发现她本人就是个秘书")

(13) They ordered the police to stop drinking after midnight. ("他们叫警察自己午夜后停止喝酒"或者"他们叫警察阻止午夜后酗酒""午夜后他们叫警察停止喝酒""他们叫警察午夜后即停止喝酒")

(14) ——Name and title, please?

——John Smith, Associate Editor and Professor. ("副主编兼副教授"还是"副主编兼教授"? 可能由于说话人故意不愿说出实情,以期抬高身价)

(15)他怎么样了? 他进去了。("进去了"可指进入某一范围或场所,也可表达被捕之意)

(16) more realistic novels ("更多的现实主义小说"或"更为现实的小说")

(17) a dancing teacher ("a teacher who is dancing" or "a teacher who teaches dancing")

(18) The Clerk (entering): Are you engaged?

Augustus: What business is that of yours? However,…

The Clerk: That isn't what I mean. Can you see a female?

Augustus: Of course I can see a female as easily as a male. Do you suppose I'm blind?

The Clerk: You don't seem to follow me somehow. There's a female downstairs…She wants to know can you see her if I let her up.

Augustus: Oh, I am disengaged…

职员：(进来)你有事吗？

奥古斯都：与你有什么相干？不过……

职员：我不是说订婚的事。你能会见一个女士吗？

奥古斯都：当然可以，我看见一个女人就像看见一个男人那样容易。你以为我是一个瞎子吗？

职员：你怎么没弄懂我的意思。楼下有一位女士……如果我让她上来，你能否接见她。

奥古斯都：啊，你的意思是，我现在是不是有空。……

 习题三

简答题

1. 简述中西思维的差异及对翻译的影响。
2. 简述英汉语言的特点及不同。

第四章 英汉互译语言转换中的辩证思维

中西两种思维方式和汉英两种语言之间既有相似之处,也有相异之点,两者关注不同,重点有别。因此,在翻译过程中,译者应注意处理好因思维方式和语言表达的差异而造成的语言转换的问题,主要表现在以下四个方面,即:动态表达与静态表达之间的转换;概略化表达与具体化表达之间的转换;有生命主语句与无生命主语句之间的转换;形合表达与意合表达之间的转换。

一、动态表达与静态表达之间的转换

在表述某一动作概念时,既可选择静态的表述方式(在英语中多以"be/系动词+名词/形容词/副词/介词短语"句式为主,在汉语中多以"是+名词/形容词"句式为主),也可选择动态的表述方式("动作动词+其他句子成分"句式)。一般来讲,英语注重静态描写,在表述动作意义时往往倾向于选择静态的表述方式;而汉语注重动态描写,在表述动作意义时往往倾向于选择动态的表述方式。因此,在进行英汉语言转换过程中,应该注意相应的动态与静态调整。

(一)化静为动

1. "be+动词的同源名词"句式

(1) In the past few years he was passive witness to the decrease of prices of our raw materials and the increase of the prices of manufactured goods.

在过去的几年中,他坐视了原料价格下跌和制成品价格的上涨。

(2) Mary is a lover of popular music.

玛莉喜欢流行音乐。

(3) She is the murderer of her husband and is to be executed for her crime.

她谋杀了自己的丈夫,因此将会被处决。

(4) He has been the ruler of this country for over thirty years.

他统治这个国家长达30多年。

2. "be+非动词同源名词"句式

(1) Don't talk nonsense here. They're all ears.

别在这里胡说八道,他们可都贴着耳朵听着呢。

(2) We were all eyes as the box was opened.

盒子打开时,我们目不转睛地看着。

(3) It was only my capacity for hard work that saved me from early dismissal.

要不是我能干重活,早就给辞退了。

3. "be+动词的同源形容词"句式

(1) All the wisdom of the ages, all the stories that have delighted mankind for centuries, are easily and cheaply available to all of us within the covers of books.

古往今来的人类智慧结晶、数百年来一直为人津津乐道的故事,这些东西我们都可以轻而易举地从书本中得到,而且也无需过多的花费。

(2) He was always critical of our improper behaviors when worked in that corporation.

在那个企业上班时,他总是批评我们的一些不合规行为。

4. "be +非动词同源形容词"句式

(1) His addiction to computer games has been a very anxious business for his parents.

他沉溺于电脑游戏,这件事情令父母十分担忧。

(2) Buffet was fanatical about following in Graham's footsteps, even in his investing.

巴菲特很崇拜格雷厄姆,对他的投资策略亦步亦趋。

(3) Our nation will be poverty-free in the recent future.

我们的国家不久将会摆脱贫困。

5. "be+副词"句式

(1) The delegation is here to see us.

代表团来这儿看我们来啦。

(2) That book will be out pretty soon.

那本书不久就要出版了。

(3) She'll be down in a little while.

她一会儿就下楼来。

6. "be+介词短语"句式

(1) The Reagan Administration is all for a big clampdown on trade with Moscow.

里根政府极力主张取缔与莫斯科的贸易。

(2) The court judgment is against Roy on the ground that the protection of religious freedom does not restrict the way the United States government chooses to run its affairs.

法庭判决否定了罗伊的要求,理由是对宗教信仰自由的保护不能限制美国政府对其内部事务的运作方式做出决断。

(3) Tom used to be into sports, but now he is into books.

以前汤姆喜欢体育运动,可是现在他却喜欢读书。

7. "be+过去分词"句式

(1) His eyes were fixed upon Della.

他的眼睛盯着德拉。

(2) He was planted squarely on his feet, with little fear on his face.

他两脚像生了根似的四平八稳地站立着,毫无恐惧之色。

(3) The academic team was well equipped for carrying out the scientific research project.

学术团队为执行这项科研任务做好了充分准备。

(二)化动为静

(1) Deep in the forest sits a luxurious royal palace.

森林深处是一座豪华的皇宫。

(2) They disagree with each other for thought differently.

他们有分歧是因为他们的想法不同。

(3) The bride and bridegroom might appreciate your presence in their wedding ceremony.

新郎新娘会为你能出席他们的婚礼盛典而感到荣幸。

二、概略化表达与具体化表达之间的转换

概略化和具体化是两种不同的语言表达方式。在英汉两种语言中,某些意义或概念既可用概略化的手法来表达,也可用具体化的手法来表达。但由于英汉两种语言的差异,在英汉语言进行转换时,需要根据具体情况进行表达方式上的调整,以此使译文达到准确、通顺和便于阅读。

(一)概略化翻译

概略化的翻译方法和表达方式可分为具体词义概略化和个别概念概略化两种情况。

1. 具体词义概略化

所谓词义概略化,是指在一种语言中,某些字面意义较明确具体的词语,转化为另外一种语言时,可以采用意义较抽象、概括的词语来表达。例如:

(1) For decades those fuels such as coal and oil have been regarded as the chief energy sources used to transport men from place to place.

几十年来,煤和石油等燃料一直被认为是交通运输的重要能源。(transport...place的字面意义是"将……从一个地方运输到另一个地方")。

（2）We attach so much importance to education because it gives full scope to the flowering of the human personality.

我们如此重视教育是因为它能充分培养人健全的品格和优秀的品质。(flowering 的字面意义为"发育")

（3）What count most in my life are health, heart and home and happiness, with nothing to do with wealth.

在我生命中,最重要的是健康、爱情和家庭,都与金钱毫无关系。

2. 个别概念概略化

例如:

（1）The economic problems to be dealt with are not our only problems. In my opinion, we still have political, cultural and social problems as well.

经济问题并不是亟待解决的全部问题。我们还有政治问题、文化问题和社会问题。(only 原意为"唯一的")

（2）Were it left to me to decide whether we should have a government without newspapers or newspapers without government, I should not hesitate a moment to prefer the latter.

如果让我决定我们要一个没有言论自由的政府还是要一个只有言论自由而无政府的国家,我会毫不犹豫选择后者。(newspaper 原意为"报纸")

（3）Mike is a clean-desk man, so it does not take him long to prepare for the trip.

麦克是一个办事有条不紊的人,因此,他并没花多长时间就做好了出行准备。(clean-desk 原意为"整洁的桌子")

(二) 具体化翻译

与概略化相对,具体化是指在翻译过程中,采用目的语中意义较为具体、明确的词语来翻译原文中意义较为抽象、概括的词语。具体化的翻译方法和表达方式分为以下几种情况。

1. 抽象概念具体化

对于在原语中含义较抽象的词语所表达的某一具体概念,应根据上下文和

具体语境,在译文中选用意义较为具体、明确的词语进行翻译。例如:

(1) Without tools man is nothing, with tools he is all.

人没有工具就一事无成,而有了工具就无所不能。(nothing 的字面意义为"无关紧要的人或物";all 的字面意义为"全体")

(2) The beauty of laser is that it can do machining without ever physically touching the material.

激光的妙处就在于它能进行机械加工而不必实际接触所加工的材料。(beauty 的字面意义为"美丽")

(3) The effectiveness and efficiency explains the preference for artificial intelligence in the world today.

效率和效益是当今世界人工智能被优先采用的原因。(preference 的原意为"偏爱")

(4) He attempted to make bribery his entre to the new administration.

他试图以贿赂作为他进入新政府的敲门砖。(entree 的字面意义为"进入")

2. 概括或笼统概念具体化

(1) The Forbidden City is a must for most foreign visitors to Beijing.

对于到北京游览的外国人来说,故宫是必不可少的参观项目。(must 字面意义为"必须")

(2) The Gestapo learned they were there, and sent the ones they found to Auschwitz, and the headmaster to a work camp.

盖世太保探知他们的下落,把搜出来的送往奥斯维辛集中营,把校长发配劳动营。(learn 字面意义为"弄明白",find 字面意义为"发现",send 的字面意义为"带到,送")

(3) He send me a surprise on my birthday.

我生日那天,他给了我一件意想不到的礼物。(surprise 的原意为"吃惊")

3. 广义词义具体化

(1) As a member of Communist Party of China, I have been well prepared to face various troubles and difficulties and devoted to the holy

and great cause at any time.

作为一名中国共产党员,我已经有了面对各种困难的充分准备,并随时准备献身于这项崇高而伟大的事业。

(2) She was a shapely well-preserved woman of forty-five.

她已是四十五岁的女人了,但身材保养得很匀称。

(3) Since liberation, the Great Wall has been well protected by governments of all level and people of various fields.

解放以来,长城已经得到各级政府和各界人士的妥善保护。

(4) In chemistry class, the teacher asks the students to shake the bottle well in order to have a good observation of the chemical reaction in it.

化学课上,教师要求学生们反复摇晃瓶子,以便更好地观察到瓶中所产生的化学反应。

(5) Check your answers well before you hand in your test paper.

交卷之前要仔细检查答案。

4. 其他情况具体化

(1) This products were in commercial use at the end of this decade (in the 1980s).

这款产品在 20 世纪 80 年代末就投入商业运行了。(this decade 具体译为 20 世纪 80 年代)

(2) You must remember that we are here to serve the people that are building a New Society. The bureaucracy has this rare opportunity to prove its worth to build a progressive nation.

你们必须记住,我们是为人民服务的,我们正在建设一个新社会,这是全体政府官员显示才干、建设一个进步国家的绝好机会。

(3) There is a definite link between smoking and heart disease and lung cancer. But this doesn't make you too uncomfortable because you are in good company.

抽烟和心脏病以及肺癌的确有联系。但这并不会使你感到多么地不安或焦虑,因为和你一样抽烟的人很多。

(4) No reproduction is granted by implication or otherwise of this information.

本资料不得私下或公开翻印。(or otherwise 具体译为"公开",以便与 by implication 相对应)

(5) You must know it, if you know anything at all.

如果你当真知情的话,就该知道这回事。

(6) His ego was of suitably gigantic proportions.

他心中的"我"字也很大,但无伤大雅。

他自尊心很强(他相当自负/自我意识很强),但并无大碍。

三、有生命主语句与无生命主语句之间的转换

一般来讲,英语多用非人称词类作主语,而汉语多用人称代词作主语。根据动作的执行者有无生命进行分类,动词可以划分为有灵动词(verbs for animate objects)和无灵动词(verbs for inanimate objects)。在英汉两种语言中,对于有灵动词和无灵动词的使用是有区别的。在英语中,一个动词往往既可用作有灵动词,又可用作无灵动词,两者没有明确的区别;而汉语则不同,一个动词或者是有灵动词,或者是无灵动词,不能既可用作有灵动词,同时还可用作无灵动词(当然,也有特殊情况,如修辞中的拟人化表达)。例如:

(1) My conscience told me that I deserved no extraordinary politeness. (无灵动词)

凭良心讲,你待我礼貌有加,我却受之有愧。

(2) Please tell me what happened to him yesterday. (有灵动词)

请告诉我昨天他发生了什么事情。

正是由于英汉语言的这种差异,在进行翻译时,需要对有灵动词和无灵动词、有生命主语句和无生命主语句进行必要的转换。要弄清英语中有无生命主语句的特点及类型,掌握对其进行翻译的方法。

(一)无生命主语句的类型

1. 以时间、地点等名词做主语的句子

(1) The May Fourth Movement produced many famous thinkers and influential works in various circles.

五四运动中,许多著名思想家脱颖而出,有影响力的著作纷纷问世。

(2) No city on American soil had known such destruction.

在美国国土上,没有一座城市曾经遭受过如此严重的破坏。

2. 具有行为和动作意义的名词做主语

(1) The same blend of humor and charm, toughness and candor, topped by no small amount of guile, characterizes his style with Congressmen and foreign leaders.

他对付国会议员和外国领导人也是用的这一套:风趣和魅力齐用,强硬与坦率并举,外加千狡百诈。

(2) The application of this new method will greatly decrease the percentage of defective products.

人们应用新方法可以大大地降低废品率。

(3) A transfer of attitude (of suspicion) had already taken place from the labor to the other columns.

人们对(该报纸的)劳工版面的不信任感已经波及其他的栏目。

3. 表示生理状态、心理状态、某种遭遇的名词做主语

(1) Her illness prevented her from attending her daughter's graduation ceremony.

她因病未能参加女儿的毕业典礼。

(2) Bitterness fed on the gentleman who devoted his whole life to the welfare of the disabled.

这位一心致力于残疾人事业的绅士自己却饱尝辛酸。

(3) Astonishment, apprehension and even horror oppressed her.

她又惊又怕,加上几分担忧,心情十分抑郁。

(4) Happiness swept over her face.

她的脸上洋溢着幸福。

4. 表示其他事物的名词做主语

(1) The event asks our close concern.

这个事件需要我们密切关注。

(2) This method runs into two difficulties.

采用这种方法会碰到两个困难。

(3) Her reputation of a hero outlives her.

她虽已牺牲,但她作为英雄的声望将永垂不朽。

(4) Despite the great age gap between them, an instant affinity asserted itself.

他们两人尽管年龄相差悬殊,但是情投意合,一见如故。

(二) 无生命主语句的译法

翻译英语中的无生命主语句,关键在于处理好主语的选择。为了使译文具有可读性,在进行无生命主语句和有生命主语句转换时,往往需要对原文的无生命主语句进行切分并调整。在此过程中,有时需要采用增词的翻译方法,有时需要采用减词的翻译方法,有时需要混合使用几种翻译方法。一般有如下几种译法。

1. 将无生命主语转换为有生命主语

将原有句子进行切分,必要时可将主语译成分句。

(1) The expression "My God" always creep into the actor's speeches.

那位演员进行演讲时,总会不经意地冒出 My God 这种表达。

(2) Absence and distance make the overseas student increasingly fond of their motherland.

留学生们背井离乡,远居国外,这使得他们愈发热爱自己的祖国。

(3) My total ignorance of the connection must plead my apology.

恕我孤陋寡闻,对此关系一无所知。

(4) Jane's kind and gentle nature could not but revolt at her sister's callous behavior.

珍妮是个温和善良的好人,对她妹妹这种冷酷无情的行为,实在看不惯。

2. 改变谓语或将无生命主语具体化

保留无生命主语,改变与之搭配的谓语动词,使谓语动词与无生命主语协调一致;或者改变主语,将无生命主语转换成表示具体事物的主语,必要时切分句子,将主语译成分句或者单句,或者调整句子的语序。

(1) Her mouth smiled to itself, with her eyes watching him gently and secretly.

她嘴边绽出一丝笑容,双目温柔而又神秘地注视着他。

(2) Give me a hand and my arms and legs go to sleep.

帮个忙,我的手脚不听使唤了。

(3) His countenance rather gained in austerity.

他的神情越发威严起来。

(4) The thought of going abroad to further his post-graduate studies never deserted him.

去国外攻读研究生的想法始终在他心头萦绕。

(5) Its gleaming sands and backdrop of pine woods and distant hills give it a pleasant and restful atmosphere.

这儿沙滩耀眼,松林掩映,远山连绵,自有着一种让人心旷神怡的感觉。

3. 将英语的无生命主语转换成汉语的状语

(1) The October 1st, 1949 saw the founding of the People's Republic of China.

1949年10月1日,中华人民共和国成立了。

(2) The news that greeted us in Shanghai, and our visits later to various places turned anxiety into joy.

通过在上海得到的消息以及随后在各地的访问,我们的忧虑已化为喜悦。

(3) Investigation has led us to the conclusion that the price will be on

the rise.

经过调查,我们得出结论,价格还会上涨。

(4) April is to take President to China for a visit.

四月,总统将前往中国进行访问。

4. 将英语的无生命主语转化为汉语的无主语句

(1) In that situation Pakistan defies any easy classification.

在那种情形下,很难把巴基斯坦简单地列入哪个类型中。

(2) The heat makes me sweat like a pig.

热得我大汗淋漓。

(3) The shouts made the whole neighborhood unrest.

吵得整个街区都不得安宁。

(4) This medicine will make you feel better.

吃了药你会舒服些。

5. 将无生命主语转化成汉语复句

(1) The publisher's rejection of his manuscript depressed him.

由于出版商拒绝接受他的手稿,他的情绪一落千丈。

(2) The arrest of the flood-waters saved many homes.

将洪水拦住后,许多家庭得救了。

(3) The loss of her daughter made Mrs. Bennet very dull for several days.

女儿走了以后,班纳特太太郁闷了好几天。

(4) His saying that he was sorry altered the case.

他表示歉意后,情况就改变了。

6. 将英语中的无生命主语转化成汉语的外位成分

把无生命主语从原句拆出来,转化成目的语的外位成分①进行翻译。这样处理可以避免汉语的主语太长,使译文结构紧凑、逻辑清晰、表达晓畅、可读性强。

---

① 汉语句子的主语可用一个代词(如"这")来替代前面或者后面的意义表述,即为外位成分。

(1) The kaleidoscope of shifting interests of the parties in the international trade made it impossible to sort out the "winners" and "losers".

国际贸易中,各方利益变化不定,好像万花筒似的,这就使人难以分辨出究竟谁是"胜者",谁是"输家"。

(2) The traditional pattern of classroom experience at the college level brings the professor and a group of 20 to 30 students together for a 45-to-50-minute class session two or three times a week.

由一位教授和二三十名学生每周会晤两三次,每次授课时间45至50分钟,这是大学课堂教学的传统模式。

7. 采用使役句式

(1) He paid an unexpected visit; it led to the change of my whole plan.

他的突然来访使我的整个计划发生了改变。

(2) Continuous rain keeps us inside the apartment with nothing to do.

阴雨连绵使我们只好待在家里,无事可做。

(3) Her stupidity began to bother me.

她笨得让我开始心烦。

(4) The snake frightened the young lady.

那条蛇把年轻女士吓坏了。

8. 将无生命主语拟人化

将无生命主语拟人化时要注意具体的语体和语境,不能滥用,以免造成不适宜的表达效果。

(1) Cancer deprived the girl of her life.

癌症夺走了这个女孩的生命。

(2) The country is in support of her pursuit of international academic position.

全国上下都支持她争取国际学术地位。

(3) Fortune favors those who are well prepared.

时运偏爱有准备的人。

(4) His heart did whisper that he had never given it up.

他确实在心里嘀咕:他从来没有放弃过。

四、形合表达与意合表达之间的转换

所谓形合表达法(hypotaxis),就是通过形合手段来显示句子内部成分之间、句子与句子以及句群中各部分间的相互关系。例如:He stayed at home because it was raining outside. 因为外面下着雨,他待在家里。而所谓的意合表达法(parataxis),则指依靠上下文或逻辑意义上的关联,来显示句子内部成分之间、句子与句子以及句群中各部分间的相互关系。例如:The door was open, so he walked in. 门开着,他走了进来。虽然英汉两种语言属不同的语系,但在句法上,二者均有形合和意合的表达方式。不过一般来看,英语句法更注重形合,而汉语句法更注重意合。正是由于两种语言存在句法上的这种差别,在进行翻译时,需要根据具体情况进行转换。

(一) 采用意合表达法

将具有形合表达特点的英语句式,翻译为具有意合表达特点的汉语句式,对汉语读者来讲,具有更强的可读性。需要采用意合表达法翻译的英语句子主要包括并列句、复合句和并列复合句。

1. 并列句

(1) John is playing for high stakes, but so is his brother.

约翰下的赌注很大,他弟弟下的赌注也不小。

(2) The economic conditions are getting better with each passing day while the international trades are getting worse daily.

国内经济形势一天天好了起来,国际贸易状况却每况愈下。

2. 复合句

(1) You tend to be forgetful when you get old.

人老了,就容易健忘。

(2) As we arrived at the small village, the rain stopped and the sun appeared.

我们到达小村庄时,雨停了,太阳出来了。

(3) The sports meeting had to be put off since it rained heavily.

雨下得很大,运动会只好延期。

(4) She is so beautiful that there are a lot of pursuers around her.

她长得非常漂亮,身边有很多追求者。

3. 并列复合句

(1) She came into the classroom, and some students were playing cards, when a big laughter burst outside.

她走进教室,几个学生正在玩牌,外面传来一阵大笑。

(2) A light burned in the upper room. His horse neighed in the gateway, and he heard a shrill little wail that sent all the blood into the apple of his throat.

楼上房间里点着一盏灯,在入口处经过的马儿开始嘶鸣,他听到一阵尖锐的哭泣声,激动得周身的血液都要涌上喉咙口了。

(二)采用形合表达法

虽然汉语是以意合为主要特点的语言,但也具备形合的特点。可以通过使用"因为……所以……、由于、因此、以至、与其……不如……、既……又……、只要……就……、才……"等表示关联作用的副词,来表达因果、目的、转折、条件等逻辑关系。形合法表达可以使汉语句子逻辑清晰、结构紧凑。具有形合法特点的汉语句子较之具有意合法特点的句子显得更加正式、更具书面语和正式文体特征。

(1) Since we live in the mountain, we can enjoy the fresh and clean air.

因为我们在山里居住,所以可以享受新鲜清洁的空气。

(2) His company went bankrupt and he became penniless but I still wanted to get married to him.

尽管他的公司破产,他也身无分文,但我依然想和他结婚。

(3) If you can get there before ten a. m. , you will get a gift from the company.

如果你能上午10点到达,你将得到一份公司送的礼物。

(4) I had hoped that he could finish this project as promised. In fact, he was a liar, and he had done nothing when time was out.

我原以为他会按照承诺完成这个项目。而事实上,他是一个骗子,当项目到了期限时,他却什么都没有做。

(5) I try my best to go over all the lessons so that I can attain a high score in the final exam.

我努力复习功课,为了期末考试能获得优异成绩。

(6) The mantle of your high office has been placed on your shoulder at a time when the world at large and this organization are going through an exceptionally critical phase.

正当全世界和本组织处于一个异常危急的时刻,这个崇高职务的重担落到了你的肩上。

(7) As soon as he came into the library, he took off that book from the shelf and read it carefully.

他一进入图书馆,就从书架上取下那本书,认真地读了起来。

此外,对于英语中带有意合特点的句子,也可以采用形合表达法进行翻译。例如:

(1) Her outstanding achievement got her off.

由于她的杰出贡献,她得到了宽恕。

(2) The sight of the car always reminds her of that accident.

一见到这辆车,她就想起那次交通事故。

(3) The treasure is to be had for the digging.

只要坚持挖下去便能得到宝藏。

(4) With all his shortcomings, he was a loyal attendant.

尽管他有缺点,但他对主人非常忠诚。

(三) 意合法和形合法混用

在进行英汉语言转换时,根据表达需要,选择形合法或者意合法,也可以将二者混合使用。例如:

(1) An old dog like him never barks in vain. Whenever he barks, he always has some counsel that is worth listening to.

像他这样老道的人是从来不会胡乱开口的。一旦开口,总有高见值得一听。

(2) I can read every word that Dr. Johnson wrote with delight, for he had good sense, charm and wit. No one could have written better if he had not willfully set himself to write in the grand style.

我读约翰逊博士的著作,每句话都使我感到愉快,因为他有头脑、有魅力、机智。任何人,如果他不是刻意要用高雅的文体写作的话,都不可能比他写得更好。

(3) Don't you feel it strange that she should be so much ungrateful to Jack, who did so much for her when she was in poverty?

尽管杰克在她困难时帮了她那么多忙,她却对杰克如此忘恩负义,难道你不觉得奇怪吗?

(4) One of the most heartwarming aspects of people who are born with a facial disfigurement, whether minor or major, is the number of them who do not allow it to upset their lives, even reaching out to help others with the same problem.

有些人生来脸上就有或大或小的缺陷,但令人欣慰的是,这些人中有相当一部分并没有让这些缺陷扰乱了他们的生活,他们甚至还主动去帮助其他有同样缺陷的人。

(5) We can only wonder why it should be claimed it (the draft) has a history of a whole week behind it.

为什么竟然有人声称草案拖了整整一个星期,对此我们不能不觉得奇怪。

(6) Their (the English) stock had gone down. But Nasser, who had brought off the arms deal with the Soviet bloc, was riding high.

英国人的本钱所剩无几了。但是,纳赛尔在和苏联集团达成军火交易之后,还洋洋得意。

翻译小贴士

1. 翻译中的欧化语言表达

2020年诺贝尔文学奖得主的官网的评语为:The Nobel Prize in Literature for 2020 is awarded to the American poet Louise Glück "for her unmistakable poetic voice that with austere beauty makes individual existence universal".

然而就是这简短的一句话,网上流传着不同的译本,例如:

(1)她用无可辩驳的诗意嗓音,以朴实的美感使个人的存在变得普遍。

(2)因为她那无可辩驳的诗意般的声音,用朴素的美使个体的生存变得普遍。

(3)表彰她朴实无华的诗意之声,以朴素的美感使个体的生存变得普遍。

(4)因为她那毋庸置疑的诗意声音具备朴素的美,让每一个个体的存在都具有普遍性。

(5)以她精确的诗的声音和不事雕琢的美使得个体的存在具有了普遍性。

略读以上几个译文感觉不像汉语,似有"欧化"现象。欧化汉语又称为西化汉语或英式汉语,是指语法、文笔、风格或用词受欧洲语过分的影响,进而导致了现代汉语中出现欧化语法现象(语法上主要表现为长句、复杂句的出现,代词的增多,主语的凸显,连词的使用等)。欧化汉语的产生,很大一部分原因就是在将英文作品翻译成汉语时采用了异化的策略,所以译文就具有了欧化的特点,而这其中的主要原因是英语与汉语之间具有差异(英语是静态语言,汉语是动态语言;英文有形态语,汉语无形态语;英语重物称,汉语重人称;英语与汉语的思维方式不同)。

下面为从网上摘录的网友的译文:

(1)她富于诗意的表达鲜明而昭彰,其中蕴含的美令人肃然起敬,她的作品使个体存在不再囿于个体本身,而是成为全人类的普遍体验。

(2)她用别具一格的诗意语言,渲染出一花一世界的朴实唯美。

(3)无可挑剔的诗意之声,以朴素的美感使个体的生存变得普遍化。

(4)晓畅诗意之音,朴素华清之美,点点滴滴,溶于沧海。

(5)她的美妙诗词既别具一格又朴实无华,即便是小人物的情感琐事经她之笔也能让人感同身受。

(6)她的诗词既别具一格又朴实唯美。即便是描绘凡人琐事,她也总能于细微处激发共鸣。

(7)她的诗性语言无与伦比,美在内敛含蓄,一粒沙中有世界。

(8)美国诗人路易斯言辞中肯,既充满诗意而又朴实无华,在她笔下,个人亦众生。

(9)为她完美准确,而又充满素雅美的诗意之声让个例的存在变得普遍。

(10)她的诗意,鲜明昭彰,朴实无华,塑造的是共同的生存体验。

(11)因为她用清晰且诗意般的语言给我们带来了朴素之美,并使我们认识到每位个体的存在都是有价值的。

(12)她诗意般的语言朴实无华,惹人共鸣,她一个人的体验获得举世赞叹。

(13)她诗意般的语言无可辩驳,朴实但不失美感,彰显了个体的存在。

(14)她的诗文有着鲜明的个人特色,带着朴实的美,彰显着个体的普世性。

(15)她诗性般的话语真切而朴实,将个人经验化作群众感受。

(16)其诗风独具,文辞质朴;其个体经验具有普遍意义。

(17)她朴实无华而美丽的语言,使个体的存在更加自然有意义。

(18)在她的笔下,精准表达与朦胧诗意毫无冲突,朴素大方与华美富丽相得益彰,个人体验与普世价值完美融合。

2. 口吻的翻译

口吻,即口气,说话时流露出来的感情色彩,比如严肃的口吻,诙谐的口吻和埋怨的口吻等。国人常说"听话要听音"意即为此。成功的译文也应该传递、保留原文的口气,或口吻。所谓"口吻",在书面语中,主要通过措辞来体现,它并非局限于"虚词"(语气助词),比如"啊""哦""咦"等。识别原文的口吻,使之毕现于译文，属于"锦上添花"的翻译技巧，属于翻译理论中的"美学"范畴。

在一篇题为 Penguins(企鹅)的短文中，有这样一段描述：

Their sole enemy is the sea-leopard, which attacks them when only in the water, and even then it is not certain that he can always catch them; the consequence is that they are quite fearless on land or ice and will march up to a man with an air of curiosity and an expression of "You're a mighty big penguin, but I am not in the least afraid." They certainly think twice before they enter the water from the rookery, because bitter experience has taught them their enemy lurks under the ice, waiting for just such careless divers.

全段弥漫着拟人的修辞气息，"拟人"口吻又成功演绎成淡淡的幽默。且不说以"You're a mighty big penguin, but I am not in the least afraid."来形容 an expression 是如何逼真地描绘出了企鹅的憨态，且不说 enemy/careless divers 等词汇是如何自然地为本段文字抹上诙谐，就连英语的著名劝世明言 think twice before you act(要三思而后行)也被巧妙地活用！

比较一下两段译文：

(1) 海豹是企鹅唯一的敌人，它只在水下发动攻击，攻击时海豹并无把握是否能够抓住企鹅；因此，无论是在陆地上还是在冰上，企鹅都没有什么害怕，而且它们会好奇地向人走去，带着一种"你是一只大企鹅，可我一点都不怕"的表情。从栖息处下水前，它们定会考虑再三，因为痛苦的经验已让它们明白：敌人潜伏在冰下，正等待着粗心的入水者呢。

从 dynamic equivalence(动态对等)的视角去审视，存在一些问题。可以想象，原文作者写到此处时，一定流露出文思泉涌与下笔有神的喜色。渗透"拟人"口吻的文笔，当属于"灵感思维"的产物，非唾手可得。可以想象，读原文不得不为作者的文笔折服，为其幽默的拟人口吻发出会意一笑。而读此译文，会产生原文读者那样的反应吗？

(2) 海豹是企鹅的唯一杀手，它只在水下发动攻击，攻击时它并无把握能否得手；因此，无论是在陆地上，还是在浮冰上，企鹅都无所畏惧。它们会好奇地大摇大摆地向人靠近，神情自得，似乎在说"你真是一只超级企鹅啊，可我一点也不怕"。从栖息处下水之前,它们懂得"三思而后行",因为,过去的经验给它们上了惨痛的一课:敌人正潜伏在冰层下面,悄悄守候着那些大大咧咧的潜水者哩。

拟人口吻的亮色在本译文中没有消失,相反,在某些地方还有所强化。比如"大摇大摆"和"大大咧咧"这些叠音词有效渲染了拟人气氛,貌似添译,却非添译。an expression of 被化成"神情自得,似乎在说",使拟人口吻得以适度夸张。

在一篇题为 Pursuit of Possessions(追求拥有)的文章中,作者批评了某些人购物成癖的社会现象。讽刺口吻十分强烈,口吻已经远远不是文采问题,而是影响或左右着读者的观点。

◀ 原文 ▶

How do we find this time? That's easy. We turn evenings, weekends, and holidays—times that used to be set aside for family and friends—into shopping expeditions.

译文

(1)那什么时间去买东西呢?这很简单。晚上,周末,还有假日,这些留给家人和朋友的时间都可以用来采购。

译笔如此规矩,以致译文的口吻"变味",竟然发展到给读者"安排"购物的时间了。原文作者的本意难道真的是为读者安排购物的时间吗?反话成为正说,讽刺成为规劝。

(2)怎么才能找到采购的时间呢?这还不简单!晚上,周末,假日,这些本该留给家人和朋友的时间,应该一律让路,毫不犹豫地投入采购大行动中。

总之,良好的翻译效果需要求得天平两侧(the response of the receptor to the translated message 和 the original receptors presumably reacted to the message when it was given in its original setting)的平衡!

 习题四

简答题
1. 英汉语言转换中的辩证思维体现在哪四个方面？
2. 在翻译实践中如何体现四个方面的辩证思维体？举例说明。

技巧篇

第五章 择词

　　所谓择词,是指在翻译过程中,在准确理解原文的基础上,进行恰当的"词义和表达方式的选择",忠实地表达原文含义,同时被目的语读者更好地理解和接受。"恰当的词语应用在恰当的地方,就会形成正确的概念或完美的修辞。"如果不能根据具体的语境和实际表达需要,选择恰当的词语展现原文的内容和信息,翻译也就不能成为不同文化间交流的可靠工具,也不能成为搭建源语作者与目的语读者之间沟通的桥梁。

　　要掌握"在适当的场合使用适当词语"的翻译艺术或表达技巧,译者首先要深刻了解中西两种文化,深度掌握中英两种语言词汇,还要坚持不懈地进行翻译实践练习,形成一种强烈的语感,以便翻译时能够信手拈来。

　　由于英汉语言的差异,在词汇内涵上存在很多不对等的情况,因此,对于措辞或择词中存在的一些问题也应该加以注意。这些问题主要包括冗余词汇、滥用词汇和伪等价词汇。比如:这是我们应该采取的正确的态度。如果我们将其翻译为"This is the correct attitude that we should adopt.",目的语读者会感到困惑,因为这不符合他们的思维习惯。如果这是一种正确的态度,我们当然应该接受;如果这是我们应该接受的态度,毫无疑问,它必然是正确的。因此,以上译文就是一个存在冗余现象的译文,可以将其改译为"This is the attitude that we should adopt."。再如,"几道淡淡的晨曦正在升起,预示新的一天的到来。"若将其翻译成"Streaks of faint light were rising, heralding the oncoming of another day.",便是忽略了 herald 这个词的内在含义,即 announce the approach of sb.

/sth.,该词本身就含有了 oncoming 的意思,因此就出现了词汇冗余的现象,可以改译为"Streaks of faint light were rising, heralding another day."

把握好词汇的真正含义,是应用择词技巧的前提条件。若将"他试图劝我参加讨论,但因我心境不好,拒绝了。"翻译成"He persuaded me to join in the discussion, but as I was in a bad humor, I refused.",便是因为没有掌握 persuade 这个词的真正含义:cause sb. to do sth. by arguing or reasoning with him,该词本身已经含有了"成功说服去做某事"的意思,所以正确的表达应该是"He tried to persuade me to join in the discussion, but as I was in a bad humor, I refused."。下面几个例子也说明了这一问题。

(1) 伤兵的病情很危险,随时可能死亡。

The wounded solider was very dangerous; he might die at any moment. (错误)

The wounded solider was in a critical condition; he might die at any moment. (正确)

分析

dangerous 表示 likely to cause danger or be a danger 对他人造成危险。

(2) 受害者一声痛苦的叫喊,似乎使那迫害他的人暗暗得到满足。

A painful cry from the victim seemed to give his prosecutor secret satisfaction. (错误)

A cry of pain from the victim seemed to give his prosecutor secret satisfaction. (正确)

分析

painful 表示 Causing pain or distress 令人痛苦的。

(3) 这个年轻人总是戴着帽子,因为他是秃头。

The young man always wears a cap, because he is bare-headed. (错误)

The young man always wears a cap, because he is bald. (正确)

分析

bald 表示(of people)having little or no hair on the scalp 指秃头的;而 bare-headed 指没有戴帽子

(4)房间里一片黑暗,只有门缝里射进一点亮光。

The room was dark except the light coming in through a crack in the door. (错误)

The room was dark except for the light coming in through a crack in the door. (正确)

分析

except for 除了具有 except 本身所含有的意义之外,还表达了先整体描述,后细节补充说明的意思。

(5)除了几所古老的庙宇外,只有很少一些古迹。

There are very few historical sites besides some old temples. (错误)

There are very few historical sites apart from some old temples. (正确)

分析

apart from 表示 in addition to "除了(某事物)以外,还有……"的意思。

(6)她痛苦叫喊,使我们心如刀绞。

She cried anguishly which pierced our hearts like daggers. (错误)

She cried in anguish which pierced our hearts like daggers. (正确)

分析

anguish 为名词,但没有 anguishly 这种表达。

(7)我们两个人除了外貌有略相似外,性格和气质截然不同。

We two, except for little resemblance in appearance, are poles apart either in character or in temperament. (错误)

Slight resemblance in appearance, we two are poles apart both in character and in temperament. (正确)

分析

不能简单地将原文中的"除了"翻译成"except for",应该从整句话上把握原文意思,否则会导致信息传递偏差。

由此可见,译者必须穿透词汇的表层意思,在词汇的真正含义上下功夫。我们再看下面一些例句及其译文:

你能给我介绍一部好的儿童作品吗?

Could you recommend a good children's work to me?

我会把新来的朋友介绍给大家。

I will introduce new friends to you all.

教授向我们介绍了一些他的科研经验。

The professor told us something about his experience in scientific research.

她热衷于为年轻人介绍对象。

She is fond of finding boy or girl friends for young people.

欢迎张主任给我们介绍一下当前的形势。

Welcome Director Zhang brief us on the present situation.

他是我的入党介绍人。

He is my sponsor when I applied for party membership.

从以上句子的翻译我们可以看到,在不同的语境中,同一个中文词汇可以翻译成不同的英语单词。如果我们将第一句话译成" Could you introduce me a good book?",这就有点滑稽,以英语为母语的读者就会感到莫名其妙,怎么能将一本书介绍给一个人呢?这就是用词不当导致译文曲解了原文的信息。

由于中英两国人民在思维习惯和语言表达方式上的差异,特别是在两种语言中存在大量一词多义与一义多词的语言现象,因此在动笔翻译之前,译者应该根据原文的语境认真地衡量和考虑每一个词汇(或单词)的真实含义。为了掌握好这一技巧,我们应该注意以下几个方面的问题。

一、根据语境选择词义

正确理解词汇在具体语境中的真实含义,精确地进行词义选择。以 accept

为例，一般认为它在汉语中对应的词汇是"接受，收受"。但根据上下文，还有以下一些含义：

Government accepted the whole affair to be an unfortunate accident.

政府<u>承认</u>这整个事件是一桩不幸的意外。

It was pouring with rain so I accepted his offer of a lift.

正下着瓢泼大雨，所以我<u>领</u>了他的情，搭了他的便车。

He had a bill of exchange accepted.

他昨天<u>承兑</u>了一张汇票。

You have to accept the consequences of your actions.

你得对你的行为后果<u>负责</u>。

The kind of surface will not accept ink.

这种表面不<u>吸墨</u>。

The telephone booths accept 10 and 20 pence coins.

电话亭可<u>使用</u>10便士和20便士的硬币。

How is his gesture to be accepted?

他这个手势<u>意指</u>什么？

Not all of them accept the idea.

并不是他们所有人都<u>赞</u>同这个想法。

Has he been accepted at Peking University?

他被北京大学<u>录取</u>了吗？

The hall can accept two thousand people.

这个大厅能<u>容纳</u>2000人。

How is this phrase to be accepted?

这一短语如何<u>解释</u>？

再以account这个单词为例，一般我们会将其理解为"计算；账户"，但根据具体的语境，还有以下的意思：

The victim gave a detailed account of what happened on that rainy night.

受害者详细<u>描述</u>了那个雨夜所发生的事情。

No satisfactory account was given of these phenomena.

对这些现象不曾提供令人满意的解释。

A newly-married couple, he thought, on account of their walking so close together.

看俩人走路时挨得这么近,他觉得他们是新婚夫妇。

It is of much account that we act on our own principles.

按自己的原则行事,这点非常重要。

The team fought hard and gave a good account of themselves.

这支队伍奋力拼搏,表现出色。

Their sleep is regularly disturbed by the sound of gunfire as criminal gangs settle their nightly accounts.

他们经常被黑帮每晚火拼的枪声所吵醒。

It is very popular for people to invest their money to good account.

用自己的钱做有利可图的投资近来很流行。

It is on this account that he gave up smoking.

正是出于这个缘故,他戒了烟。

The firm is one of our best accounts.

这家商行是我们最佳客户之一。

The cosmetics account has been awarded to a new agency.

化妆品广告业务已委托给一家新的代理公司。

同样,汉语中也存在类似的情况。以"问题"这个词为例,一般会将它对等译为英语单词中的 question 和 problem,但实际情况并不尽然。例如:

他的人品和能力没问题。

Not to worry about his personality and ability.

这是个原则和立场问题。

This is a matter of principle and position.

重要的问题是我们应该站在哪一方。

The important thing is which side we should stand in line with.

他们对这个问题进行了开诚布公的讨论。

They had a frank discussion about the issue.

一路上没出问题。

The trip went off without mishap.

工作还行吗？没问题。

How is your work getting on? All right.

还有"电话"这个词，一般在英语中表达为 phone 和 telephone，但也要考虑实际情况，例如：

咨询电话

Information/ inquiries

投诉电话

Call... to complain

救援电话

Emergency Helpline

订票电话

Ticket Service Line

再看"情况"这个词，一般认为它的英语对等词是 circumstances 和 situation，但需要根据实际情况，具体问题具体分析。例如：

现在情况不同了。

Now things are different.

这种情况必须改变。

This state of affairs must be changed.

他们的情况怎么样？

How do matters stand with them?

前线有什么情况？

How is the situation at the front?

前面有情况，做好战斗准备。

There is enemy activity ahead, prepare for combat.

再看一个我们更为熟悉的、颇具汉语特色的词——"意思",分析一下该词在不同语境中的含义及其在英语中对应的表达。

甲:这一点小意思,请务必收下。

乙:你这人真是有意思,怎么也来这一套?

甲:哎,只是意思意思。

乙:啊,真是不好意思。

A:This is a little gift as a token of my appreciation. Please take it.

B:Oh, Aren't you a bit too polite? You shouldn't do that.

A: Well, it just conveys my gratitude.

B:Ah, thank you then, though I really don't deserve it.

二、根据搭配习惯进行择词

英汉两种语言中的词汇,各有一套自己的习惯用语搭配体系。这些比较固定的说法,有时可以逐字翻译,但在大多数情况下不可以逐字对应。所以,翻译时必须摆脱原语词汇含义的束缚,按照目的语的搭配习惯来处理原文中的某些搭配。

(一) 动词和宾语的搭配

以英语动词 take 为例,说明不同情境中的翻译用词选择:

take office 就职

take one's eye 看中了

take second place 获得第二名

take a master degree 取得硕士学位

take a deep breath 深呼吸

take a wife 娶妻

take a message 捎个口信

take a hint 会意

take offense 生气

take the part of the hero 扮演男主角

take the blame 承担过错

take poison 服毒

take one's ease on the porch 在门廊上休息

take cold 着凉

take a walk 散步

take a bath 洗澡

take sb's advice 采纳某人建议

take a bribe 受贿

take a seat 就座

以汉语动词"实现"为例,说明不同情境中的翻译用词选择:

实现高增长率 notch up high growth rates

实现自己的诺言 fulfill one's promise

实现平衡预算 achieve a balanced budget

实现改革 bring about a reform

实现祖国统一 reunify the motherland

实现利润 make profit

实现夙愿 long-cherished wish comes true

实现九年义务教育 implement the system of nine-year compulsory education

实现自己的理想 realize one's ideal

实现计划 carry out a plan

实现"四个"现代化 accomplish the modernization of agriculture, industry, national defense, and science and technology

再以汉语中的动词"取消"为例,说明不同情境中的翻译用词选择:

取消会议 cancel (call off) a meeting

取消会员资格 deprive sb. of his membership

取消决定 rescind a decision

取消禁令 lift a ban

取消诺言 kill the promise

再来看汉语"送"形成的一些搭配及其在英语中对应的表达：

送某人一本书 give sb. a book

送礼 present a gift to sb

送信 deliver a letter

送客 see a visitor out

送行 see sb. off

送雨伞 bring sb. an umbrella

送命 lose one's life

送孩子上学 take a child to school

送某人回家 escort sb. home

送卫星上天 launch a satellite

(二) 定语和中心词的搭配

现以英语形容词 heavy 为例，说明不同情境中的翻译用词选择：

a heavy load 重负

heavy frost/rain/snow 严重霜冻/暴雨/大雪

heavy crop 丰收

heavy schedule 排得很紧的日程表

heavy digging/lifting 费力的挖掘/提举

heavy applause 热烈的掌声

a heavy buyer 大主顾

a heavy drinker/smoker 酒瘾/烟瘾大的人

heavy silence 沉寂

heavy groan/sigh 深沉的呻吟/叹息

a heavy politician 显耀的政治家

a heavy play 一出严肃的戏

a heavy curtain/coat 厚窗帘/外衣

heavy bread 发得不好的硬面包

heavy lorries/trucks 重型卡车

a heavy thinker 深邃的思想家

a heavy news 令人难过的消息

heavy footsteps 沉重的脚步

以汉语形容词"好"为例,说明不同情境中的翻译用词选择:

好年成 a good year

好姑娘 a nice girl

好父母 a loving parent

好儿女 an obedient child

好妻子 a virtuous wife

好丈夫 a dutiful husband

好领导 a competent leader

好教徒 a faithful Christian

好汉 a brave man

好话 word of praise

好脸 a smiling face

好感 favorable impression

好天气 lovely weather

好半天 quite a while

以汉语形容词"淡"为例,说明不同情境中的翻译用词选择:

淡茶 weak tea

淡酒 light wine

淡季 slack season

淡水 fresh water

以汉语形容词"烈"为例,说明不同情境中的翻译用词选择:

烈风 strong gale

烈日 burning sun

烈火 raging fire

烈性子 fiery disposition

三、以目的语的表达习惯和表达方式为依据选择词汇

(1) A small quantity of aspirin relieves pain and inflammation. It also reduces fever by interfering with some of the body's reaction.

(动词 relieve 意指"缓和""消除",英文中后接两个宾语,但中文很少用一个动词与两个名词搭配,一般医学术语中习惯称"消炎止痛",否则不符合中文表达习惯。)

少量阿司匹林可以消炎止痛,还可以通过干扰肌体的某些反应而退热。

(2) He realized that where labors and materials were in short supply, he would have to work harder.

(在从句中,主语 labors 和 materials 只有一个介词短语 in short supply 做表语,若两者都翻译成"供应不足",有些欠妥。)

他意识到在这缺人短物的地方,他应该更加努力地工作。

(3) Around each corner of a city block, around each bend in a country road, there is something new to greet the eyes, the ears, the nose.

(原文中的 greet 一词译成汉语时应根据汉语的搭配习惯,分译成三个动词,这样译文就更加生动活泼。)

在城市街区的每一拐角处,在乡村街道的每个拐弯处,总有什么新的东西映入我们的眼帘,窜入我们的耳朵,吸入我们的鼻子。

四、根据词类确定词义,在此基础上进行择词

通读一个句子,首先判断分析重点单词在句子中的作用,属于哪一词类,再根据词类选择或猜测它的确切词义。

现以 right 为例,它有以下几种词类及相应的意义:

(1) 形容词:正当的;准确的;合适的;良好的;对的
(2) 副词:直接地;彻底地;恰当地;立即
(3) 名词:正义;权利;正确
(4) 感叹词:行了;好了吧
(5) 动词:纠正;整理;为……申冤

形容词的译法：

You were quite right to criticize him.

你批评他批评得很对。

副词的译法：

The car spun right off the track.

汽车完全开出了车道。

The pear was rotten right through.

这个梨烂透了。

名词的译法：

Education is provided by the state as of right.

受教育是国家赋予每一个人的权利。

Do the police have the right of arrest in the case?

在此情况下警方有逮捕权吗？

感叹词的译法：

"You may find it hurts a little at first." "Right."

"开始时，你会觉得有点疼。""噢。"

Right, open your mouth, let's have a look.

行了，把嘴张开，咱们来瞧瞧。

动词的译法：

Righting the economy will demand major cuts in expenditure.

恢复经济需要大量削减开支。

再以 well 为例，它有以下几种词类及相应的意义：

(1)副词：好；对；令人满意地；完全地；很；相当；大大地

(2)形容词：健康的；身体/状态/情况良好的；明智的；可取的；好的

(3)感叹词：哎呀；哟；啊；好啦；唉；好吧；嗯

(4)名词：水井；楼梯井；电梯井道；(法庭中的)律师席；来源，源泉

(5)动词：涌出；冒出；流出；溢出；涌起；迸发

副词的译法：

He's well able to take care of himself.

他完全能够自理。

形容词的译法：

All's well that ends well.

结果好就算一切都好。

感叹词的译法：

Well, well —I would never have guessed it!

哟,哟,我怎么也不会猜到那儿去!

名词的译法：

The knowledge is a well of progress.

知识是进步的源泉。

动词的译法：

Hate welled up inside him as he thought of the two of them together.

他一想到他们俩在一起就恨得咬牙切齿。

下面是有关择词这一翻译技巧的更多例句：

(1) 建设文化强国、教育强国、人才强国、体育强国、科技强国、制造强国、质量强国、网络强国、交通强国。

China will become a strong country in culture, education, talent, sports, science and technology, build itself into a manufacturer of quality, and enhance its strength in cyberspace and transportation network.

(2) 全面建设社会主义现代化国家、全面深化改革、全面依法治国、全面从严治党(全面建成小康社会)。

Fully build a modern socialist country, comprehensively deepen reform, law-based governance in all fields, comprehensively strengthen Party discipline (build a moderately prosperous society in all respects).

(3) 到2035年人均国内生产总值达到中等发达国家水平,中等收入群体显著扩大。

By 2035, China's per capita GDP will reach the level of moderately developed countries, and the size of the middle-income group will be significantly expanded.

(4) 对港珠澳大桥这样的重大工程，既要高质量建设好，全力打造精品工程、样板工程、平安工程、廉洁工程，又要用好管好大桥，为粤港澳大湾区建设发挥重要作用。

The Hong Kong–Zhuhai–Macao Bridge should not only be a high-quality and well-managed project but also serve as an example of work safety and transparent operation, in a bid to contribute to the development of the Guangdong-Hong Kong-Macao Greater Bay Area.

(5) 从历史上看，不管遇到什么风险、灾难、逆流，人类社会总是要前进的，而且一定能够继续前进。

Looking back at history, humanity has always been able to forge ahead despite risks, disasters and headwinds, and humanity shall and will continue to stride forward.

(6) 坚持农村土地农民集体所有制不动摇，坚持家庭承包经营基础性地位不动摇。扎实推进第二轮土地承包到期后再延长30年工作，保持农村土地承包关系稳定并长久不变。

We need to unwaveringly uphold farmers' collective ownership of rural land while continuing the fundamental practice of rural families exercising their right to contract and manage land in rural areas. It is important to ensure rural land contracting practices remain stable and unchanged on a long-term basis and adopt concrete steps to extend the current round of contracts for another 30 years when they expire.

(7) Kind words, kind looks, kind acts and warm handshakes, these are means of grace when men in trouble are fighting their unseen battles. (John Hall, American musician and politician, b. 1948)

友好的话语，亲切的目光，善意的行动，温暖的握手。这就是人们陷入困境时，该如何优雅地打响看不见的战斗。（约翰·霍尔，美国音乐家、政治家，生于1948年）

第五章 择词

翻译小贴士

"一词多义"和"一义多词"现象在中英两种语言中都大量存在,这对两种语言转换造成了障碍,"择词"是解决这一障碍的重要技巧。但这一技巧的掌握,必须基于大量实践练习之上,下面是采用该技巧进行的中译英翻译实例。

(1) 坚持公有制为主体、多种所有制经济共同发展和按劳分配为主体、多种分配方式并存,把社会主义制度和市场经济有机结合起来,不断解放和发展社会生产力。

Upholding the dominant role of the public sector and common development of economic entities under diverse forms of ownership, the distribution system whereby distribution according to labor is dominant and a variety of other modes of distribution exist alongside it, the synergy between the socialist system and the market economy, and continuously unlocking and developing the productive forces.

(2) 坚持德才兼备、选贤任能,聚天下英才而用之,培养造就更多优秀人才。

Selecting officials based on integrity and ability and on the basis of merit regardless of background to cultivate more talented individuals.

(3) 坚持党的集中统一领导,坚持党的科学理论,保持政治稳定,确保国家始终沿着社会主义方向前进。

Upholding the centralized and unified leadership of the CPC, following the CPC's scientific theories, maintaining political stability and ensuring that the country keeps advancing in the direction of socialism.

(4) 坚持人民当家作主,发展人民民主,密切联系群众,紧紧依靠人民推动国家发展。

Seeing that the people run the country, promoting the people's democracy, maintaining close ties with the people and relying on them to push forward the country's development.

(5) 坚持全面依法治国,建设社会主义法治国家,切实保障社会公平正义和人民权利。

Ensuring law-based governance in all fields, building a country of socialist rule of law, and guaranteeing social fairness and justice and the people's rights.

(6)坚持以人民为中心的发展思想,不断保障和改善民生、增进人民福祉,走共同富裕道路。

Adhering to the vision of making development people-centered, and continuously guaranteeing and improving people's livelihoods and improving people's wellbeing to achieve common prosperity for everyone.

(7)坚持改革创新、与时俱进,善于自我完善、自我发展,使社会充满生机活力。

Continuing reform and innovation, moving with the times, and promoting self-improvement and development to build a society full of vitality.

(8)坚持党指挥枪,确保人民军队绝对忠诚于党和人民,有力保障国家主权、安全和发展利益。

Keeping the armed forces under the Party's command and ensuring that the people's armed forces are completely loyal to the Party and the people so as to safeguard China's sovereignty, security and development interests.

(9)我们要坚持团结协作,合力克服疫情挑战。

We need to enhance solidarity and coordination, and come together to meet the COVID-19.

 习题五

汉译英

1. 他开始意识到他是跟一个淹死的鬼说话。

2. 我不想失掉机会。

3. 健康对每个人都是宝贵的。

4. 他们不顾天冷,目不转睛地盯着电视屏幕。

5. 随着岁月的流逝,我们的热情逐渐减退了。

6. 毫无疑问,他走路淋着雨了。但他浑身湿透,光是雨是不能解释的。

7. 我从来没有这样深刻地感到自己知识的肤浅。

8. 她那蓬乱的头发上闪耀着雨滴的光。

9. 我的姑母在乡下过着简朴平静的生活。

10. 又下雨了,这回也带来了寒风。

第六章 增词

汉英两种语言在词法和句法结构方面存在着极大差别,例如:英语中有词形的变化,汉语中没有;英语中大量使用连词、介词、关系代词等,而汉语中各成分往往通过内在语义关系贯穿在一起,不一定或很少使用连词和介词。所以,要通顺、正确地译出原文含义,逐词翻译是行不通的。进行翻译时,译文必须以原文为基础进行必要的调整,其中,增词便是经常采用的一项翻译方法。例如:

◀ 原文 ▶

(1) Histories makes men wise; poets witty; the mathematics subtle; natural philosophy deep; moral grave; logic and rhetoric able to contend.

译文

读史使人明智;读诗使人灵秀;数学使人周密;科学使人深刻;伦理使人庄重;逻辑与修辞使人善辩。

◀ 原文 ▶

(2) 班门弄斧

译文

This is like showing off one's proficiency with the axe before Lu Ban, the master carpenter.

在以上两句话的翻译中,为了更符合目的语的语言表达习惯和目的语读者的文化接受程度,在译文中增加了原文隐含的意义,使得译文更加明确,更有可

读性。再看更多的例子及分析:

◀ 原文 ▶

(3)后半夜,他感到了十分的寒冷,肚子里咕噜咕噜响着,好像有无数屁要放,但一个屁也放不出来。

译文

It was past midnight(增加形式主语及系动词,形成完整的系表结构句子), and(增加并列连接词) he was getting cold; as(增加连接词) his(增加代词) stomach growled, he(增加主语) felt an immense buildup of gas(注意"屁"这个词在不同语境中的应用), which(注意 which 的作用和功能,形式上为定语从句,实际上表达转折) he couldn't pass, no matter how he tried(增加原文形式上无,但实际意义上有的内容).

◀ 原文 ▶

(4)他咕嘟咕嘟地喝着,一口气喝下去大半瓶。

译文

Tipping the bottle back a second time(基于原文信息,增加了时间顺序词,使译文更加符合逻辑), he gulped about half of the remaining urine(基于原文信息,增加了"喝"的对象).

◀ 原文 ▶

(5)大道之行,天下为公。和平与发展是时代主题,也是不可抗拒的历史潮流。面对人类面临的挑战,世界各国应该加强团结而不是制造隔阂,推进合作而不是挑起冲突,携手共建人类命运共同体,造福世界各国人民。

译文

As the Chinese saying goes(增加背景信息表达), "The Universal Way leads to the greater good of all." Peace and development are the theme of our(增加代词) times. They are the unstoppable trend of history. Given the challenges facing humankind, countries need to strengthen solidarity, not create estrangement; they need to advance cooperation, not provoke conflicts. Let us（增加动宾结构）join hands to build a community with a shared future for mankind and bring greater benefit to people of our world.

◀ 原文 ▶

（6）秉持正义,维护和平。我们应该坚持和平共处,尊重各国发展权利,尊重各国自主选择的发展道路和模式,坚持多边主义,反对单边主义、霸权主义、强权政治,反对各种形式的恐怖主义和极端暴力行径,维护世界公平正义与和平安全。

译文

Let us（增加动宾结构）uphold justice to（引出目的）jointly safeguard world（增加修饰语）peace. We（增加主语）need to adhere to peaceful coexistence. We（增加主语）need to respect other countries' right to development and their independent choice of development paths and models. We（增加主语）need to uphold multilateralism, oppose unilateralism, hegemony and power politics, and（增加连词）reject all forms of terrorism and acts of extreme violence. We（增加主语）need to work together to safeguard equity, justice, peace and security in the world.

◀ 原文 ▶

（7）党的十八大以来,通过全社会共同努力,我国科技事业取得了历史性成就、发生了历史性变革。重大创新成果竞相涌现,一些前沿领域开始进入并跑、领跑阶段。

译文

Since the 18th CPC National Congress, China（主语发生改变,原文的主语是"我国科技事业",译文改为China）has made historic achievements and（增加连词）transformations in science and technology thanks to the joint efforts of the whole society. China（增加主语）has seen major innovations （原文的"成果"可以理解为"范畴词",其内涵意义已经包含在innovation之

中) emerge in large numbers and the country is now leading or co-leading(原文的"阶段"可以理解为"范畴词",可以略去不译) the world in some frontier areas.

◀ 原文 ▶

(8)事实证明,将疫情政治化、污名化,搞"甩锅"、推责,干扰的是全球合作抗疫大局。我们要推动以团结取代分歧,以理性消除偏见,扫除"政治病毒",凝聚各国携手抗疫的最大合力。

译文

What has happened shows that acts(增加表面无、实际有的内容,使原文信息的呈现更具体) of politicization, stigmatization, blame-shifting and scapegoating only serve to disrupt overall global cooperation against the virus. We need to overcome division with unity, replace bias with reason and stamp out the "political virus". In this way(增加连接词), we(增加主语) will pool the maximum global synergy to beat the virus.

◀ 原文 ▶

(9)国家文物局11月18日在新闻发布会上表示,得益于中英两国的共同努力,68件流失英国数十年的文物近日回国。这些文物时间跨度达千年,从春秋到清代,质地以陶瓷居多,地域分布江西、安徽、福建、河南、陕西、河北、贵州等。国家文物局副局长关强表示,这批文物的回归,为中国政府持续25年的跨国文物追索行动画上了圆满句号。

译文

After(增加表示时间的介词) being abroad for decades, 68 Chinese cultural relics that(增加从句引导词) had been taken to the UK recently were returned to their homeland(增加代词their,homeland这个词用得非常好,将重新回到原生地的内涵翻译了出来) thanks to joint efforts of the two countries, the National Cultural Heritage Administration said at a news conference on Wednesday(中文惯用日期,英文惯用星期几). Some of the relics span millennia, dating（根据实际内容进行词义补充）from the Spring and Autumn Period (770-476 BC)（对朝代的起止时间加以说明）to the Qing Dynasty (1644—1911)（对朝代的起止时间加以说明）, and they encompass a variety of items（增加表面无、内涵有的意义和信息）, mainly ceramics. They（增加主语）are from a variety of provinces（先总后分，符合英语表达习惯）, including Jiangxi, Anhui, Fujian, Henan, Shanxi, Hebei and Guizhou. Their return brings an end（短语 bring...to an end 已经含有完全结束的意思，因此不必再译出"圆满"这层意思，否则造成信息冗余。将"句号"这一具象，直接翻译成了其所表达的"结束，完成"这一概念意义）to a quarter-century of efforts for repatriation, said Guan Qiang, deputy director of the administration（调整语序，符合英语新闻报道的表达规范和习惯）。

◀ 原文 ▶

（10）While not everyone will have pondered the subject while staring out of the window during a flight, the question as to why aeroplanes have circular windows rather than square ones is interesting. Over the years, aerospace engineering has made huge leaps in aeroplane technology, meaning planes can carry more passengers and go faster. The planes have also changed shape to increase safety – including the windows. Where there's a corner, there's a weak spot. Windows, having four corners, have four potential weak spots, making them likely to crash under stress – such as air pressure. By curving the window, the stress that would eventually crack the window corner is distributed and the likelihood of it breaking is reduced.

译文

虽然不是每个人都会在飞行中凝视窗外的时候思索一个问题：（增加标点符号）为什么舷窗是圆形的而不是方形的。但（增加转折连词）这个问题很有趣。多年来，航空航天工程在飞机技术上取得了巨大的飞跃，这（增词形成外位成分）意味着飞机可以运载更多的乘客，飞行速度更快。同时（增加时间连词），为了提高安全性，飞机在外形上也做出了相应的（增加逻辑成分）改变。舷窗便是变化之一(增加逻辑成分)。哪里有拐角,哪里就有弱点。方形舷窗有四个角,就有着四个潜在的薄弱点,所以它们很可能在压力作用下破裂,比如大气压力。因此(增加结果连词),让窗缘线条弯曲,来分散窗口四角的压力,从而降低了窗户破碎的可能性。

◀ 原文 ▶

(11) First, we need to uphold multilateralism, and safeguard peace and stability in our world. History teaches us that multilateralism, equity and justice can keep war and conflict at bay, while unilateralism and power politics will inflate dispute and confrontation. Flouting rules and laws, treading the path of unilateralism and bullying, and withdrawing from international organizations and agreements run counter to the will of the general public and trample on the legitimate rights and dignity of all nations.

译文

我们要坚持多边主义,维护世界和平稳定。历史昭示我们,恪守(增加动词)多边主义,追求(增加动词)公平正义,战乱冲突可以避免;搞(增加动词)单边主义、强权政治,纷争对抗将愈演愈烈。如果(增加象征形合的连词)无视规则和法治,继续大搞(增加动词)单边霸凌、"退群毁约",不仅(增加象征形合的连词)违背世界人民普遍愿望,也是(增加象征形合的连词)对各国正当权利和尊严的践踏。

由此看来,所谓增词,并不是不顾原文意义随意增加;而是以原文为基础,增加原文表面无、实际有的含义表达。一般来讲,在以下几种情况下可以采用增词的翻译方法。

一、根据语言特色结构需要进行增词

第一,英译中时,增加原文语义上有而形式上无的成分、原文省略的成分、表时态的词、名词复数的词、连词等。

(1) With great achievements in her research, she had never the

slightest change of the habit of staying up late.

她在研究领域虽然取得了很大成就,但熬夜加班的习惯没有丝毫的改变。

(2) "I'll make a man of him," said Jack. "College is the place."

"我要把他培养成一个堂堂的男子汉,"杰克说,"大学就是一个理想的地方。"

(3) So teaching gives me pace, and variety, and challenge, and the opportunity to keep on learning.

所以说,教学使我的工作有了节奏,生活变得丰富多彩,教学给我提出了挑战,使我有了不断学习的机会。

(4) He allowed the father to be overruled by the judge, and declared his own son guilty.

他以法官的职责战胜父子的私情,判决他儿子有罪。

(5) This plan with all its disadvantages is considered to be one of the best.

尽管有种种不周全之处,这个计划仍被认为是最佳计划之一。

(6) I had thought it was a coincident, but it seems it is a trap on purpose.

我原以为是一种巧合,但现在看来是故意设下的一个陷阱。

(7) The men squatted in their dark-colored logis, the ever-present cheroots clenched between their teeth.

男人们穿着深色的袍裙,蹲坐在那里,嘴里总是叼着烟。

(8) There lay one of the chief difficulties.

这就是当时的主要困难之一。

(9) The dust, the uproar and the growing darkness threw everything into chaos.

烟尘滚滚,人声嘈杂,夜色愈浓,一切都陷入混乱之中。

(10) The subsequent generations of this family grew impoverished by a combination of drought, extortion, and too many gifts to opera girls, all of

which led to their losing face and their property.

在接下来的几代中,因为遭遇旱灾,被人勒索,再加上给优伶的封赏太多,这个家族便最终资财耗尽,风光不再了。

(11) A gas exerts the same pressure in a mixture of gases as it would exert if it were in the container alone.

在混合的几种气体中,每一种气体所产生的压力都与它单独在容器中的压力一样。

(12) They won victories in the past two years.

在过去的两年里,他们取得了一次又一次的胜利。

(13) The middle-aged teacher carried on teaching work in spite of the diseases.

尽管那位中年教师身患种种疾病,他仍然坚持进行教学工作。

(14) Day after day he came to his work—sweeping, scrubbing, cleaning.

日复一日,他做着同样的工作——扫地,擦桌椅,清理房间。

(15) She finally fell ill after many continuous days of hard work.

在数日的艰苦工作之后,她终于累病了。

(16) Demand will be higher for individuals in modern society. Those who can think, collaborate, create, problem-solve, communicate and lead are welcomed.

现代社会对个人的要求会更高。它需要的是有思想、能与人合作、勇于创新、善于解决问题、懂得交流并具备领导才能的人。

(17) A man may usually be known by the book he reads as well as by the company he keeps; for there's a companionship of books as well as of men; and one should always live in the best company, whether it be of books or of men.

可以通过读书来认识人,亦可交友结识人;既有因书而产生的友谊,也有因人而出现的良友;人们应当永远生活在真情之中,无论它来自于书还是来自于人。

(18) Which do you like better, dictation or translation exercises?

你喜欢听写练习,还是翻译练习?

(19) He never drinks before driving.

他开车前从不喝酒。

(20) Censorship has been in force since early in World War II.

审查制度从第二次世界大战初期实行一直到现在。

(21) He dismissed the meeting without a closing speech.

他没有致闭幕词就宣布结束会议.

第二,中译英时,根据具体情况,增补主语、宾语、物主代词、并列连词、从属连词、系动词、介词、冠词等。

(1) 得寸进尺。

If you give him an inch, he will take a mile.

(2) 没有调查,就没有发言权。

He who makes no investigation has no right to speak.

(3) 把这些故事看完以后,用你自己的话讲一遍。

After you have read these stories, tell them in your own words.

(4) 你越是隐藏缺点,它们就越会暴露。

The more you try to hide your shortcomings, the more they will be exposed.

(5) 我们认为尽快建立一所学校是十分重要的。

We think it more important to set up a new school as soon as possible.

(6) 他耸耸肩,摇摇头,两眼看天,一句话不说。

He shrugged his shoulders, shook his head, cast up his eyes, but said nothing.

(7) 冬天来了,春天还会远吗?

If winter comes, can spring be far behind?

(8) 留得青山在,不怕没柴烧。

As long as the green mountains are there, one should not worry about firewood.

(9) 她冒着生命危险去抢救那个溺水儿童。

She risked her life trying to save the drowning child.

(10) 有志者,事竟成。

Where there is a will, there is a way.

(11) 其实地上本没有路,走的人多了,也便成了路。

For actually the earth had no roads to begin with, but when men pass one way, a road is made.

(12) 只许州官放火,不许百姓点灯。

The magistrates are free to burn down houses while the common people are forbidden even to light lamps.

(13) 他走进屋来,大衣上全是雪。

He entered the room, his coat covered with snow.

(14) 送君千里,终有一别。

Although you may escort a guest a thousand miles, yet must the parting come at last.

(15) 这些动物喜欢白天休息,晚上活动。

These animals tend to have a sleep in the daytime and go out to search for food at night.

(16) 我们要做充分准备,才能实施这个工程。

We must make ample preparations before the project can be properly carried out.

(17) 礼拜天我们不上课。

On Sundays we have no school.

(18) 活到老,学到老。

No one is too old to learn.

(19) 改过不嫌晚。

It is never too late to mend.

(20) 昨天周末，我们全家去野炊。

It was weekend yesterday, and my family went for a picnic.

二、根据文化特点需要进行增词

原文中有些关键词语与特定的历史背景或其他文化情况有关，用来象征与历史背景或文化相关的某种特殊意义，翻译时往往需要增加适当的词语加以表达，弥补目的语读者因源语文化背景的缺失而造成的阅读障碍。

(1) The terrorists had been caught and jailed. But the two leaders had escaped with machines guns. This fact hung like the sword of Damocles over the police commissioner's head.

那些恐怖分子已被入狱，但两个头头却携带机关枪逃脱了。这件事使警察局长仿佛头悬达摩克利斯之剑，时刻坐立不安。

文化背景：达摩克利斯（Damocles）是锡拉库扎（Syracuse）暴君狄俄尼索斯（Dionysius）的廷臣。狄俄尼索斯在一次宴请达摩克利斯时，在达摩克利斯头上用一根头发悬挂着一把剑。在宴会过程中，达摩克利斯坐在剑下，恐惧万分。狄俄尼索斯意在告诉他，当国王并不享福，而是时刻都有生命危险。所以在译文中加上了"时刻坐立不安"。

(2) The blond boy quickly crossed himself.

那个金发小男孩立刻在胸前画十字架，祈求上帝保佑。

文化背景：基督教徒在祈祷或祝福时，会在胸前划十字，这一手势起源于基督教的标志十字架。相传耶稣是被钉死在十字架上的，人们为了纪念耶稣，便将十字架定为基督教的标志。后来，基督教徒们开始在胸前划十字以表示对耶稣的虔诚，祈求耶稣宽恕他们的"原罪"，帮他们消灾解难，保佑他们平安。所以在译文中加上了"祈求上帝保佑"，使译文表达的意义更加明确。

(3) It was Friday and soon they'd go out and get drunk.

星期五发薪日到了，他们马上就要上街喝个酩酊大醉。

文化背景：英国每逢星期五发工资，而这点与我国的文化背景不同。译文加"发薪日"三字,读者就会明白英国人为何要在这一天上街去大吃大喝。

(4) It was a Herculean task, but he managed to do it.

那是赫拉克勒斯式的任务,非常艰巨,但他终于完成了。

文化背景:Herculean(赫拉克勒斯)是希腊神话中的身材魁梧、力大无穷的英雄。他曾被罚去完成12项极为艰巨的任务,成功后,被封为神。赫拉克勒斯式任务指需要巨大的体力或智力才能完成的任务,故译文中增加"非常艰巨"。

(5) People considered that what he had played on that occasion was no more than a Judas Kiss.

人们认为他在那种场合所表演的不过是犹大之吻,居心险恶。

文化背景:在圣经故事中,犹大原为耶稣十二门徒之一,后来背叛了耶稣,为了三十块银币以亲吻耶稣的方式把他出卖给犹太教当权者。故犹大在西方成为叛徒的代名词;"犹大之吻"指口蜜腹剑的伪善阴险行为,故增加"居心险恶"。

(6) This great scientist was born in New England.

这位伟大的科学家出生在美国东北部的新英格兰。

文化背景:英国本土也可称作"英格兰",但"新英格兰"在美国东北部的一个地区,通过增词,就让不了解英美文化的读者知道了所谈论的地方不在英国本土,而在美国东北部的某个地方。

中译英时,需要增加必要的词语,以解释相关的历史与文化背景。

(1) 不要重复叶公好龙那个故事,讲了多少年的社会主义,临到社会主义跑来找他,他又害怕起来了。

The story of Lord Ye who professed to love dragons should not be repeated, one must not just talk about socialism for years and then suddenly turn pale when socialism comes knocking at the door. (增加词语,解释了"叶公好龙"这一成语的意思,更清楚地表达了原文实际的内涵意义)

(2) 铁饭碗。

"Iron rice bowl", China's system of lifetime job and income security. (增加词语,以对"铁饭碗"这一具有典型中国文化特色的负载词进行解释)

(3) 三个臭皮匠,胜过诸葛亮。

The wit of three cobblers combined surpasses Zhuge Liang the master mind. (增加词语,对"诸葛亮"这一中国文化中妇孺皆知,但西方却可能鲜有人知的人物进行解释,为译文提供原文历史背景知识)

(4) 她在戏中扮演包公。

In the opera, she played the male role of Judge Bao, <u>the just and impartial judge in Chinese history</u>. (增加词语,对"包公"这一文化负载词进行解释)

(5) 他们都晓得两点,为什么我们只提一点?

They all know there are <u>two aspects to everything</u>, why do we only mention one? (增加词语,对哲学术语"两点论"进行解释)

增加必要的词以适应修辞的需要

(1) Poor little tender heart! And so it goes on hoping and beating, and longing and trusting.

可怜这温柔的小姑娘,一颗心<u>抖</u>跳个不停,她<u>左盼右盼</u>,一直想念情人,对他深信不疑。(译文并没有将 hoping and beating 简单地译为"盼望着、跳动着",而是增加了一些描述性的词语来描写少女思念情人的心情,使人如见其人,产生了一种可触可摸的立体感觉)

(2) Their host carved, poured, served, cut bread, talked, laughed, proposed health.

他们的主人,又是切肉<u>啊</u>,又是倒酒<u>啊</u>,又是上菜<u>啊</u>,又是切面包<u>啊</u>,又是说<u>啊</u>,又是笑<u>啊</u>,又是祝福<u>啊</u>,<u>忙个不停</u>。(增加语气助词和概括词语)

(3) Only very slight and very scattering ripples of half-hearted hand-clapping greeted him.

欢迎他的只有几下<u>零零落落</u>、<u>冷冷淡淡</u>的掌声。(增加了汉语特有的叠词)

(4) Ambition is the mother of destruction as well as of evil.

野心不仅是罪恶的<u>根源</u>,同时也是毁灭的<u>根源</u>。(增加了原文排比省略的部分)

(5) Whether to use tests, other kinds of information, or both in a particular situation depends, therefore, upon the evidence from experience concerning comparative validity and upon such factors as cost and availability.

因此,究竟是使用测试,还是使用其他种类的信息,抑或在特定情况下两种都使用,取决于相对效度来自于经验的证据,同时还取决于成本和可获得性这样的因素。(增加了原文省略的动词)

(6)新旧社会真是两个社会。

The new and the old societies are really two different worlds. (增加表面无、内涵有的内容)

(7)十二年的延安岁月,中国共产党人已经适应了当地的风土和季节,也适应了农民的气质。

In the twelve Yanan years the Chinese Communists had fitted themselves to the land, the rhythm of its seasons, the mood of its peasants. (增加表面无、内涵有的内容)

翻译小贴士

1. 增词翻译实例赏析

◀原文▶

12月1日,圆明园马首铜像正式回归。160年前,英法联军抢掠焚毁圆明园后,该文物流失海外。马首铜像是圆明园流失海外重要文物中第一件回归并入藏原址的文物。十二生肖兽首铜像原本是圆明园海晏堂前水力钟的主要构件,铸造于清朝乾隆年间。1860年,第二次鸦片战争期间,圆明园被英法联军抢掠焚毁,12尊兽首流失海外。马首铜像由意大利艺术家郎世宁设计,由宫廷匠师精工制作,融合东西方艺术风格。澳门亿万富豪何鸿燊购得马首铜像并决定将其捐赠给国家文物局,让它回归故里。

译文

A bronze horse head sculpture, a treasure of China's Old Summer

Palace that went missing after an Anglo-French allied forces' looting 160 years ago, returned to its original palace home Tuesday. It is the first time that a lost important cultural relic from the Old Summer Palace, or "Yuanmingyuan", has been returned to and housed at its original location after being repatriated from overseas. Twelve animal head sculptures once formed a zodiac water clock in Beijing's Yuanmingyuan, built by Emperor Qianlong of the Qing Dynasty (1644—1911). The originals were looted from the royal garden by Anglo-French allied forces in 1860 during the Second Opium War (1856—1860). The horse head, designed by Italian artist Giuseppe Castiglione and crafted by royal craftsmen, is an artistic blend of East and West. Macao billionaire Stanley Ho bought the bronze horse head and decided to donate it to the National Cultural Heritage Administration and return it to its original home.

赏析：这篇材料中涉及很多人名、地名、年代、事件等专有名词和术语的翻译，如"圆明园""英法联军""十二生肖""海晏堂""水力钟""清朝""乾隆""鸦片战争""郎世宁""何鸿燊"，如何将这些专有名词翻译成英语，而且被目标语读者所接受，需要采用一定的翻译技巧，如增词，增加一些解释性信息，补充完善时间 the Qing Dynasty (1644—1911)、the Second Opium War (1856—1860)，专有名称 the Old Summer Palace, or Yuanmingyuan 等，更完整地再现原文信息。此外，在翻译中还需要对原文进行一些语序上的调整，如将原文的前几句话打乱顺序，对原有信息重新排列组合，使译文符合目的语表达习惯，也便于目的语读者能更好地理解原文。

2. 翻译实践

◀ 原文 ▶

Opera is expensive: that much is inevitable. But expensive things are not inevitably the province of the rich unless we abdicate society's power of choice. We can choose to make opera, and other expensive forms of culture, accessible to those who cannot individually pay for it. The question is: Why should we? Nobody denies the imperative of food, shelter, defence, health and education. But even in a prehistoric cave, mankind stretched out a hand not just to eat, drink or fight, but also to draw. The impulse towards culture, the desire to express and explore the world through imagination and representation is fundamental. In Europe, this desire has found fulfillment in the masterpieces of our music, art, literature and theatre. These masterpieces are the touchstones for all our efforts; they are the touchstones for the possibilities to which human thought and imagination may aspire; they carry the most profound message that can be sent from one human to another.

译文1

聆听歌剧是一种奢侈,你必须为此支付昂贵的票价。但是,享用昂贵的东西并非一定是富人的特权,除非我们放弃社会权利的选择。我们有权利让歌剧或其他昂贵的文化形式面向大众,面向那些不具备个人支付能力的人。然而,问题是我们为什么要这样做?没人会否认食物、居所、防护、健康与教育的不可或缺性。但即便是在史前的穴居时代,人们伸出手来,也不仅仅是为了吃喝,为了搏杀,而且还有一个目的,那就是动手画画。人们对于文化的冲动,即人们通过想象和再现手段来表现探索这个世界的愿望,才是最根本的。在欧洲,人们通过音乐、艺术、文学和戏剧等方面的不朽作品的创作,实现了这一愿望。这些杰作是衡量人们努力程度的试金石,是检验人类思维和想象潜能的标准,它们有着最深厚的寓意,并在人们之间彼此传播。

译文2

聆听歌剧,无疑昂贵至极。但是,昂贵的事物并非只是属于富人的范畴,除非我们放弃社会的选择权。我们可以选择去使歌剧以及其他某些昂贵的文化形式也能为那些不具备个人支付能力的人所享受。但问题是,我们有必要这么做吗?没人会否认食物、居所、防护、健康与教育的不可或缺性。但即便是在史前时代的洞穴中,人类伸出手来,就不单纯是为了吃、喝或搏杀,而且亦进行绘画创作。人类对于文化的冲动,通过形象思维和再现手段来表现探索世界的欲望,乃亘古有之。在欧洲,这一欲望在我们的音乐、艺术、文学和戏剧杰作中寻找到了其实现形式。这些杰作成为我们全部努力的试金石。作为试金石,它们能衡量出人类思想和想象力所可能企及的高度。它们携带着最寓意深刻的主题,可在人类彼此间相互传递。

通过以上两个译文的对比,不难发现,增加一些原文"表面无、内在有"的信息,对于译入语读者更好理解和接受原文,是非常必要的。

习题六

一、英译汉

1. I had imagined it to be merely a gesture of affection, but it seems it is to smell the lamb and make sure that it is her own.

2. After the football match, he's got an important meeting.

3. He dismissed the meeting without a closing speech.

4. Basically, the theory proposed, among other things, that the maximum speed possible in the universe is that of light.

5. Ideally, one day, researchers will know enough about the genesis of earthquakes and the nature of particular faults to predict quakes directly.

二、汉译英

1. 他喜欢指出别人的缺点,但用意是好的。
2. 你越讲空洞的大道理,人家越感到讨厌。
3. 这个小孩饭前都洗手,然后用餐巾纸擦干。
4. 只有晚上躺在床上时,她才感到神志清醒。
5. 还有些人也不能进领导班子或者不能重用,例如,革命意志严重衰减的人,饱食终日、无所用心的人,等等。

第七章 减词

由于英汉语言差异,在进行英汉语言转换过程中,难以实现形式和意义上的一一对等。出于目的语的要求,有时候需要进行必要的调整,省略或减掉原语中的一些冗余或没有实际价值的表达。如:"教育部12月1日表示,今冬明春发生局部聚集性疫情风险加大,高校放寒假要坚持'错峰'原则,安排学生分批次有序离校,妥善安排留校师生寒假生活。"在这句表达中,"错峰"和"分批次有序离校"实际上是一个意思,没有必要对两种表达进行重复翻译,只需要翻译"分批次有序离校"或"错峰离校"这个信息即可,译文为"Universities in China should make sure departures of students heading home for winter vacation are staggered and make proper arrangements for those staying on campus amid increasing risks of COVID-19 cluster infections, the Ministry of Education said on Tuesday."。再如,"Our aim is to turn the China market into a market for the world, a market shared by all, and a market accessible to all."这句中的 market 属于重复,在译文中可以根据实际需要省去部分表达,翻译为"让中国市场成为世界的、共享的、大家的市场。"当然,若是为了修辞上的强调,也可以复制原文的重复。再看下面两个例子:"这绝不是封闭的国内循环,而是更加开放的国内国际双循环,不仅是中国自身发展需要,而且将更好造福各国人民。"这句话可以翻译为"What we envision is not a development loop behind closed doors, but more open domestic and international circulations. We will do so not only to meet China's own development needs but also for the greater benefit of people in all countries.",其中"双"这一词的信息已经包含在 circulations 之中。还有,"Louis Cha Leung-yung, one of the most influential Chinese novelists, and better known under the pen name Jin Yong, died on Tuesday afternoon in Hong Kong Sanatorium and Hospital. He was 94. Readers across China pay tribute to the grandmaster of wuxia",在这句话中,人称代词 he 根据汉语的表达习惯略去不译,翻译成"中国最有影响力的小说家之一、武侠小说泰斗金庸(原名查良镛)于 10 月 30 日下午在香港养和医院逝世,享年 94 岁。国内读者纷纷缅怀金庸。"

一般来讲,省略或减词这种翻译方法或翻译技巧主要应用于以下这些情况:

一、省略范畴词

在某种情况下,有些汉语词汇并没有实际的意义,比如,在"为……作准备工作"这个表达中,"工作"这个词并没有什么实际意义,仅是汉语中的一种表达习惯而已。类似情况的表达还有:问题、情况、态度、状态、范围等,这些词被称为"范畴词"。在进行中译英的过程中,由于这些范畴词不具有实际意义和价值,可以省去不译。

(1)不仅对人如此,就是国与国之间相处,中国人也秉持着谦虚的态度。

In addition to personal relationships, Chinese people are modest in relationship with other countries.

(2)优势在我们方面,不在敌人方面。

It is we, not the enemy, who are in the superior position.

(3)他在我不知道情况下私自拿走了那东西。

He took it away without my knowledge.

(4)前怕狼,后怕虎的态度不能造就干部。

"Fearing wolves ahead and tigers behind" will not produce cadres.

二、省略自我暗示词

因英汉两种语言表达的差异,有些意义重复,或者已经被包含在其他词语的表达中,翻译时可以省去不译。

(1)小栓依他母亲的话,咳着睡着了。

Obediently, Little Shuan coughed himself to sleep.

(obediently 这个词本身就有"顺从,依附"的意思,依据上下文的提示,"依他母亲的话"就可以省略不译了。)

(2)反对党领袖的演讲在报纸上大出风头,使政府相形见绌。

The opposition leader's speech stole the headlines from the government.

(3)他们从地上爬起来,擦干身上的血迹,掩埋好同伴的尸首,他们又继续战斗了。

They picked themselves up, wiped off the blood, buried their fallen comrades and went on battle again.

(4)你说的话总是最正确的。

What you say is always correct.(按照常规的逻辑,一个事物或概念正确与否,没有程度之分,谈不上"最"正确这种程度上的修饰。)

三、减去对偶同义词中的某一个词

在英语的某些表达中,存在所谓的"对偶同义词",即同时并用所指意义相同或相近的两个词,中间用连接词连接在一起。在翻译过程中若遇到这种情况,就可以采用减词或省略译法,即不重复地译出同义词,而是仅译出其中一个词的意思。表面看从数量上减少了一个词,而原文所包含的信息和内在意义却没有任何消减。

(1) Less than two weeks, the agreements of the two countries were pronounced null and void.

不到两周时间,双方签订的多份协议被宣布无效。(null 和 void 都是"无效的,作废的,过期的"意思,出于简洁,因而略去一词不译。)

(2) The bold and courageous struggle of the working class and its Communist Party carried the day.

工人阶级及其共产党的英勇斗争取得了胜利。(bold 和 courageous 为同义词,意指"英勇的,勇敢的",可以略去一词不译,只译其一)

(3) If the arteries become hard and stiff, the heart has to work much harder.

如果动脉硬化,心脏负担就得加重。(英文 hard 与 stiff 为同义词,在中文只要用一个词就可以了)

(4) With a tiresome journey a whole day, my arms and legs go to sleep.

一整天疲惫的跋涉之后,我的四肢麻木,不听使唤。

(5) Neither party shall cancel the contract without sufficient cause or reason.

双方均不得无故解除合同。

(6) The most amazing and inspiring part of the tale came after that.

这之后才是故事最惊心动魄的部分。

四、省略四字结构中意义重复的词汇

四字结构短语(特别是成语)是汉语的特色表达。有些四字结构(特别是成语)短语的前半部分与后半部分意义相同,而后半部分仅仅是出于对前半部分的强调而已。因此,在对这类四字结构(特别是成语)进行翻译时,只需翻译出它的真实意义即可,不必进行逐字翻译。

(1) 解放前,他们被迫离乡背井,给城里的一个大资本家干活。

Before liberation they were forced to leave their native place and worked for a capitalist in the city.

(2) 这是九月的一个晴朗的下午,纽约的大街上,人来人往,五光十色。

It was a bright September afternoon, and streets of New York were brilliant with moving men.

(3) 我的回答完全是坦坦荡荡,直言不讳。

I have been completely honest in my replies, with holding nothing.

(4) 欢迎他的只有几下轻轻的、零零落落、冷冷淡淡的掌声。

Only a very slight and very scattering ripples of half-hearted hand-clapping greeted him.

(5) 他一坐下来就讲开了,滔滔不绝地讲个没完。

As he sat down and began talking, words poured out.

(6) 因为他们很注意处理各方面的关系,所以八面玲珑,到处结缘。

Sensitive in their dealings with others, they are well liked everywhere.

五、省略原文表达中重复使用的词、词组或句子成分等

重复是一种修辞表达。为了修辞效果,或者出于强调或其他目的,在语言表达中往往使用重复。但由于英汉语言的差异,未必需要在译入语中复制原有的重复,应省略或减去源语中的重复,使用其他手段加以代替,从而产生更好的表达效果。

(1) 我书架上的小说你最喜爱哪一本,你就可以借哪一本。

You may borrow whichever novel in my bookcase you like best.

(2) 青年人的觉悟程度如何,道德品质如何,知识水平如何,直接关系着社会主义建设的速度,关系着祖国的未来。

How the youth comes up in political consciousness, in moral qualities and in intellectual attainments has a direct bearing on the speed of socialist construction and the future of our motherland.

(3) 雪花撒落在水池上,田野里,撒落在河边湖畔,撒落在山峦和山谷中。

The snow falls on every pond and field; by the river and lake, on the hill and in the valley.

(4) 他不再梦见风涛,不再梦见惊人的遭遇,也不再梦见大鱼、搏斗和角力。

He no longer dreamed of storms, nor of great occurrences, nor of great fish, nor of fights, nor of strength.

(5) 亚洲经济管理向来不以完美取胜,而是以务实和灵活性取胜。

Asia's strength of economic management, however, has not been its perfection, but its pragmatism and flexibility.

(6) 他成为一个石油大亨——一个白手起家的石油大亨。

He became an oil baron, all by himself.

(7) 质子带正电,电子带负电,而中子既不带正电,也不带负电。

A proton has a positive charge and an electron has a negative charge, but a neutron has neither.

(8) 夺取这个胜利,已经是不用很久的时间,不用花费很大的力气了。巩固这个胜利,却是需要很久的时间和花费很大的力气的事情。

To win this victory will not require much more time and effort, but to consolidate it will.

(9) 她是一个漂亮的女人,一个时尚的女人,一个睿智的女人,一个充满人情味的女人。

She is a woman of beauty, fashion, wit, and humanity.

(10) 俄国人民的革命曾经依照了这条规律,中国人民的革命也依照了这条规律。

The Russian people's revolution followed this law, and so has the Chinese people's revolution.

六、省略句子中的连接词、人称代词

英语是一种具有形合特征的语言,而汉语则主要是一种具有意合特征的语言。形合语言的一个主要特征就是连接词的使用。另外,英语是逻辑性很强的语言,逻辑性首先表现为语言形式的完整。因此,在进行英汉翻译时,需省略或减去原文中的一些连接词、人称代词等,以此符合汉语的表达习惯。

(1) The audience waited almost one hour before the speaker suddenly stepped out on the balcony and waved his hand towards the audience.

观众们等了将近一个小时,突然演讲者走了出来,站在阳台上,向大家挥手。

(2) The sun is bright, and the sky is clear.

阳光灿烂,晴空万里。

(3) As I lay awake, I realized that I was in trouble.

我醒来,躺在地上,明白自己的处境不妙。

(4) I was like that ship before my education began, only I was without compass or sounding-line, and had no way of knowing how near the harbor was.

我在开始受教育之前,就像这样一条船,没有罗盘,没有测深绳,也无法知道离海港有多远。

(5) We took this opportunity to inform you that we are now in a position to make a prompt shipment of the merchandise.

兹奉告,该商品可即期装运。

(6) Outside it was pitch dark and it was raining cats and dogs.

外面一片漆黑,大雨倾盆。

(7) We have 365 days a year and 24 hours a day and 60 minutes an hour.

一年有365天,一天有24小时,一小时60分钟。

(8) Friction manifests itself as a force that opposes motion.

摩擦表现为阻碍运动的力。

(9) Although pure science usually has no apparent connection with technology, it does lend itself to the development of applied science.

纯理论科学虽然通常与技术没有明显的联系,但确实有助于应用科学的发展。

翻译小贴士

1. 针对美国驻华使领馆用 PS 图片抹黑中国的做法,7月13日,外交部发言人华春莹做出回应。

◀ 原文 ▶

他们侮辱自己的智慧我不反对,但是我们坚决反对美方以如此低劣的谎言来污名化、污蔑攻击中国。这种恶劣行径应该遭到谴责和追究。这也再次证明,美方一些人现在为了诋毁攻击中国,已经到了没有任何下限的地步。

译文

I have no problem with them insulting their own intelligence, but we firmly oppose them using this to tarnish China's name. The US should be condemned and held accountable for such egregious acts. It once again proves that for some people in the US, nothing is not up for use in its fanatic bid to attack and smear China.

分析

"没有任何下限"指的是美方一些人为了诋毁中国,"无所不用其极",因此这里译成"nothing is not up for use",后面接"in its fanatic bid to attack and smear China",形容词 fanatic 表示"狂热的",用在这里形象地描绘了美方一些人的嘴脸。"侮辱自己的智慧"在这里直译成 insult their own intelligence。

2. 7月15日,有记者就英国封禁华为一事提问,华春莹向英国发出了灵魂拷问。

◀ 原文 ▶

中国有句俗话,"种瓜得瓜,种豆得豆",任何决定和行为都需要付出代价。

译文

We have a saying in China which basically means "you reap what you sow". All the decision and actions come with price tags.

◀ 原文 ▶

英方究竟能否保持其独立自主地位,还是甘心沦为美国附庸、为美国火中取栗?

译文

Does it want to act in its own way of its own volition or is it OK with being a subordinate and a cat's paw for the US?

分析

"种瓜得瓜,种豆得豆"的译文采用了"归化"的策略,译成了英文中类似的谚语"you reap what you sow",你播种了什么,就会收获什么。

火中取栗是一个舶来的成语,出自 17 世纪法国寓言诗人拉·封丹的寓言。猴子骗猫从火中取栗子,结果猫爪上的毛被火烧掉,栗子却全被猴子吃了,比喻"为他人冒险出力,自己却一无所获"。为他人火中取栗的人就是 cat's paw,猫爪。

习题七

一、英译汉

1. If I learn to drive a motorcycle, I will certainly buy a new one.

2. It is better to do well than to say well.

3. That dishonest boy is not at all ill. He is alive and kicking in the swimming pool. We all saw him.

4. If you don't go there tomorrow, they'll get angry.

二、汉译英

1. 总理在出席音乐会之前,还有许多工作要做。

2. 她连续讲了两小时的法语,没有出现任何错误。

3. 可怜两个强徒,不过做了南柯一梦。

4. 现在有少数人就是做官当老爷,有些事情实在不像话。

5. 语言这个东西,不是随便可以学好的,非下苦功夫不可。

6. 自周秦以来,中国是一个封建的社会,其政治是封建的政治,其经济是封建的经济。

第八章 词类转换

词类转译是指在翻译过程中,为了表达通顺,一种词类可以转译为另一种词类。词类的转译没有什么严格的限制和规定,主要是根据上下文,有时依据词语固定搭配,有时是根据译文语言的表达习惯。例如:史蒂文森有口才,有风度,但很软弱。

对于这句话,可以有以下两个不同的英文译文:

(1) Stevenson has skills of speaking and a graceful manner, but is very weak.

(2) Stevenson was eloquent and elegant-but soft.

译文(1)完全按照原文的结构和词类进行翻译,而译文(2)在保留原文含义的基础上,将原文中的动宾结构转换为系表结构,将名词"口才""风度"转译为形容词 eloquent 和 elegant。两个译文相比较,显然译文(2)更加简洁,更加具有表现力。

翻译中的词类转换主要有以下几种情况。

一、英语的非动词转译为汉语的动词

(一) 英语的名词转译为汉语的动词

英语中经常使用大量具有动作意义的名词和动词派生出来的名词,在译成汉语时,这类词往往可以译成动词。

(1) It's my conviction that complacency is at the root of our troubles.

我深信自满情绪是我们各种问题的根源。

(2) For all her thoughts were still with her lover, whom she intended to seek in the disguise of a page.

因为她一心一意还是惦记着她的情人,她打算扮成一个儿童去找他。

(3) Those small factories are also lavish consumer and waster of raw materials.

那些小工厂还在极大地消耗和浪费原材料。

(4) The new situation requires the formation of a new strategy.

新形势要求制定新战略。

(5) A view of the village can be obtained from the tower.

从塔上可以看见这个村庄。

(6) In the recent several decades, the abuse of guns has become one of the most serious social problem in that country.

在近几十年,滥用枪支已经成为那个国家最严重的社会问题之一。

(7) He is never a non-smoker, but a chain-smoker.

他非但抽烟,抽起烟来还一根接一根。

(8) There were various possible candidates for the position.

有好几个人竞聘这个职务。

(9) Language does not exist in isolation—it is the preservation of our past and the record of our present civilization.

语言并不是孤立地存在着,它保存了昔日的文明,也记载了当今的文明。

(二)英语的介词转译为汉语的动词

英语中的介词或介词短语在许多情况下可以译成汉语的动词,尤其当它们用作表语或状语时。

(1) The People's Republic of China has been firmly on the road of opening and reform since 1978.

自1978年以来,中国已经坚定不移地走上了改革开放的道路。

(2) Heat sets these particles in random motion.

热量使这些粒子做随机运动。

(3) Up the street they went, past stores, across a broad square, and then went a huge building.

他们沿着大街走去,经过一家家店铺,穿过一个宽广的广场,然后走进一栋大楼。

(4) ...this nation under God, shall have a new birth of freedom, and that government of the people, by the people, for the people shall not perish from the earth...

这个国家在上帝的保佑下,要获得自由的新生,而这个民有、民治、民享的政府将永远不会从地球上消失。

(5) But then another policeman appeared, this time in uniform, and I was left in no doubt.

但又有一个警察出现在我面前,这次是身着警服,这一下使我确信无疑了。

(6) Soon, he was on his way in his new 16-metre boat.

不久,他就驾着那艘16米长的新船出发了。

(三) 英语的形容词转译为汉语的动词

英语中的形容词,常常与系动词搭配构成"系表结构"。"系表结构"作谓语,从而使这些形容词具有了动作意味,翻译成汉语的时候需要转换为动词。这些词常常表示状态、知觉、情感、态度等意义,在句中作表语的形容词,以及同介词搭配构成句子表语或定语的形容词,通常可译成汉语中的动词。

(1) He made a very informative lecture yesterday, and all of us benefited a lot.

他在讲座中透露了很多消息,我们都感到获益匪浅。

(2) The fact that she was able to send a message was a hint. But I had to be cautious.

她能够给我带信儿这件事就是个暗示,但是我必须小心处理。

(3) He is always being indifferent to our advice and customers' complaints.

他从来不在乎我们的建议和顾客的投诉。

(4) Integrity means you do what you do because it's right and not just fashionable or politically correct.

诚实意味着去做你认为对的事,而不仅是为了赶时髦或在政治上不出错。

(5) Yet the public has every reason to be wary of professional deception.

但是公众完全有理由对职业性欺骗保持警惕。

(四)英语的连词转译为汉语动词

(1) Nine and four is thirteen.

9加4等于13。

(2) The book will be published by one of the publishing houses in America in two weeks or fourteen days.

这本书将在两周后,也就是14天后由美国的一家出版社出版。

(3) He is the fourth and last person in this interview.

他是这次面试中第四个也是最后一个。

(4) This distance is four kilometers or 2.485 6 miles.

这段距离为四公里,合2.486 5英里。

(5) Further outlook, rain and snow.

未来天气雨夹雪。

(五)英语的副词转译为汉语的动词

英语当中的副词在做表语或宾语补足语时也经常转译为汉语中的动词。

(1) Our wedding ceremony is only ten days away, but I still keep a secret from my parents.

距离我们的婚期只有10天的时间了,但我还没有告诉我的父母。

(2) The boy opened the door, telling me that his father was out.

那个男孩打开门,告诉我他的父亲出去了。

(3) The little boy had been up with a packet of mints.

小男孩上楼来,送来了一盒薄荷糖。

(4) As soon as the piston reaches the top of the exhaust stroke,

it starts down on another intake, compression, power, and exhaust cycle.

活塞一到达排气行程的顶端,它便开始向下运动,进入另一个进气、压缩、做功和排气的工作循环。

(5) She opened the window to let fresh air in.

她把窗子打开,让新鲜空气进来。

二、英语的非名词转译成汉语的名词

(一) 英语的动词转译成汉语的名词

(1) The volume of trade has increased tremendously to the advantage of both countries.

贸易量有了很大的增加,这给两国都带来了利益。

(2) Formality has always characterized their relationship.

他们之间的关系,有一个特点,就是以礼相待。

(3) He thought the gentleman looked and talked a little wildly.

他觉得那位先生的神情和言谈有些不可思议。

(4) He acted as though he was the host of the house.

他的一举一动似乎显得他是这里的主人。

(5) As the war progressed, he would symbolize their frustration, the embodiment of all evils.

随着战争的进行,他成了他们受挫的象征,成了一切坏事的化身。

(二) 英语的形容词转译成汉语的名词

(1) This issue is no more serious than that one.

这个问题的严重性不亚于那个问题。

(2) Since silver and gold are inconvenient to carry and to assay for purity and for weight, it became customary for each state to stamp out in coin form a specified number of ounces of gold carrying the seal of the state to guarantee purity and weight.

由于携带金银以及给金银的纯度和重量进行鉴别均不方便,因此,以往通常的做法是,每个国家把特定数量盎司的黄金冲压成金币,同时印上该国的印记以保证纯度和重量。

(3) With the development of society, government is getting more efficient these days.

随着社会的发展,近日来,政府的工作效率越来越高了。

(4) Out of the corner of his eye he could see the landscape. It was industrial and at that hour, sad.

他眼角的余光还能瞥见窗外的景色。这里是工业区,此刻一片萧条景象。

(5) Beg filed an urgent story to his newspaper in London, little realizing that he was about to become part of a new journalistic legend on Fleet Street.

贝格往伦敦报社发了一条急电,当时根本没想到自己会成为舰队街新闻界一件奇闻中的相关人物。

(三) 英语的副词转译成汉语的名词

(1) The paper said editorially that this area has successfully survived a destructive natural disaster.

该报的社论说,这个地区成功地抵御住了一场毁灭性的自然灾害。

(2) They have not done so well ideologically, however, as organizationally.

但是,他们的思想工作没有组织工作做得好。

(3) He is well known to be strong physically, but weak mentally.

众所周知他体力很强,可智力很弱。

(4) What is the fare to Nanjing and back?

去南京一个来回车费是多少?

(5) Sodium is very active chemically.

钠的化学特性很活泼。

三、英语的非形容词转译成汉语的形容词

(一) 英语的副词转译成汉语的形容词

(1) They were widely and deeply influenced by what happened at that moment.

那一刻所发生的一切对他们产生了深刻而广泛的影响。

(2) She has stupidly committed such a mistake.

她真笨,竟然犯了这样一个错误。

(3) Earthquakes are closely related to faulting.

地震与地层断裂有密切的关系。

(4) He routinely radioed another agent on the ground.

他跟另一个地勤人员进行了例行的无线电联络。

(5) The engineer had prepared meticulously for his design.

工程师为这次设计做了十分周密的准备。

(二) 英语的名词转译成汉语的形容词

(1) If he should fail, what a concern it would be to his teacher!

万一他真的没通过,他老师该多难过呀!

(2) A newly-elected President is a power, I know that.

一个新当选的总统的确是威风十足,那我是知道的。

(3) The pallor of her face indicated clearly how she was feeling at the moment.

她苍白的脸色清楚地表明了她那时的情绪。

(4) Oh, he is all generosity and tolerance.

他非常大方也很包容他人。

(5) He talked for some time with Bundy, and his questions reflected the enormity of his doubts.

他同邦迪谈了一会,他提出的问题反映出他有很大的怀疑。

四、英语的非副词转译成汉语的副词

(一) 英语的名词转译成汉语的副词

(1) The hero received the gangster's attack with the most undaunted intrepidity.

面对歹徒的袭击,那位英雄一往无前,毫不畏缩。

(2) Quasi-stars were discovered in 1963 as a result of an effort to overcome the shortcomings of radio telescopes.

类星体是 1963 年发现的,是人们努力克服射电望远镜的缺点所取得的一项成果。

(3) Her younger brother with great cheerfulness told her that he had much good news to communicate.

弟弟兴高采烈,他带来了非常好的消息。

(4) Each sample must be submitted with full particulars of its source.

每个样品均应详细标明其来源。

(5) The new mayor earned some appreciation by the courtesy of coming to visit the city poor.

新市长有礼貌地前来访问城市贫民,获得了他们的好感。

(二) 英语的形容词转译成汉语的副词

(1) In case of use without conditioning the electrode, frequent calibrations are required.

如果在使用前没有调节电极,使用时则需要经常校定。

(2) His avid history study had taught him that the people are the real creator of the history of human beings.

他学习历史知识如饥似渴,这让他了解到人民才是人类历史的真正创造者。

(3) This is sheer nonsense.

这完全是胡说。

(4) Please give an accurate account of the whole affair.

把整个事情确切地讲述一下。

(5) A further word of caution regarding the selection of standard sizes of materials is necessary.

必须进一步提醒关于选择材料的标准规格之事宜。

五、汉语的动词转译为英语的名词

一般来讲，汉语表达惯用动词，而英语表达少用动词；也就是说，汉语的一句话中可能包含几个动词，而英语的一句话中却只能有一个主体动词。由于名词用法更为简洁，便于表达较为复杂的内容，而且因为语法的限制，英语中名词使用频繁，而汉语则更倾向于使用动词，所以汉译英过程中，经常将一些动词或动词短语转换成英语的名词。例如：

他对总统声明为保住其职位而决心奋斗表示钦佩。

在这句话中，出现了四个动词，而我们将其翻译成英语之后：

He admires the President's stated decision to fight the job.

仅有一个谓语动词和一个不定式后面的原形动词。

汉译英过程中，汉语的动词转换为英语的名词主要存在以下几种情况。

(一) 汉语的动词转译为由动词派生出的英语名词

(1) 电影明星是大部分少女崇拜的对象。

Film stars are objects of admiration for most girls.

(2) 人工智能已经用来探索和开发海洋资源了。

Artificial intelligence has found application for exploration and development of the marine resources.

(3) 我们也认识到越来越需要使某些经济部门工业化。

We also realized the growing need and necessity to industrialize certain sectors of the economy.

(4) 在中国，人们非常注重讲礼貌。

In China, there is a lot of emphasis on politeness.

(5) 发言人一个接一个表示要打倒帝国主义,要消灭人剥削人的制度,要解放世界上的被压迫人民。

One after another, speakers called for the downfall of imperialism, abolition of exploitation of man by man, liberation of the oppressed of the world.

(二)汉语动词转译为具有动作意义的英语名词

(1) 她一看见自己的丈夫和另一个女人走在一起就勃然大怒。

She flared up at the sight of her husband walking with another woman.

(2) 他一生的真正的使命是通过各种途径为推翻资本主义社会而做出贡献。

His real mission in life was to contribute, in one way or another, to the overthrow of the capitalist society.

(3) 听见孩子的哭声,她一下子冲出门外。

The sound of baby's cry had her rush out of the room.

(4) 一周快结束时,敌人彻底溃退了。

As the week drew to a close, the enemy's rout was completed.

(5) 仔细研究原文,你会翻译得更好。

A careful study of the original text will give you a better translation.

(三)汉语动词转译为构成短语的英语名词

(1) 汽车猛地刹住,停在悬崖边上。

The car braked sharply, coming to rest on the edge of the cliff.

(2) 昨天的新闻报道没有提到教育改革的事情。

The news report yesterday made no mention of the education reform.

(3) 我们大家都得克制一下自己,我知道车子陷到泥里去了,但我们是可以把它弄出来的。

Now let's just take a firm grip on ourselves, I know the car's truck in the mud, but we should be able to get it out again.

(4) 他们最后看了铁麦克一眼——它依旧安然无恙地耸立在黑暗中。

They took a final look at Iron Mike, still intact in the darkness.

六、汉语的动词转译为英语的介词

英语中广泛使用介词。有些介词仅表示静态的时间、地点,而有些介词却含有动态词义。因此,我们在进行汉英翻译时,可以将汉语中的动词转换为英语中含有动态词义的介词。

(1) 有个首领管辖他们。

They had a captain over them.

(2) 代表们将投票决定这项议案。

The representatives are going to vote on the motion.

(3) 我笔直向前高速飞行,越过港口,飞临海面。

I barreled straight ahead, across the harbor, and out over the sea.

(4) 我完全赞成你的意见。

I'm all for you opinion.

(5) "来啦!"她转身蹦着跳着跑了,越过草地,跑上小径,跨上台阶,穿过凉台,进了门廊。

"Coming!" away she skimmed over the lawn, up the path, up the steps, across the veranda, and into the porch.

(6) 欧洲共同体是服务于这一目的的最好工具。

The European Community is the best instrument for this purpose.

七、汉语的动词转译为英语的形容词

英语中的一些形容词或形容词性的分词具有动态的含义,可以用来表达汉语中的动作。因此,汉译英时,可以将某些动词翻译成具有动作含义的形容词或形容词性的分词。

(1) 刘晓乐木木地看着她,茫然不解。

A puzzled man, Liu Xiaole gazed at her dumbly.

（2）理论上讲，油和金子都不能溶解于水。

Theoretically, neither oil nor gold are soluble in water.

（3）风湿病和某些传染病常引起心脏瓣膜疾患。

Rheumatic and certain infectious diseases are commonly responsible for diseases of the heart valves.

（4）他们非常关心国家的前途。

They are very much concerned about the future of their country.

（5）我们都熟悉这样一个事实，自然界中没有一个物体会自行开始或自行停止运动的。

We are familiar with the fact that nothing in nature will either start or stop moving of itself.

（6）她能够给我带个信儿这件事就是暗示，但是我必须小心谨慎。

The fact that she was able to send me a message was a hint. But I have to be cautious.

八、汉语的动词转译为英语的副词

（1）他出门，忘了穿袜子。

As he left, he forgot to have his socks on.

（2）油箱里的油用完了。

The oil in the tank is up.

（3）经理让专家们进来，让其他人出去。

The manager let the experts in and others out.

（4）那天他在日出前就起来了。

That day he was up before sunrise.

九、汉语的名词转译为英语的动词

（1）他的怒吼声把敌人吓跑了。

He roared, which threatened his enemies away.

(2) 我们的时代是深刻政治变化的见证。

Our age is witnessing a profound political change.

(3) 这份租赁合同有效期为8年。

The new lease would expire in 8 years.

(4) 黎明时,天空映出了瞭望塔的轮廓。

In the early dawn, the guard towers were silhouetted against the sky.

十、汉语的名词转译为英语的形容词

(1) 而我们这些小国终将发现,资本主义就其本性而言,就是帝国主义,就是剥削,我们小国会变成欧美资本主义国家的卫星国。

And our small states will discover that capitalism is, by its very nature, imperialistic and exploitative, and that we will become satellites to the capitalist states of Europe and America.

(2) 这两个工作都没有弹性。

This workpiece is not more elastic than that one.

(3) 在一定条件下,坏事可以变成好事。

Under given conditions, the harmful can be transformed into the beneficial.

十一、汉语的形容词或副词转译成英语的名词

(1) 我们深信这一政策是正确的,并有坚定的决心继续奉行这一政策。

We are deeply convinced of the correctness of this policy and firmly determined to pursue it.

(2) 在国际贸易中,有时候一定程度的妥协是绝对必要的。

In international trade the compromise to some extent is an absolute necessity on some occasions.

(3) 河下游的情况是多种多样的。

The lower stretches of rivers show considerable variety.

(4)我们感到,解决这个复杂的问题是困难的。

We found difficulty in solving this complicated problem.

十二、汉语的形容词或副词转译成英语的介词

(1) 他在城里到处乞讨。

He went begging about the town.

(2) 屋子又脏又乱。

The house is in a mess.

(3) 拖拉之风是一切习惯中最应该避免的。

Procrastination is of all habits to be avoided.

(4) 特别是你,没有要嘀咕的理由。

You of all people, have no cause for complaint.

十三、汉语的副词转译成英语的形容词

(1) 无论是在城市还是在农村,托儿所和幼儿园都在大量地增加。

There has been a tremendous expansion of nurseries and kindergartens in both towns and villages.

(2) 计算机的特点是计算准确而迅速。

The computer is chiefly characterized by its accurate and quick computation.

(3) 所有一切证明我们必须深入地研究金属的特性。

All of this proves that we must have a profound study of properties of metals.

(4) 他每年去北京一次,让他接触到许多国内有名的作家。

His annual visits to Beijing brought him into contact with many well-known writers of our country.

翻译小贴士

网络新词汇的翻译

1. 甜野男孩（young man with ruggedly handsome appearance）

请看例句：

厌倦了娱乐男星精致的外表和妆容，很多网民被一位藏族小伙粗犷俊俏的模样吸引。

Sick of male entertainment stars' delicate looks and heavy use of make-up, many Chinese netizens are attracted by a Tibetan's ruggedly handsome appearance.

近日，四川省甘孜藏族自治州（Garze Tibetan Autonomous Prefecture）理塘县20岁藏族小伙丁真因一条视频走红。黝黑的皮肤（swarthy skin）、大大的眼睛、长长的睫毛（long eyelashes）、浓密而凌乱的头发（thick but messy hair），这都构成扎西丁真吸引人的特质（winning features）。他走在雪上脚下的家门口，对着镜头羞涩地微笑（smile shyly towards the camera）。网友从丁真原生态的美中得到灵感，创造了新词——"甜野男孩"。丁真的走红带热了游客们对其家乡的兴趣。在线旅行社携程的数据显示：丁真家乡理塘的搜索量激增（the number of searches for Litang soared）。携程平台上11月20日起"理塘"的搜索量开始上升，11月23日至29日，"理塘"搜索量较前一周猛增620%（the searches shot up 620% compared with the previous week），是国庆假期搜索量的4倍。丁真如今已经成为理塘县文旅体投资发展有限公司的员工，为理塘县做旅游推广（promote tourism for the county）。他的工作包括拍摄宣传甘孜州和理塘县美丽风景的短片（shoot short videos that promote the beautiful scenery of Litang county and Garze prefecture），以及运营社交媒体平台（operate social media platforms）等。

2. 爷青回（my youth is making a comeback）

请看例句：

12月1日，"哔哩哔哩"（以下简称"B站"）发布了2020年度最火弹幕榜单,"爷青回(爷的青春又回来了)"荣登第一。

Bilibili released its annual ranking of most popular danmus on Tuesday. The danmu of the year goes to "yeqinghui", which colloquially translates to "my youth is making a comeback".

"爷青回"的使用场景通常是:当某个视频或电视剧集反映出一种怀旧情结或是唤醒了某人青春的回忆(a certain video or TV episode reflects a sense of nostalgia or awakens reminiscences of one's youth)。用户观看经典戏剧作品的翻拍版或改编版(watch video remakes or adaptations of classical theatrical works)时尤其爱发送"爷青回"的弹幕。

入选年度弹幕前五的还有:

武汉加油:Come on Wuhan

有内味了:Finally getting it right(有那个味道,有那种感觉了,形容某种事物是否地道、正宗,或一个人的操作或言行有某个人的既视感)

双厨狂喜:an expression of the excitement to see two favorite idols appear in the same work(形容看到一个作品中同时融合了自己喜欢的两件事物时的激动心情)

禁止套娃:No old tricks please!(来源于俄罗斯著名的传统玩具套娃,意思是制止别人一直套一个素材、话题的无限循环行为)

这是B站第四年发布年度弹幕(danmu of the year),前三年的年度弹幕分别为"囍(double happiness)""真实(real)""AWSL(I'm dying)"。弹幕(bullet-words/short live comments)是一种在视频播放时允许用户评论同步出现在视频上的评论系统(a commentary system allowing users to leave synchronized messages that scroll directly over videos)。每年的年度弹幕既是对过去一年流行文化趋势的总结,也是对这一年中最具共鸣的社会情绪的呈现。

3. 视频相关新词汇

视频分享平台:video-sharing platform

流行语:catchphrase

动漫表情包:anime meme

动漫游戏视频网站:ACG (animation, comics, games) video portal

 习题八

一、英译汉

1. The government called for the establishment of more technical schools.

2. I am so grateful to my father for his continuous encouragement during my childhood.

3. It was officially announced that Pairs is invited to the meeting.

4. He is both a bibliomaniac and a lover of calligraphy.

5. He roared, which threatened his enemies away.

二、汉译英

1. 他长期以来习惯于在最后一分钟做出决定。

2. 十一点钟时,他已睡在被窝里。

3. 他在读书时不加选择。

4. 她非常漂亮。

5. 你说他傻不傻?

第九章 附属成分的翻译

英汉两种语言的基本区别之一在于句法层面。汉语的句法重意合,句中的各意群、成分往往通过内在联系贯穿在一起,至于内在的主从或并列关系须由读者自己去体会。而与此相反,英语的句法重形合,句中的各意群、成分往往通过外在联系(连接词、语法功能等)贯穿在一起。例如:

总工程师急躁不安,两手插在裤子口袋里,踱来踱去。

表面来看,这句中文表达似乎是由三个并列部分组成的一个句子,但这三个部分之间果真是并列关系吗?看下面两个译文:

(1) The chief engineer was vexed and restless. He put his two hands into his trousers pockets and paced back and forth.

(2) Vexed and restless, the chief engineer paced back and forth, hands in his trousers pockets.

显然,译文(1)将原文理解并表达为三个并列的动作或状态,似乎没有主次的区别。而译文(2)将原文中状态描写的部分视为附属成分,主要的动作视为主体部分,使得译文不仅简洁、逻辑清晰、主次分明,还更好地传达了原文的意思,便于目的语读者阅读和理解。

可见,分清句子的主次结构,理解句子中主体和附属的关系,对于英汉翻译具有重要的作用。在汉英转换中,英语的从属部分主要有以下四种处理方式。

一、独立主格结构处理从属部分

(一) 名词+现在分词

(1) 你到处都可以看到人们穿着节日的服装,满面笑容。

Everywhere you can see people in their holiday dresses, their faces shining with smiles.

(2) 天气要是合适的话,我们明天要到西山去玩。

Weather permitting, we'll go on an excursion to the Western hill tomorrow.

(3) 暑假要来了,我的同学都在计划如何去放松自己。

Summer holiday coming, my classmates are planning how to relax themselves.

(4) 黑夜笼罩大地,谁也看不清远处黑压压的一片是什么东西。

Night enshrouding the earth, nobody could make out what the dark mass was from a distance.

(二) 名词+过去分词

(1) 他脸朝天,头枕着手躺着。

He lay on his back, his face up and his hands crossed under his head.

(2) 他做完作业后回家了。

His work done, he went home.

(3) 阿瑟走后,他就会像其他熟人一样被允许拜访了。

Arthur gone, he would only be allowed to make visits like other acquaintances.

(4) 雨不断地下,车辆陷入泥沼,桥梁被水冲走。

It rained and rained, vehicles bogged clown and bridges washed out.

(三) 名词+形容词短语

(1) 他鼻子冻得通红地走进房来。

He came into my room, his nose red with cold.

(2)老头坐了下来,由于痛苦脸色发白,两颊上还带着泪痕。

The old man sat down, his face pale with pain and traces of tears on his cheeks.

(3)他们坐在那里,门窗开着,还是热得受不了。

Although they sat with doors and windows open, they were overpowered by heat.

(4)母亲坐在厨房里,脸色阴沉而忧郁。

My mother sat in the kitchen, her face dull and heavy.

(四)名词+副词短语

(1)散会了,校长很快就离开了会议室。

The meeting over, our headmaster soon left the meeting room.

(2)灯熄了,我们不能继续工作了。

The lights off, we could not go on with the work.

(3)她坐在桌前,衣领已解掉,头低了下来,拿好钢笔,准备开始写一封长信。

She sat at the table, collar off, head down, and pen in position, ready to begin the long letter.

(五)名词+名词

(1)他第一枪没击中,又打了一枪。

His first shot failure, he fired again.

(2)两百人死于事故,其中有许多儿童。

Two hundred people died in the accident, many of them children.

(3)他的书成了畅销书,他对一切都满意了。

His book now a bestseller, he felt pleased with the world.

(六)名词+不定式

(1)借助于一些旧零件,他要做一个飞机模型。

He is going to make a model plane, some old parts to help.

(2)他们道别后,一个回了家,一个去了书店。

They said good-bye to each other, one to go home, the other to go to the bookstore.

(3)来客也不少,有送行的,有拿东西的,有送行兼拿东西的。

We also had quite a number of visitors, some to see us off, some to fetch things, and some to do both.

(4)他为这家出版社写了两本书,一本即将在本月出版,另一本将在下月出版。

He has written two books for this publishing house, one to be published in this moth, the other to come out in next month.

(七)名词+介词短语

(1)他们欢快地一手拿着鞭子,一手扯着缰绳,催马向前。

In jolly spirits, they urged the horses on, whip in one hand and reins in the other.

(2)他端着枪,走进那间黑屋子。

He entered the dark room, gun in hand.

(3)他的脊背朝天,四肢伸展,头枕着左臂,直挺挺地趴伏着。

He lay at full length upon his stomach, his head upon his left forearm.

(4)每天下午,一个背着一大捆柴火的老妇人都会从那间破旧的房屋前蹒跚着走过。

Every afternoon a very old woman hobbled past the old house, a vast load of firewood on her back.

(八)介词 with+以上各种形式

(1)他枕着自己的胳膊入眠。

He was asleep with his head on his arms.

(2)约翰走了,我们得到了更大空间。

With John away, we have got more room.

(3)有这么多的名胜可参观,小孩很激动。

The kid feels excited with so many places of interest to visit.

(4) 全班都瞧着他,他更感到不自在了。

He felt more uneasy, with the whole class staring at him.

(5) 你必须告诉我真实情况,既不要夸大,也不要缩小。

You must give me a true account, with nothing added and nothing removed.

(6) 我们上午参观了博物馆,中间匆忙地吃顿午饭,就去参观艺术馆。

We visited the museum in the morning and the art gallery later, with a hurry lunch in between.

二、分词结构处理从属部分

(一) 用现在分词处理从属部分

(1) 我强做均匀的呼吸,努力使自己镇静下来。

I tried to compose myself, forcing deep, even breath.

(2) 在城市里搜查小偷,花费了警察很长一段时间。

Searching for the thief in the city, it had taken the policemen a long time.

(3) 夕阳西下,把金色余晖洒在矮矮的西山上。

The sun was setting, spilling golden lights on the low western hills.

(4) 丝绸之路延伸6 000多公里,得名于古代中国的丝绸贸易。

Extending more than 6,000 kilometers, the Silk Road got its name from the silk trade of ancient China.

(二) 用过去分词处理从属部分

(1) 错误与挫折教训了我们,让我们变得聪明起来,我们的事情就办得好一些。

Taught by mistakes and setbacks, we have become wiser and handle our problems better.

(2) 我一直坐到十一点多钟,全神贯注地看书。

I sat until eleven, absorbed in a book.

(3)当被问及这件事时,班长说这是他的职责。

Asked why he did it, the monitor said it was his duty.

(4)尽管受到警察的殴打,被关入监狱,甘地却首创了非暴力抵抗的原则。

Beaten by the police and sent to jail, Gandi created the principle of nonviolent resistance.

三、短语结构处理从属部分

(一) 用形容词短语处理从属部分

(1)华盛顿是个坚毅、勇敢,而又谨慎的军人。

Washington was a great soldier, firm, brave and cautious.

(2)那位外籍老师博学、诚实、平易近人,却是一个不平凡的人。

Learned, honest and easy to approach, he was an unusually great man.

(3)周总理是那样谦逊、随和、易于接近,大家很快就不紧张了。

Modest, unassuming, easy to approach, Premier Zhou soon put everyone there completely at ease.

(4)这些艺术品丰富多彩,栩栩如生,而且别出心裁,具有鲜明的民族特色和地方特色。

Colourful, lifelike and original, these works or art had distinctive national and local characteristics.

(二) 用名词短语处理从属部分

(1)他是一位多产的作家,撰写了几百部作品。

A versatile writer, he has written hundreds of works.

(2)中国是个发展中的国家,属于第三世界。

A developing country, China belongs to the Third World.

(3)秋瑾既是诗人,又是革命家,她不但用刀而且用笔进行战斗。

A poet and revolutionary, Qiu-jin fought with her pen as well as her sword.

(三)用不定式短语处理从属部分

(1)幕开了,展现出了集市场景。

The curtain parted, to reveal a market scene.

(2)即使走遍天涯海角,也找不到像这样的东西。

To go to the ends of the earth, you could not find another like it.

(3)如果听到他讲英语,人们会以为他是英国人。

To hear him speak English, one would take him for an Englishman.

(4)有一天纳尔逊先生在城里不见了,以后再没有人看见他。

One day Mr. Nelson disappeared from the town, never to be seen again.

(四)用相应的短语处理从属部分

(1)运动会照常进行,风雨无阻。

The sports meet will be held, rain or shine.

(2)不管成功与否,我要试一下。

Sink or swim, we'll have a try.

(3)时间一秒一秒嘀嗒嘀嗒地过去了。

Time ticked away, second by second.

(4)他们手挽手,走过来。

They came over, hand in hand.

(五)用解释或描述的短语处理从属部分

(1)他的妻子料理一切大大小小的事务。

His wife manages all affairs, big and small.

(2)他光头赤脚,气喘吁吁地冲进我的房间来。

He dashed into my room, hatless, barefooted and out of breath.

(3)她一只手提个篮子,内中有个破碗,空的,另一只手拿着一根比她自己还高的竹竿,下端开了裂。

In one hand she carried a basket in which was broken bowl, empty. In the other she held a bamboo pole, longer than herself, split at the bottom.

(4) 国家不论大小、强弱、贫富,都应该平等对待。

All countries, big or small, strong or weak, rich or poor, should be treated equally.

四、用连续否定处理从属部分

(1) 周围没有村庄,甚至连一棵可供掩蔽的大树也没有。

There are no villages around, not even a big tree to take shelter under.

(2) 中国不做超级大国,现在不做,永远也不做。

China will not be a superpower, not either today or even in future.

(3) 老太太是个管家能手,更是个好厨师。

The old lady is not a poor housekeeper, not to speak of a good cook.

(4) 在全球化的世界中,没有一个国家可以独善其身,没有一个国家可以摆脱责任。

In the globalized world, no country is immune, nor can it shrink its responsibility.

附属成分翻译的关键是区分原句的主要成分和附属成分,并在译文中体现。以下原则将帮助我们理解并区分主要成分和附属成分:虚指内容(the non-essential)附属于实指内容(the essential);方式(manner)附属于行为(action);条件(condition)附属于影响(effect);原因(cause)附属于结果(result);背景信息(background information)附属于判断信息(judgment)或主要动词(the main verb);否定部分(negative part)附属于肯定部分(affirmative part)。

翻译小贴士

重要词汇学习

1. 人民至上:put the people in the first place

◀ 原文 ▶

中共中央总书记、国家主席、中央军委主席习近平参加十三届全国人大三次会议内蒙古代表团审议时指出,党在任何时候都把群众利益放在第一位,为保护人民生命安全和身体健康可以不惜一切代价。

译文

President Xi Jinping said that the Party puts the people's interests in the first place under any circumstances and is willing to protect the people's life and health at all costs. Xi, who is also general secretary of the Communist Party of China Central Committee and chairman of the Central Military Commission, made the remarks in a deliberation with fellow deputies from the delegation of Inner Mongolia autonomous region, at the third session of the 13th National People's Congress.

◀ 原文 ▶

在重大疫情面前,我们一开始就鲜明提出把人民生命安全和身体健康放在第一位。

译文

Since the very beginning of the novel coronavirus outbreak, the Party has upheld the principle of putting the people's lives and health as the top priority.

——2020年5月22日,习近平参加十三届全国人大三次会议内蒙古代表团审议时表示

◀ 原文 ▶

我们党没有自己特殊的利益,党在任何时候都把群众利益放在第一位。

译文

The CPC does not have any exclusive interests for itself, and it has put the people's interests in first place all the time.

——2020年5月22日,习近平参加十三届全国人大三次会议内蒙古代表团审议时表示

2. 脱贫攻坚重大胜利:major victory in poverty alleviation

◀原文▶

中共中央政治局常务委员会12月3日召开会议,听取脱贫攻坚总结评估汇报。中共中央总书记习近平主持会议并发表重要讲话。习近平指出,经过8年持续奋斗,我们如期完成了新时代脱贫攻坚目标任务,现行标准下农村贫困人口全部脱贫,贫困县全部摘帽,消除了绝对贫困和区域性整体贫困,近1亿贫困人口实现脱贫,取得了令全世界刮目相看的重大胜利。

译文

Xi Jinping, general secretary of the Communist Party of China (CPC) Central Committee, said on Dec 3 that China has accomplished its poverty alleviation target of the new era as scheduled and achieved a significant victory that impresses the world. Through eight years of sustained work, China has lifted all rural poor population under the current standard out of poverty and nearly 100 million poor people have shaken off poverty, Xi made the remarks while presiding over a meeting of the Standing Committee of the Political Bureau of the CPC Central Committee. China has removed all poor counties from the poverty list, and eradicated absolute poverty and regional poverty, Xi said.

◀原文▶

脱贫攻坚的重大胜利,为实现第一个百年奋斗目标打下坚实基础,极大增强了人民群众获得感、幸福感、安全感,彻底改变了贫困地区的面貌,改善了生产生活条件,提高了群众生活质量,"两不愁三保障"全面实现。

译文

The great victory in poverty reduction has laid solid foundations for the fulfillment of the first centenary goal – to finish building a moderately prosperous society in all respects by the time the CPC celebrates its centenary in 2021 – and has boosted the people's feeling of gain, happiness and security. The livelihood of the people in poverty-stricken areas has been greatly improved, and the people have sufficient food and clothing, as well as access to compulsory education, basic medical services and safe housing.

——2020年12月3日,中共中央政治局常务委员会召开会议听取脱贫攻坚总结评估汇报,习近平发表重要讲话

3. 疫情防控阻击战:the battle of epidemic prevention and control

◀ 原文 ▶

2月3日,中共中央政治局常务委员会召开会议。中共中央总书记习近平在主持会议时强调,要同时间赛跑、与病魔较量,坚决遏制疫情蔓延势头,坚决打赢疫情防控阻击战。

译文

Xi Jinping, general secretary of the Communist Party of China Central Committee, urged concrete efforts on Feb 3 to race against time in combating the novel coronavirus and winning the battle of epidemic prevention and control. Xi made the remark while presiding over a meeting of the Standing Committee of the Political Bureau of the CPC Central Committee in Beijing.

◀ 原文 ▶

做好疫情防控工作,直接关系人民生命安全和身体健康,直接关系经济社会大局稳定,也事关我国对外开放。

译文

The outcome of the epidemic prevention and control directly affects people's lives and health, the overall economic and social stability and the country's opening-up.

——2020年2月3日,习近平主持中共中央政治局常务委员会会议时发表的讲话

◀ 原文 ▶

疫情防控不只是医药卫生问题,而是全方位的工作,各项工作都要为打赢疫情防控阻击战提供支持。

译文

The epidemic prevention and control is not only a health issue but comprehensive work which requires all-round support.

——2020年2月3日,习近平主持中共中央政治局常务委员会会议时发表的讲话

4. "十四五"规划编制:14th Five-Year Plan formulation

◀ 原文 ▶

中共中央总书记、国家主席、中央军委主席习近平对"十四五"规划编制工作网上意见征求活动作出重要指示强调,要更好发挥互联网在倾听人民呼声、汇聚人民智慧方面的作用。

译文

President Xi Jinping has urged the better use of the internet to heed people's views and pool their wisdom. Xi, also general secretary of the Communist Party of China Central Committee and chairman of the Central Military Commission, recently gave an instruction on the work of soliciting public views and suggestions online to formulate the country's 14th Five-Year Plan for economic and social development.

◀ 原文 ▶

谋划"十四五"时期发展,要贯彻以人民为中心的发展思想,坚持发展为了人民、发展成果由人民共享,努力在推动高质量发展过程中办好各项民生事业、补齐民生领域短板。

译文

When making plans for the 14th Five-Year period (2021-2025), we must insist that development is for the people with the benefits shared by the people, and more efforts should be made to improve weak links concerning people's livelihood, while striving for high-quality development.

——2020年9月17日,习近平在基层代表座谈会上强调

5. 区域全面经济伙伴关系协定:Regional Comprehensive Economic Partnership

◀ 原文 ▶

经过八年谈判,亚太地区15个国家于11月15日签署《区域全面经济伙伴关系协定》(RCEP)。该协定是全球最大的贸易协定,参与国家包括东盟十国及其五个主要贸易伙伴:中国、日本、韩国、澳大利亚及新西兰。

译文

After eight years of negotiations, 15 Asia-Pacific countries signed the Regional Comprehensive Economic Partnership (RCEP) on Nov 15, the world's biggest trade pact. The agreement involves all 10 member countries of the Association of Southeast Asian Nations and five of its major trading partners–China, Japan, South Korea, Australia and New Zealand.

◀ 原文 ▶

中国愿同更多国家商签高标准自由贸易协定,推动尽快签署区域全面经济伙伴关系协定,加快中欧投资协定、中日韩等自由贸易协定谈判进程,加强同世界高标准自贸区交流互鉴。

译文

China stands ready to conclude high-standard free trade agreements with more countries in the world. We will work for the early signing of the Regional Comprehensive Economic Partnership (RCEP) and speed up negotiations on a China-EU investment treaty and a China-Japan-ROK free trade agreement. We look forward to more exchanges and mutual learning with high-standard free trade zones in other parts of the world.

——2020年11月4日,第三届中国国际进口博览会开幕式举行,习近平以视频方式发表主旨演讲

6. "双循环"发展格局:a "dual circulation" development pattern

◀ 原文 ▶

中共中央政治局召开会议,分析研究当前经济形势,部署下半年经济工作。会议指出,当前经济形势不稳定性不确定性较大,我们遇到的很多问题是中长期的,必须加快形成以国内大循环为主体、国内国际双循环相互促进的新发展格局。

◀ 译文 ▶

At a meeting held to analyze the economic situation and plan for the second half of the year, the Political Bureau of the Communist Party of China Central Committee said China still faces uncertain situations and problems that are likely to exist in the medium and long run, and urged the country to accelerate the establishment of a "dual circulation" development pattern in which domestic economic cycle plays a leading role while international economic cycle remains its extension and supplement.

◀ 原文 ▶

在当前保护主义上升、世界经济低迷、全球市场萎缩的外部环境下,我们必须集中力量办好自己的事,充分发挥国内超大规模市场优势,逐步形成以国内大循环为主体、国内国际双循环相互促进的新发展格局。

◀ 译文 ▶

In the face of an external environment characterized by rising protectionism, global economic downturn, and a shrinking international market, we need to pool resources and concentrate on managing the country's affairs well, and give full play to the advantage of a huge domestic market, so that a new development pattern will gradually be created whereby domestic and foreign markets can boost each other, with the domestic market as the mainstay.

——2020年7月21日,习近平主持召开企业家座谈会并发表重要讲话

7. 基础研究:basic research

◆原文▶

科技部表示,我国通过政府引导、央地联动等方式大幅提升基础研究投入。基础研究投入从2015年的716亿元增长到2019年的1 335.6亿元,年均增幅达到16.9%,大大高于全社会研发投入的增幅。

译文

Through government support and coordination of enterprises and social entities, China has substantially increased funding for basic research. China's investment in basic research increased from 71.6 billion yuan in 2015 to 133.56 billion yuan in 2019, with an average annual growth rate of 16.9 percent, much higher than that of the spending on research and development, according to the Ministry of Science and Technology.

◆原文▶

要持之以恒加强基础研究,加大基础研究投入,给予必要政策支持,创造有利于基础研究的良好科研生态。

译文

We should persist in strengthening basic research by increasing funding and providing more resources and policies to create a favorable atmosphere for basic research.

——2020年9月11日,习近平在科学家座谈会上发表的重要讲话

8. 光盘行动:"Clean your plate" campaign

◆原文▶

国家主席习近平作出重要指示强调,要坚决制止餐饮浪费行为,切实培养节约习惯。他指出,餐饮浪费现象,触目惊心、令人痛心!尽管我国粮食生产连

年丰收,对粮食安全还是始终要有危机意识,今年全球新冠肺炎疫情所带来的影响更是给我们敲响了警钟。

译文

President Xi Jinping has stressed resolutely putting an end to wasting food and called for promoting thrift. Xi made the requirement in an instruction. Calling the issue of food waste shocking and distressing, Xi highlighted the need to maintain a sense of crisis regarding food security, especially amid the fallout of the COVID-19 epidemic, despite the fact that China has scored consecutive bumper harvests.

◀原文▶

要进一步加强宣传教育,切实培养节约习惯,在全社会营造浪费可耻、节约为荣的氛围。

译文

It is necessary to further enhance public awareness of the issue, effectively cultivate thrifty habits and foster a social environment where waste is shameful and thriftiness is applaudable.

——2020年8月,习近平对制止餐饮浪费行为作出重要指示

9. 嫦娥五号:Chang'e-5 mission

◀原文▶

12月17日,嫦娥五号首次实现了我国地外天体采样返回。中共中央总书记、国家主席、中央军委主席习近平发来贺电,代表党中央、国务院和中央军委,向探月工程任务指挥部并参加嫦娥五号任务的全体同志致以热烈的祝贺和诚挚的问候。

译文

President Xi Jinping on Dec 17 congratulated the complete success of the Chang'e-5 mission that brings back the country's first samples collected from the moon. On behalf of the Communist Party of China (CPC) Central Committee, the State Council and the Central Military Commission (CMC), Xi, also general secretary of the CPC Central Committee and chairman of the CMC, extended warm congratulations and sincere greetings to all members who participated in the Chang'e-5 mission in a congratulatory message.

◀ 原文 ▶

嫦娥五号任务作为我国复杂度最高、技术跨度最大的航天系统工程,首次实现了我国地外天体采样返回。这是发挥新型举国体制优势攻坚克难取得的又一重大成就,标志着中国航天向前迈出的一大步,将为深化人类对月球成因和太阳系演化历史的科学认知作出贡献。

译文

As China's most complicated space project, the Chang'e-5 mission has achieved the extraterrestrial sampling and returning for the first time. It is another major achievement in overcoming difficulties by giving full play to the advantages of the new nationwide system, marking a great step forward in China's space industry. This will contribute to deepening the understanding of the origin of the moon and the evolution history of the solar system.

——2020年12月17日,习近平致电代表党中央、国务院和中央军委祝贺探月工程嫦娥五号任务取得圆满成功

10. 只争朝夕,不负韶华:seize the day and live it to the fullest

◀ 原文 ▶

新年前夕,国家主席习近平发表了2020年新年贺词。贺词指出,2020年是具有里程碑意义的一年。我们将全面建成小康社会,实现第一个百年奋斗目标。

译文

President Xi Jinping delivered a New Year speech in Beijing to ring in

2020, pledging to achieve the first centenary goal of building a moderately prosperous society in all respects in the "milestone" year.

◀ 原文 ▶

2020年也是脱贫攻坚决战决胜之年。冲锋号已经吹响。我们要万众一心加油干,越是艰险越向前,把短板补得再扎实一些,把基础打得再牢靠一些,坚决打赢脱贫攻坚战,如期实现现行标准下农村贫困人口全部脱贫、贫困县全部摘帽。

译文

2020 will also be a year of decisive victory for the elimination of poverty. The bugle has sounded. United as one, we shall work harder. The greater the difficulties are, the further we advance, strengthening our weak links even more and laying a more solid foundation to win the hard battle against poverty with determination, to lift all impoverished rural residents and counties out of poverty by current standards as scheduled.

——2019年12月31日,习近平发表2020年新年贺词

◀ 原文 ▶

让我们只争朝夕,不负韶华,共同迎接2020年的到来。

译文

Let's seize the day and live it to the fullest, and greet the arrival of the year 2020 together.

——2019年12月31日,习近平发表2020年新年贺词

 习题九

汉译英

1. 他们向前门走去,伙伴们在后面跟着。

2. 两个人一肥一瘦,闯进我的房间来。

3. 他写了许多诗,其中有些还是十四行诗。

4. 吃过午饭后,小张和小李匆忙地离开学校,前者去赶火车,后者去车站接朋友。

5. 她脸上带着温暖的微笑走出来迎接我,两个大大的眼睛闪闪发光。

6. 他对其中几个问题进行了深入分析,澄清了许多混乱思想。

7. 桂林素以美丽的山水著称,吸引了越来越多的游客。

8. 他扑通一声地跳进河里,再也没有浮起来。

9. 时而这里,时而那里,在小山上,在草原中,有村落隐现。

10. 他看到前后左右四周都是棺材。棺材有大的,有小的;有黑色的,有白色的;有做好了的,有尚未竣工的;有镀金的,有镀银的。

第十章 肯定句与否定句转译

由于历史传统和社会文化的差异,中国人和以英语为母语的人有不同的思维方式和语言表达方式。有些英语表达在形式上看似是肯定的,但在意义上却是否定的;反之亦然。对于母语为汉语的学习者来讲,从语法上理解这些形式与意义不一致的句子是不容易的,而在对它们进行语言转换时,则更为困难。为了便于目的语读者更好地理解和传达原文意义,翻译过程中,英语中的肯定陈述可以被翻译成汉语中的否定陈述,反之亦然,这种翻译方法被称为"正说反译"或"反说正译"。例如:

我不理解这件事。

这是一个否定句,若将其译成英语,可以得到以下9个不同的译文:

I can't understand it.

I fail to understand it.

I am at a loss to understand it.

I am all at sea about it.

I am in the dark about it.

It is beyond my comprehension.

It beats me.

It is a sealed book to me.

It's all Greek to me.

毫无疑问,以上9个译文都是翻译正确的译文,但除了第一个译文在形式上仍然为否定句外,其余8个译文均是肯定句。这说明,形式上的差异和变化并没有影响信息和意义的传达。

再比如,如果将"I am no more mad than you are."翻译成"我和你一样不疯。"那么就完全错了,因为它真实的意思是"I am as sane as you are.",即"我和你一样神志正常。"显然,原文形式上是否定的,而译文形式上是肯定的,但译文完全准确地表达了原文的内容。

以上例子说明,"正说反译"或"反说正译"的翻译方法在英汉翻译中用于很多种表达形式,而且这些形式还存在很大差异,下面就其中的具体情况进行讨论。

一、形式肯定但意义否定的表达

英语中有相当多的词汇、短语、成语、俚语,甚至谚语,虽然形式上是肯定的,但实际上意义是否定的。人们在日常交流中经常使用这些表达,以获得生动的效果。非英语为母语的人们如果不了解这些用法,就不能地道、准确地进行信息转换和语言表达。例如:

His words and actions ill consort together.

他的言行很不一致。

His work is still a long way off perfection.

他的工作还远远不够完美。

两个形式肯定、意义否定的英语句子都被翻译成了形式和意义都为否定的句子,更符合汉语的表达习惯。

(一) 含有否定意义的名词或名词短语的翻译

(1) 我宁要自由,而不贪苟且的生命。

I have the preference for freedom to life without dignity.

(2) 马上出发,一刻也不能耽搁。

There is a crying necessity for setting off.

(3) 绝对的自由就是无拘束。

Absolute liberty is absence of restraint.

(4) 不修边幅。

Negligence of dress.

(5) 我深信他对你没有任何成见。

I am deeply convinced that he has a completely open mind towards you.

(二) 含有否定意义的动词或动词短语的翻译

(1) 他是不到黄河心不死。

He refused to give up until all hope is gone.

(2) 你负责这件事情,怎么能对此不置可否呢?

You are in charge of the job, how could you evade this issue?

(3) 公共场所不得大声喧哗。

Loud noise is prohibited in the public places.

(4) 雨下得太大了,我们根本不能启程。

The heavy rain hindered us from setting off.

(5) 此处风景秀美,虽有笔墨不能绘之。

The beauty of the scenery here defies any description of painters.

(三) 含有否定意义的形容词或形容词短语的翻译

(1) 历史没有记载这件事。

History is silent about this event.

(2) 报纸的报道远非事实。

The newspaper accounts are far from being truth.

(3) 用煤不如用油合算。

The use of coal is poor economy as compared with that of oil.

(4) 他一点儿也察觉不到她的错误。

He is completely blind to her faults.

(5) 她是这个球队中最没有经验的球员。

She is the least experienced in the football team here.

(6) 这种解释,理由很不充分。

The explanation is pretty thin.

(四) 含有否定意义的副词的翻译

(1) 我可不这么想。

I scarcely think so.

(2) 他没有脱衣服就跳入水中,把孩子们救出来。

He dived into the water fully clothed and rescued the children.

(3) 他情绪激动得连话都说不出来。

He is too excited to utter any word.

(4) 要不是你的帮助,我就掉进河里了。

But for your help, I should have fallen into the river.

(5) 你们那样做,不会有问题。

You may safely do in that way.

(6) 不管我怎样表扬他都不过分。

I can't praise him too much.

(五) 含有否定意义的连词或连词短语的翻译

(1) 他几乎每次开口说话都离不开抱怨。

He hardly opens his mouth but complain.

(2) 若他不能做此事,就没有人能做了。

He can do it if anyone can.

(3) 他们还来不及关开关,事故就发生了。

The accident had happened before they turned off the switch.

(4) 她根本不漂亮。

She is anything but beautiful.

(5) 缴枪不杀。

Lay down your arms, or die!

(6) 他宁愿为国捐躯也不苟且偷生。

He would rather die a martyr than drag out an ignoble existence.

(六)含有否定意义的介词或介词短语的翻译

(1) 她凡事都要全力以赴,不计成败。

She is always doing his best, against all odds.

(2) 他认为她的行为是无可指摘的(不容批评)。

He assumed that her conduct is above criticism.

(3) 若无意外事情发生,我们将中午到达。

We shall arrive at noon barring accident.

(4) 春游的时间还未确定。

The date of the spring outing is still in the air.

(5) 这篇文章不合格。

This essay is below mark.

(6) 她的美丽是无与伦比的。

Her beauty is beyond compare.

(7) 她昨天的发言是不切题的。

The speech she made yesterday was beside the mark.

(8) 有时这是塞翁失马,焉知非福。

This, sometimes, is a blessing in disguise.

(9) 若不是党的领导,我们是不会成功的。

But for the leadership of the Party, we could not have succeeded.

(七)其他含有否定意义的表达翻译

(1) 在关键时刻,他为何不帮你说句公道话呢?

He might have done you a favor to stand on your side at the critical moment.

(2) 他根本不笨。

He is anything but stupid.

(3) 谁也不知道明天会发生什么事。

Who knows what will happen tomorrow?

(4) 你用不着用那种眼神看着我。

Why should look at me in that way?

(5) 我绝不会忘掉以前那段日子。

Shall I ever forget those previous days?

二、形式否定但意义肯定的表达

(1) 向她赔礼道歉的想法始终在他心头萦绕着。

The thought of making an apology to her never deserted him.

(2) 这里摆放的所有展品都禁止触摸。

All the articles to be exhibited here are untouchable.

(3) 他的观点简直是天衣无缝。

His argument leaves no room to be desired.

(4) 此曲只应天上有。

Your song is like nothing on earth.

(5) 她年纪虽大,却风韵犹存。

She is none the less charming for her age.

(6) 狮子与老虎一样的残忍。

The lion is no less cruel than the tiger.

(7) 学校是进行教育的最好的地方。

There is no place like school for education.

(8) 一成百成。

Nothing succeeds like success.

三、双重否定的表达

(1) 除了贫穷,没有什么是不劳而获的。

Nothing could be got without pains but poverty.

(2) 巧妇难为无米之炊。

You can't make something out of nothing.

(3) 正如毛主席所讲,没有调查就没有发言权。

Just as Chairman Mao put it, there is no right to speak without investigation.

(4) 无风不起浪,万事皆有根源。

Nothing comes out of nothing (or, no smoke without fire).

(5) 听到这种谎言,我不得不予以反驳。

I could not refrain from retorting to hear such a lie.

(6) 尽管借债越来越多,但很少有人不能偿还欠款。

In spite of the increased debts, few fail to repay.

(7) 人非圣贤,孰能无过。

To err is man (or, there is no man but as his faults).

(8) 这里的雨"不下则已,下则倾盆"。

It never rains but it pours here.

四、否定式语法结构表达差异

英汉两种语言的否定式结构在使用习惯上也存在不同之处,在翻译时要注意肯定结构与否定结构的转译。

(1) ——你父亲从来没有打过你,是吧?

——是的,从来没有。

—Your father has never beaten you, has he?

—No, he hasn't.

(2) ——你不参加我明天的生日会吧?

——不,我参加。

—Are you not going to take part in my birthday party tomorrow?

—Yes, I am.

五、修辞转译

汉译英时,为了更确切表达原文含义,或为了加强语气以获得更好的修辞效果,可采用肯定句与否定句的转译方法。

(1) 法律面前,人人平等。(肯定句)

Law is no respecter of persons. (否定句)

(2) 本证书加盖钢印方能生效。(肯定句)

The certificate is invalid, if not under the steel seal. (否定句)

(3) 请勿大声喧哗。(否定句)

Keep quite! (肯定句)

(4) 他对美国提出的行动要求完全不理不睬。(否定句)

He turned a resolutely deaf ear to American demands for action. (肯定句)

翻译小贴士

1. 9月24日,在回应美方指责中国人权状况时,外交部发言人汪文斌做了回应。

▶ 原文 ▶

美方习惯于充当"人权教师爷",对别国人权状况指手画脚。

译文

The US is feeling very comfortable with playing the role of "a human rights preacher", condescendingly harping on others' human rights conditions.

分析

"教师爷"的译文借助了英文中的 preacher 一词,也就是布道者、传道士,来体现美国宣扬鼓吹人权,并对他国进行说教的形象,十分生动准确。

"指手画脚"暗指美国盛气凌人的态度,译文加上了副词 condescendingly,即"居高临下"。Harp on 指的是反复不断地提及(某个话题)直至令人生厌,表达出了美国反复指责他国人权状况,令人反感的意思。

例句:I don't want to harp on this issue any longer, but I really need it to be resolved today.

我也不想反复说这个问题,但我在今天之内必须把它解决了。

▶原文◀

2. 美国个别政客企图置TikTok、WeChat和华为等中国企业于死地,其根源就是患了"逢中必反症",强行将意识形态标签打在中国企业身上。这些人打着"国家安全"的幌子"围猎"TikTok等中国企业,充斥着谎言和污蔑,其性质是欺行霸市、强取豪夺。

译文

Some US politicians are working to crush such Chinese companies as TikTok, WeChat and Huawei because they are down with an anti-China syndrome and will strike at anything Chinese. That explains their frantic attempts to hunt down TikTok and other Chinese companies by pinning the ideological label on them under the pretext of "national security". All the lies and smears are just disguise for their daylight bullying and robbery.

分析

"逢中必反症"是一个比较新鲜的词,英文中没有直接对应的固定说法,译文采用了"拆分"的方法进行处理:把"逢中必反症"拆分为"反中国症"(anti-China syndrome)和"逢中必反"(strike at anything Chinese),表达简洁的同时,也保证了意思清晰完整。

"患上某种疾病"可以用 be down with/come down with 来表达。

例句:I didn't do much this weekend because I came down with a cold.
这周末我没做什么事情,因为我感冒了。

 习题十

一、英译汉

1. She never does more work than she can help.

2. You might as well burn the book than give them to her.

3. Please keep the news dark.

4. There is no material but will deform more or less under the action of forces.

5. The beauty of the park is more than words can describe.

二、汉译英

1. 你做实验要特别小心。

2. 能不跟他讲就尽量不要跟他讲。

3. 我没有学那项新技术。

4. 那座木桥一点也不安全。

5. 让我感到惊奇的是每只蚂蚁回来都带回一些东西。

第十一章 被动语态翻译

作为英语的一种语言特征,被动语态在英语中应用广泛。被动语态的应用具有一定的条件,例如:行为主体(主语)不明确、不为人所知、不便于提及或故意隐含时,常常借助于被动语态。有时因为考虑到句型转换,也会使用被动语态。

相对而言,汉语更倾向于使用主动语态,所以,在进行英汉双语转换时,要注意在被动语态与主动语态之间进行转换。如"用以衡量一生的不是我们呼吸的次数,而是那些让我们屏息的精彩时刻。"这一主动语态的中文表达译成英语时,需要转换为英语的被动语态表达:"Life is not measured by the number of breaths we take, but by the moments that take our breath away."再看下面几个例句:

(1)不得简单地以刊物、头衔、荣誉、资历等判断论文质量。

The quality of a thesis should not be judged simply by the journal on which it is published or the author's title, honor and credentials.

(2)不得将在学术期刊上发表论文作为授予学位的唯一标准。

The publishing of theses in academic journals should not be taken as the only criterion for awarding academic degrees.

(3)不得将学历、职称等作为在教育系统学术期刊发表论文的限制性条件。

Diploma and academic titles should not serve (be served) as restrictive conditions for theses publishing in educational journals.

下面我们了解一下被动语态翻译的情况和常用的翻译技巧。

一、英译汉

(一) 保留原主语,被动改主动

(1) He was told yesterday that his former girl friend had got married to one of his classmates.

他昨日获悉,他的前女友已经和他的一位同学结婚了。

(2) The speed of the molecules is increased when they are heated.

当分子受热时,分子运动的速度就加快。

(3) Those rest tasks must be completed as soon as possible.

剩余任务必须尽快完成。

(4) Early fires on the earth were caused by nature, not by man.

地球上早期的火是大自然而不是人类引起的。

(5) Better my life should be ended by their hate, than hated life should be prolonged to live without your love.

我宁可死在他们的仇恨之下,也不愿长久地活在他们的仇恨中而得不到你的爱。

(二) 译成汉语中的无主句

(1) That mad lady in that village was never mentioned again.

后来再也没提起过村子里的那个疯女人。

(2) The educational reform must be carried through to the end.

必须把教育改革进行到底。

(三) 如果施动者在原文中没有出现,可增加适当的主语

(1) She was seen taking away my bag from my office.

有人看见她从办公室里拿走了我的包。

(2) A large quantity of cases was cited to sustain this point of view that the plan was impractical.

这个计划不切实际。为了证明他的这个观点,他们举出了大量的案例。

(四) 译成判断句

(1) This English-Chinese dictionary is compiled by some famous linguists at home and abroad.

这本英汉双语词典是由多位著名的国内外语言学家编纂的。

(2) The old age of protagonist in this novel was spent in the loneliness.

小说中主人公的晚年是在孤独中度过的。

二、汉译英

广泛应用被动语态,是英语的特点之一,而在汉语中被动语态的使用较少。从语法上讲,英语被动语态的各种应用都具有一定的理由,这些理由也恰恰是在汉译英时使用被动语态的依据。从汉英对比的角度看,下述几方面值得译者特别注意。

(一) 简化被动语态

汉语中的简化被动语态是由主语和谓语搭配而成,自然表示被动意义,其中不需要任何表示被动的词语。这种简化被动语态的特点是:不带表示被动的词语;不带施动者;受动者多为物,也可以是人或动物;主动形式而具有被动意义。具有这几类特点的汉语句子进行英译时一般要用被动语态来处理。

(1) 这个事情处理得很好。

This matter was well dealt with.

(2) 这个科研项目今年年底结项。

This scientific research project will be completed by the end of this year.

(3) 你的提议会后讨论。

Your proposal will be discussed after the meeting.

(4) 根据能量守恒定律,宇宙中的能量既不能创造也不能消灭。

According to the law of energy conservation, energy in the universe can never be created nor be destroyed.

(5) 参赛人员请出示入场券。

Candidates are requested to show their tickets when entering.

(6) 这本书是为儿童写的。

Such books are written for children.

(7) 狡兔死,走狗烹;飞鸟尽,良弓藏;敌国破,谋臣亡。

When the cunning hares are killed, the good hound is thrown into the cauldron; when the soaring birds have been caught, the good bow is put away; when the enemy states are overthrown, the wise minister is killed.

(二) 完全被动态

汉语中的完全被动态(也称为真正的被动态)用表示被动的助词"被"或与"被"意义相同的连接词(如"受""由""遭""给""挨""叫""让""为……所"等)构成。完全被动态的汉语句子一般要相应地译成英语的被动句。如:

(1) 转瞬之间,这家银行被抢劫一空。

This bank was ransacked in a blink.

(2) 这个男孩因经常撒谎受到了批评。

This boy is criticized for his frequent lying.

(3) 这些小孩每天早晨由母亲替他们穿衣服。

These children are dressed by their mother every morning.

(4) 天色渐渐地暗下来,大地又被灰色吞噬着。

In the deepening dusk, the whole earth was shrouded in grey.

(5) 听说那个富豪昨晚让人给绑架了。

It was said that the rich man was kidnapped last night.

(6) 这里所需的并不多。

What is needed here is not much.

(三) 某些解释性句子译为被动语态

汉语中凡着重说明一件事是怎样的,或在什么时候、什么地点做的,常用"是……的"或"为……所"。这种结构的句子带有一种解释的语气,也属于被动,英译时常使用被动语态。如:

(1) 这个孤儿是由一个聋哑人养大的。

The orphan was brought up by a blind and deaf man.

(2) 这艘火箭是中国20世纪90年代制造的。

This rocket was made in China in 1990s.

(3) 我为计算机的高效和快捷所折服,对计算机的兴趣也越来越浓厚。

I was overwhelmed by the computer's high efficiency, and my interest in computer was greatly enhanced.

(4) 茅屋为秋风所破。

The thatched house was destroyed by the autumn storm.

(四) 无主句译为被动语态

在主语的应用上,汉语和英语存在一定的差异。在英语中,一般一个句子要求有一个主语,没有主语是例外。但汉语不同,在主语显然可知①的情况下,主语往往被省略,被称为无主句。汉语的这种无主句英译时一般要用被动语态。例如:

(1) 寒暄之际,已摆了酒水饭菜。

Meanwhile the greetings dinner had been served.

(2) 经过双方妥协,最后达成了停战协议。

With compromises of the two parties, a ceasefire agreement was arrived at eventually.

(3) 绝不能以破坏自然环境为代价发展经济。

The economy should be developed at the expense of the natural environment.

(4) 如果不按时将书归还图书馆或到期前不续借,就得按规定罚款。

If books are not returned to the library on time or not renewed before they are due, a fine must be paid in accordance with the regulations.

(5) 随着人工智能的迅速发展,人类的生活水平将得到更大的提高。

---

① 所谓显然可知,多指主语是"我"、"我们"或"你"、"你们";或在语言环境能暗示或说话人双方能意会时,就不必说出。

With the rapid development of artificial intelligence, the life of human beings will be greatly improved.

(6)无论多么艰难,必须保证一日三餐。

No matter how hard it is, the three meals per day must be guaranteed.

(7)必须维护生态环境的平衡。

The ecological environment should be kept in balance.

(五)主动句的被动译法

在汉语中,如果一句话有两个分句,或上下两句话在意思上紧密相关,英译时用被动结构可以给予连接上的便利,以及加强上下文的连贯性。如:

(1)市长站起来讲话,到会听众报以热烈掌声。

The mayor rose to speak and was warmly applauded by the audience present.

(2)他不知道这件事,也没有人同他商讨过这些传闻的计划。

He had no knowledge of this and had not been consulted on these reported plans.

(3)伟大艺术的美学鉴赏和伟大科学的理解都需要智慧。

Wisdom is required both in appreciating great artistic works and in understanding great scientific concepts.

(六)模糊语句的被动译法

汉语中有许多习惯用语,其中有的是用"有人""人们""大家"等作主语,有的是无主句,有的则是句中的独立结构,如"据悉""应该说""必须承认""由此可见"等等。这类汉语的主动句,英译时需要译为以 it 作形式主语的被动句。例如:

(1)当时有人建议保留这些古老的建筑。

It was suggested then these ancient buildings should be preserved.

(2)人们发现橡胶是很好的绝缘材料。

It was found that rubber is a good insulating material.

(3)必须承认,她对中国的医疗事业做出了重大贡献。

It must be acknowledged that she has made great contribution to the medical cause in China.

（4）众所周知，中国一个具有五千年文明的大国。

It is known to all that China is a big country with a history as long as 5 000 years.

翻译小贴士

1. 11月16日，在回应加拿大外交官涉疆谬论时，外交部发言人赵立坚说道："我也建议这位大使，在刷存在感的同时，是不是事先要做好家庭作业，以免贻笑大方。"

A piece of advice for him: do some homework before crafting a publicity stunt, so as not to make a fool of himself.

分析

"刷存在感"通常指的是做出某事、发表某种言论，以吸引他人注意力的行为，类似 attention seeking。这里被译为 craft a publicity stunt。publicity stunt 是市场营销中的一个常见概念，即利用各种噱头、花招吸引眼球的活动，往往带有贬义。这里的 craft 也用得十分巧妙，作名词时，craft 指手艺、工艺或手工艺品；作动词时，指的是精心制作，尤指技术含量较高的制作。用在此处，就点出了加方炮制上述指控的"煞费苦心"。make a fool of himself 即"出洋相，贻笑大方"。

2. 11月17日，外交部发言人赵立坚回应英国驻重庆总领事史云森跳水救人："这是一个好事，我也看到了有关的报道。他见义勇为的举动值得赞扬，我也要为他点个大大的赞。"

We have seen relevant reports. Such a brave act is commendable and I'd like to give him a big thumbs-up.

分析

点赞最早指的是点击社交媒体平台的大拇指标志，表示"赞成或支持"，a sign of approval or support。可以翻译成 give...a like/thumbs-up。现在"点赞"

一词的应用更为广泛了,可以用来表示各种语境下的"赞赏",翻译时可以灵活处理。

例句:广大女性医务人员、疾控人员、科技人员、社区工作者、志愿者等不畏艰险,日夜奋战,坚守在疫情防控第一线。我们要为她们点赞。

Female medical and epidemic control workers, researchers, community workers and volunteers, braving danger and working around the clock, have fought at the front line of the battle. They truly deserve our admiration.

3. 中国人从来不惹事,也从来不怕事。

The Chinese people will not provoke troubles, but we never flinch when trouble comes our way.

我们对有关国家公然违反国际法和国际关系基本准则,对属于中国内政的香港事务说三道四、指手画脚,表示强烈不满和坚决反对。

We deplore and firmly oppose relevant country's finger-pointing over China's Hong Kong affairs, which is a flagrant violation of international law and basic norms governing international relations.

分析

"惹"有"挑衅"的意思,因此"惹事"可以是 provoke/cause troubles。"没事不搞事,有事不怕事",可以说:"Don't ask for trouble, but when trouble really occurs, don't be afraid of it." 在这里将"从来不怕事"翻译成"we never flinch when trouble comes our way",非常形象,当麻烦挡住了你的去路,也从不退缩,flinch 是"退缩、畏惧"的意思。

习题十一

一、汉译英

1. 一开始只能学习少数句型。因此,教师要把这堂课上得有趣而且自然,那是不容易的事。

2. 刚才有人在这里讲了一些不该讲的话。

3. 人生的道路虽然漫长,但紧要处常常只有几步,特别是当人年轻的时候。

4. 马路两旁是整齐的梧桐树。

5. 安化已普遍地减了息,他县亦有减息的事。

二、英译汉

1. Many voices have been raised demanding the setting up of an Arab common market.

2. Memoranda were prepared in advance of private meeting on matters to be discussed.

3. A boy crossing the road was run over by a motorcar.

4. The new Command having been installed, my work there was done, and I returned to give my report to the House.

5. The visitor was flattered and impressed.

第十二章 语序调整

英语和汉语在语法结构上有着许多差别,在两种语言进行转换时,我们经常需要调整原文词语的前后顺序,以符合目的语表达要求。对原文的词序照抄照搬,丝毫不顾译语的表达习惯,机械性地翻译,译文便无通顺可言。翻译时根据译文的语言表达习惯,对原文的词序进行调整,使译文做到最大程度上的通顺,这就是语序调整。例如:

首都经济贸易大学外国语学院刘教授

Professor Liu, School of Foreign Studies, Capital University of Economics and Business

汉语的语序与英文的语序完全相反。

在英汉双语转换过程中,在以下情况需要进行语序调整。

一、习惯表达的语序

(1) 我,你,他 You, he and I

(2) 先生们,女士们 Ladies and gentlemen

(3) 衣,食,住 food, clothing and housing

(4) 东南西北 North, South, East and West

(5) 男女老少 men and women, young and old

(6) 中小学 elementary and high school

(7) 分清敌我 draw a clear distinction between ourselves and the enemy

(8) 钢铁工业 the iron and steel industry

(9) 迟早 sooner or later

(10) 救死扶伤 heal the wounded, rescue the dying

二、多项定语的情况下要进行顺序调整

(一) 英语中多项定语的一般次序

(1) 冠词、指示代词、不定代词、名词所有格、序量词等充当的定语

(2) 表达判断的定语

(3) 描述客观表象的定语

(4) 国别定语

(5) 原材料定语

(6) 用途定语

(7) 中心词

(二) 汉语中多项定语的一般次序

(1) 限定性定语

(2) 国别定语

(3) 时间、地点定语

(4) 数量、种类、次第等定语

(5) 判断性定语

(6) 陈述性定语

(7) 本质性定语

(8) 中心词

正是由于英汉语言修饰成分之间的顺序差异,在进行英汉翻译时,必须进行适当的顺序调整,以满足目的语的表达特点和要求。例如:

(1) He witnessed ①the sixth ②post-war ③economic crisis, ④ of serious consequence ⑤that prevailed in various fields ⑥in the USA.

他亲眼见证了⑥美国②战后①第六次④后果严重的⑤波及各领域的③经济危机。

(英语原文定语顺序：①次第定语②时间定语③本质定语★中心词④判断性定语⑤陈述性定语⑥国别定语)

(汉语译文定语顺序：⑥国别定语②时间定语①次第定语④判断性定语⑤陈述性定语③本质定语★中心词)

（2）It was ①an old woman, ②tall and ③shapely still, ④though withered by time, ⑤on whom his eyes fell ⑥when he stopped and turned.

他站住，⑥转过身来，⑤定睛一看，①原来是个年迈的妇女。②她身材修长，④虽受岁月折磨而略显憔悴，③但丰韵犹存。

(英语原文定语顺序：①本质定语★中心词②描述性定语③陈述性定语④转折性定语⑤非限定性定语⑥)时间性定语)

(汉语译文定语顺序：⑥时间性定语⑤非限定性定语①本质定语★中心词②描述性定语④转折性定语③陈述性定语)

三、多项状语的情况下要进行顺序调整

如果一个句子中有时间副词、方式副词和地点副词，在汉语中通常会把时间副词放在前面，然后是地点副词，最后是方式副词。英语中状语的顺序正好与汉语相反，通常方式状语紧跟在主要动词之后，然后是地点状语，最后是时间状语。例如：

教授这个学期每月都会在课堂举行一次研讨。

The professor would hold a seminar at class once a month this term.

以上例子说明了英汉句子结构中时间、地点、方式状语位置的差异。

(一)英语中状语成分的顺序

(1)条件状语

(2)目的状语

(3)主语

(4)程度状语

(5)谓语

(6)方式状语

(7)频度状语

(8)时间状语

(9)宾语

(二)汉语中状语成分的顺序

(1)主语

(2)目的状语

(3)时间状语

(4)条件状语

(5)方式状语

(6)频度状语

(7)程度状语

(8)谓语

(9)宾语

例句(1)①For this reason, our company explained ②solemnly ③to your company ④many times ⑤in February ⑥ last year.

我公司①为此⑥于去年⑤二月②郑重地④多次③向贵公司表示。

(英语原文状语的顺序:①目的状语☆主语★谓语②方式状语③指涉状语④频度状语⑤时间状语中的月份⑥时间状语中的年份)

(汉语译文状语的顺序:☆主语①目的状语⑥时间状语中的年份⑤时间状语中的月份②方式状语④频度状语③指涉状语★谓语)

例句(2)我们①为顾全大局②于同年③秋末④在第三方的调停下⑤开诚布公地⑥多次⑦强烈要求贵方赔偿我们的一切损失。

④With the third party acting as an intermediary, ① to make the interest of the whole into account, we ⑦ strongly demand ⑤ with frankness and sincerity ⑥ many times ③ at the end of the autumn ② of the same year that you should compensate for all our losses.

(汉语原文状语的顺序:☆主语①目的状语②时间状语中的年份③时间状语中的季节④条件状语⑤方式状语⑥频度状语⑦程度状语★谓语△宾语)

(英语译文状语的顺序:④条件状语①目的状语☆主语⑦程度状语★谓语⑤方式状语⑥频度状语③时间状语中的季节②时间状语中的年份△宾语)

四、层次性的排列顺序

(一)重要性排序

在汉语句子结构中,层次性的排序一般是由重到轻,为递减式排序;而在英文表达中恰恰相反,层次性的排序是由轻到重,为递增式排序。例如:

(1)许多这样的探险都以死亡、灾难、失败和失望而告终。

Many such expeditions ended in disappointment, failure, disaster and death.

(2)我们要培养学生的创新意识、创新能力、创业精神和实践能力。

We should foster students' ability to apply skills, their enterprising spirit, their innovative awareness and their ability to innovate.

此外,在中文句子的结尾提到总数时,最好颠倒顺序,在英文表达中先提到总数,以确保句子重点的清晰。

(3)意大利在华投资主要分布于中国东部沿海地区,涉及汽车、机电、仪表、航空、首饰和租赁等6个行业。

Italian investment is mostly located along the east coast in six sectors as automobiles, machinery and electronic products, instruments aviation, jewelry and leasing.

(二)时间排序

语言本身有一个和时间相关的基本特征,即线性(linearity)。正是由于语言的线性,衔接顺序才会对交际的时间选择有重要作用。由于时间顺序与语言选择中线性顺序的匹配,我们又面临语言象似性(iconicity)特征。一般而言,英汉两种语言中都存在着象似性语序和非象似性语序。但汉语中使用语言象似性语序的程度比英语要高。

(1)我写完作业后,再和你一起去踢球。

I can go to play football with you after I have finished my homework.

(2)款到发货

The goods won't be delivered before the arrival of fund.

(3)他本来在天津开会,会议一结束,他就去北京度假了,昨天才坐飞机回来。

He had flown yesterday from Beijing where he spent his vacation after finishing the meeting that he had taken part in Tianjin.

(4) Nothing has happened since we are parted.

我们分别后,一直没有什么事情发生。

(三) 空间排序

就空间顺序而言,英汉语言基本上都呈现出"上—下""大—小""近—远"和"整体—部分"等顺序。

(1) Just outside our office window is a fire-escape with a little iron balcony.

在我们办公室窗外是一个紧急出口,有铁栏杆围起的阳台。

(2) The man's swarthy face was placed and still; his black hair and beard were slightly, very slightly, discomposed. His eyes stared wide-open, glassy and vacant, at the ceiling. The filmy look and fixed expression horrified me.

那个人黑黝黝的脸一动也不动;他黑色的头发和胡子都稍微,只是稍微有点凌乱。他的两只眼睛睁得大大的,正茫然而无神地瞪着天花板。那呆滞的眼神和凝滞的表情把我吓坏了。

(四) 逻辑顺序

英语的因果顺序较为灵活,表示原因的从句可以在主句之前,也可以在主句之后。而汉语通常是原因在前,结果在后。英语表示目的的行为,通常是行为在前,目的在后,而汉语有时为了强调目的,往往将目的放在行为之前。

(1) The sports meeting was cancelled because of the rain.

因为下雨,运动会取消了。

(2)为了能提前完成任务,我们要更加努力地工作。

We must work harder so that we can complete our task ahead of schedule.

五、倒装句

在翻译"从来没有""从未""没有任何""都不"等否定句或其他表示强调的汉语表达方式时,我们通常在英语翻译中用倒装句型。

(1)他几乎没时间和朋友一起喝茶。

Hardly does he have time to have a cup of tea with his friends.

(2)我永远不会忘记我参军的日子。

Never shall I forget the day when I joined the army.

(3)直到昨天晚上,我才发现我的戒指被偷了。

Not until last night did I find out that my ring was stolen.

(4)只有调动一切积极因素,才能顺利实现中华民族伟大复兴的中国梦。

Only by mobilizing all positive factors can the Chinese dream of nation rejuvenation come true smoothly.

(5)箭嗖的一声射向空中。

Up went the arrow into the air.

(6)知足者常乐。

Happy is the man who is contented.

(7)数百位烈士长眠于此。

Here lie hundreds of revolutionary martyrs.

翻译小贴士

◀ 原文 ▶

1. 今年是决胜全面建成小康社会、决战脱贫攻坚之年,全国广大教师用爱心和智慧阻断贫困代际传递,点亮千万乡村孩子的人生梦想,展现了当代人民教师的高尚师德和责任担当。

译文

This year is the time to secure a decisive victory in building a moderately prosperous society in all respects and achieve the goal of poverty alleviation. Teachers across the country devoted their love and wisdom to stopping poverty from being passed on to the next generation and inspiring millions of rural children to pursue their dreams, which demonstrates the noble ethics and sense of responsibility of contemporary teachers.

原文

2. 提振雄心,形成各尽所能的气候治理新体系。各国应该遵循共同但有区别的责任原则,根据国情和能力,最大程度强化行动。同时,发达国家要切实加大向发展中国家提供资金、技术、能力建设支持。

译文

We need to raise ambitions and foster a new architecture of climate governance where every party does its part. Following the principle of common but differentiated responsibilities, all countries need to maximize actions in light of their respective national circumstances and capabilities. Developed countries need to scale up support for developing countries in financing, technology and capacity building.

原文

3. Tesla and SpaceX founder Elon Musk has some advice for CEOs: Make better products, seek negative feedback and ditch those Power Points presentations. "Are CEOs from corporate America focused enough on product improvement? I think the answer is no," Musk said Tuesday at the WSJ CEO Summit. But that is vital, so CEOs should spend less time focusing on things like financials, according to Musk, and spend more time "just trying to make your product as amazing as possible." "I just honestly would recommend to anyone listening…just spend less time in meetings, less time

on PowerPoint presentations, less time on spreadsheets and more time on the factory floor or time with customers," Musk said.

译文

特斯拉和SpaceX创始人埃隆·马斯克有一些建议要送给首席执行官们："做更好的产品，寻找负面反馈信息，抛弃PPT。"马斯克12月8日在WSJ CEO峰会上表示："美国公司的CEO们足够专注于改善产品了吗？我认为没有。"但是马斯克认为，这至关重要，所以CEO们应该在财务等事情上少花些时间，把更多时间用于"完善你的产品"。马斯克说："我真心地建议在座所有人……在开会上少花点时间，在PPT上少花点时间，在财务报表上少花点时间，把更多时间花在厂房里或者与顾客交流上。"

习题十二

一、英译汉

1. The isolation of the rural world because of distance and the lack of transport facilities is compounded by the paucity of the information media.

2. The first two must be equal for all who are being compared, if any comparison in terms of intelligence is to be made.

3. Mr. Bennet was among the earliest of those who waited on Mr. Bingley. He had always intended to visit him, though to the last always assuring his wife that he should not go; and till the evening after the visit was paid, she had no knowledge of it.

4. Have I not described a pleasant site for a dwelling, which I speak of it as bosomed in hill and wood, and riding from the verge of a stream?

5. I then sat with my doll on my knee, till the fire got low, glancing round occasionally to make sure that nothing worse than myself haunted the shadowy room.

二、汉译英

1. 半轮晓月渐渐西沉，月光透过小床旁边一个窄窄的窗子照进来，我趁着月光穿上衣服。

2. 严志和一见了土地,土地上的河流,河流两岸的洼田,洼田上青枝绿叶的芦苇,心里就充满了喜气。

3. 对于康塔来说,即使是家乡的野兽,都比这些人有尊严。

4. 我们于1959年离开了中国。此后,中国连续两年遭遇了自然灾害,当我们在国外读到这方面的消息时,我们的心情十分悲痛。

5. 全世界人民在社会主义阳光下过幸福生活的一天是会来到的。

第十三章 长句翻译

长句的翻译主要是在对源语中的长句进行句法分析的基础之上,进行语义再现。

一、翻译技巧

由于英汉两种语言结构的差异,翻译时,有时需要对原文中的长句进行恰当的分析和适当的调整,以便更好地理解。下面介绍六种常用的长句翻译技巧。

切分法(cutting)

内嵌法(embedding)

倒置法(reversing)

拆分法(splitting)

重组法(recasting)

逻辑思维(logic thinking)

(一)切分法

在进行长句切分之前,首先要分析辨别长句的主要思想与布局,将其切成单独的部分,一个一个地进行翻译。对从属结构中的动词形式进行相应的变化,必要时为切分后的句子添加主语。

(1)这种床垫工艺先进,结构新颖,造型美观,款式多样,// 舒适大方,携带方便。

The technological design of this bed cushion is advanced with novel structure, beautiful shape and various patterns. // They are comfortable and convenient to carry.

(2) 人们实际上几乎无法将蓄意行窃的盗贼拒之门外,// 所能做的只是设法阻拦他片刻,/ 从而使其暴露在巡警或附近溜达的人面前。

Actually it is almost impossible to keep a determined burglar out. // All you can do is discourage him for a few minutes, / thus exposing him to police patrols or those wandering around.

(3) With electronic X-ray equipment, we seem finally to have figured out a way / to hold the terrorists, real and imagined, at bay; // it was such a relief to solve this problem / that we did not think much about what such a state of affairs says about the quality of our lives.

凭借着电子透视装置,我们似乎终于想出妙计,/ 让恐怖分子无法近身,无论是真的恐怖分子还是臆想的。// 能解决这一问题真是如释重负,/ 于是我们就不再多想这种状况对我们生活质量意味着什么。

(4) A portion of the hall which has been under construction for 18 months / was unveiled to the public Tuesday, //marking the close of the first stage of extensive renovations.

经过一年半的修葺,/ 镜厅的一部分已于本周二重新对公众开放。// 这标志着大规模修缮的第一阶段工作已经结束。

(5) Children play with dolls equipped with personality chips,// computers with inbuilt personalities will be regarded as workmates rather than tools,// relaxation will be in front of smell television,//and digital age will have arrived.

儿童将与装有个性芯片的玩具娃娃玩耍,//具有个性化内置的计算机将被视为工作伙伴而不是机器,//人们将在气味电视前休闲,//这时数字时代就到来了。

(6) Interest in historical methods had arisen //less through external

challenge to the validity of history as an intellectual discipline//and more from internal quarrels among historians themselves.

人们对历史研究方法产生了兴趣,//这与其说是来自外部的对历史作为一门科学知识的有效性提出的挑战,//还不如说是历史学家内部发生了争吵。

(二) 内嵌法

内嵌是指在句子中把修饰词放到被修饰词之前,它常用于将英语长句翻译成紧凑连贯的汉语。该种方法常用于定语从句和同位语从句的翻译。

(1) Congress has made laws requiring most financial groups to give <u>information</u> about how much they spend and how they spend it, the amount and sources of funds, membership, and names and salaries of their representatives.

国会已制定法律,要求大部分金融集团呈报他们花费了多少钱,怎样花的,款项的总额以及来源。成员人数、代表的姓名和薪金等情况。

(2) History has proved that <u>man's understanding of natural resources</u> and his developing and utilizing of them, as well as <u>his capability of making tools of production to make use of these sources</u>, are very <u>important signs to indicate the developing level of social productive forces</u>.

历史业已证明,人类对资源的<u>认识</u>、开发和利用,以及制造生产工具利用资源的<u>能力</u>,是社会生产力发展水平的重要<u>标志</u>。

(3) <u>The controversy</u> surrounding the effects of modern farming methods on the rural landscape <u>has created bitter conflict</u> between farming and environmental interests in recent years.

近年来,围绕现代农耕方式对乡村地貌环境影响的<u>争论</u>,引起了对于农业和环境关系问题之间的<u>激烈矛盾冲突</u>。

(4) What is harder to establish is <u>whether the productivity revolution</u> that businessmen assume they are presiding over <u>is for real</u>.

难以确认的是,商界人士认为他们所主导的<u>生产力革命</u>是否真的存在。

(5) Our wish is to establish <u>a government</u> that is willing to work for you,

giving you what you've paid for, said the incoming president at the inauguration.

在就职典礼上,即将上任的总统说:"我们要建立一个尽心竭力为民众服务的<u>政府</u>,对大家的付出给予应有的回报。"

(三)倒置法

倒置是指在翻译中调整句子的顺序,使其符合目的语的用法。在复杂句的主句、状语从句、定语从句和强调结构的翻译中经常使用。

(1)①<u>Such is human nature</u> in the West that ②a great many people are often willing to sacrifice higher pay for the privilege of becoming white-collar workers.

②许多人常常愿意牺牲比较高的工资换取白领工人的社会地位,①<u>这在西方倒是人之常情</u>。

(2) Many times I have felt a sadness when exposed to modern children so immersed in the electronic media that they have little or no awareness of <u>the marvelous world</u> to be discovered in books.

多少次,当我看到如今的孩子们如此沉迷于电子媒体时,我不由得深感悲哀,他们很小,或许根本不了解书中所能发现的<u>神奇世界</u>。

(3)<u>We take heart from the fact</u> that the experiment for a new medicine, which has been carried on for months, has come to signs of promising effect.

进行了几个月的新药试验总算显现出迹象表明可能良好疗效,<u>这一事实使我们增强了信心</u>。

(4)在感恩节的气氛中,①乔治②没有跟朋友们一起庆祝节日,而是沉浸于阅读他父亲留给他的日记。// 他的父亲在连续两次环球旅行后在海上去世。

Amid the atmosphere of Thanksgiving, ②rather than joining his friends in celebrating the holiday , ①George was immersed in the diary left to him <u>by his father</u>, <u>who died</u> at sea after completing successive trips around the world .

(5) Our main aim in producing the magazine is to give readers inspiration and ideas for their homes and it's heart-warming to learn about the success we've had.

我们创办这本杂志的主要目的,是为读者营造温馨和提供灵感与思考的家。当得知这一目标已实现时,<u>我们感到十分欣慰</u>。

(四)拆分法

拆分翻译法主要用于英汉翻译,是指从一个句子中提取子句、短语或单词等语素,分别进行分析与考虑(根据事件中句子顺序的优先等级,可以将拆分元素放在句子的后置或前置位置)。当采用切割法和嵌入法很难得到合适的翻译文本时,可以采用拆分法进行翻译,以达到准确、通顺的效果。

(1) An outsider's success could even <u>curiously</u> help two parties to get the agreement they want.

<u>说来奇怪</u>,一个局外人取得的成功竟然能够促使双方达成一项他们企盼的协议。

(2) <u>Covering a large population and vast area</u>, it's difficult for China to impose a single solution to reform of household registration.

中国人口众多、地域辽阔,户籍改革问题复杂,不宜搞"一刀切"。

(3) Thousands of Parisians watched <u>in horror</u> from behind police cordons as a ferocious blaze devastated Notre Dame Cathedral.

数千名巴黎人在警戒线后眼睁睁地看着一场猛烈的大火吞噬了巴黎圣母院,<u>惊恐万分</u>。

(4) Sue feared Johnsy would, indeed, <u>light and fragile as a leaf herself</u>, float away, when her slight hold upon the world grew weaker.

约翰西身体就像一片叶子又瘦又弱,苏担心要是她那本已脆弱的生存意志再动摇下去的话,真的会凋零飘落。

(5) The land, <u>which once barred the way of weary travelers</u>, now has become a land for winter and summer vacations, a land of magic and wonder.

这个地方已经成了冬夏两季的休假胜地,风光景物,蔚为壮观;而从前的旅游者们只能到此止步,<u>望洋兴叹</u>。

(6) The dropout is <u>partly the effect of</u> farmers' selling down existing pig stocks and holding back from expanding herds.

养猪户减少现有库存,抑制生猪数量扩大,这是生猪数量下降的<u>部分原因</u>。

(7) A <u>growing minority</u> of Western intellectuals agreed.

越来越多的西方知识分子开始接受这种看法,<u>尽管从数量上说,他们仍然是少数</u>。

(8) 他的身材魁梧,生一副大长方脸,嘴巴阔大,肌肤呈着紫檀色。

<u>He</u> was a giant of a man with a long square face, a wide mouth and a complexion suffused with the color of red sandalwood.

(9) A <u>persistent</u>, cold rain was falling, mingled with slow.

外面冷雨夹雪,淅淅沥沥下个不停。

(10) Those Chinese scientists in Silicon Valley are <u>understandably</u> proud of their achievements.

这些在硅谷工作的中国科学家们对他们取得的成就感到自豪。<u>这是可以理解的</u>。

(五) 重组法

重组,亦称为合成,是指对原作进行准确理解,灵活调整和重新排序。译者应结合原文的语序和不同的翻译技巧,通过重组,将原文的意思准确地传达给读者。

(1) He felt different – was different – from the kids who rushed about in
        ①   ②   ③
the halls and//planned dances he would never attend.
                ④

他觉得自己不同于那些在过道里东奔西跑的孩子——事实上也的确与众不同。
        ①   ③   ②
//那些孩子安排的舞会他永远也不可能参加。
        ④

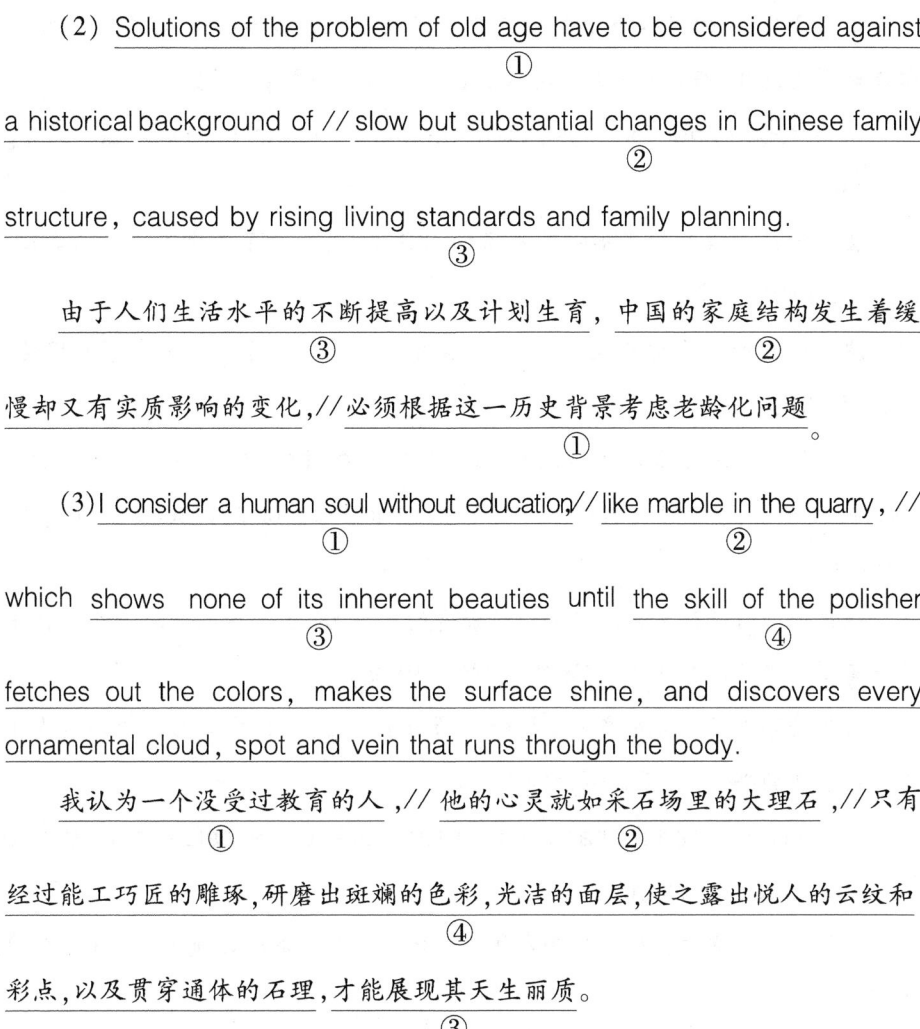

(六) 逻辑思维

逻辑思维能力是在翻译过程中不可缺少的一种能力。为了避免语言逻辑上的谬误,最重要的是要在语境中运用逻辑思维对原文进行分析,从而清晰地理解作者想表达的意思、原作的逻辑序列和修饰成分之间的语法关系。

(1) For more than two years two unyielding men, equally determined, mutually hostile, supposedly allies, wrestled over the fate of China.

在长达两年多时间里,他们为中国的命运搏斗着,他们两人的意志一样坚定,互相敌视,不肯屈服,与此同时却又是名义上的朋友。(不符合逻辑的译文)

两年多来,他们为争夺中国命运的主宰权而殊死较量。两人都下定决心,都视对方为仇敌,而表面上却是公认的盟友。(符合逻辑的译文)

(2) It took Porter four false starts before he found the courage to ring the first doorbell.

在波特鼓起勇气按了第一户人家的门铃之前,他做了四次不成功的尝试。(不符合逻辑的译文)

波特一开始四次都没敢敲门,第五次才鼓起勇气按了第一户人家的门铃。(符合逻辑的译文)

(3) A Chinese liquor stock has captured the imagination of global investors as a proxy for affluent consumers in the world's second-largest economy.

一只中国白酒股票激发了全球投资者的想象力,在世界上第二大经济体中作为富裕阶层的消费代表。(不符合逻辑的译文)

作为世界上第二大经济体富裕阶层的消费代表,一只中国白酒股票激发了全球投资者的兴趣。(符合逻辑的译文)

(4) Very wonderful changes in matter take place before our eyes to which we pay little attention.

我们很少注意的物质中那些奇异的变化都经常在我们眼前发生。(不符合逻辑的译文)

物质中那些奇异的变化常常就发生在我们眼前,尽管我们很少注意到这一点。(符合逻辑的译文)

二、翻译实例与分析

(一)英译汉

◀ 原文 ▶

(1) The election which has led to you being chosen to president over this Assembly — a very wise choice indeed — is a tribute to your great

country, which has contributed to the development of the history of free nations a tradition of peace that serves as an example for the legal community that we constitute, a country which has always commanded respect and admiration from all corners of the world.

分析

此句为复合句,采用切分法进行分析。一个主句和五个定语从句。主句为 election…is a tribute to your great country,第一个从句 which has had led 修饰 election,第二个从句 which has contributed to 修饰 your great country,第三个定语从句 that serves as 修饰 a tradition of peace,第四个从句 that we constitute 修饰 legal community,第五个从句 which has always commanded 修饰 a country(your great country 的同位语)。从句四隶属于从句三,从句五隶属于同位语,破折号之间的 a very wise choice 是插入语对 election 做进一步解释。

译文

这次选举你为本届大会的主席,实为明智的选择,这是对你伟大的国家的敬意。贵国对自由国家的历史发展贡献了一种和平传统,这一传统是我们法制社会的榜样。全世界一贯对贵国表示尊重和敬佩。

原文

(2) There are several reasons why he (Kissinger) no longer appears to be magician which the world press had made him out to be, an illusion which he failed to discourage because, as he would admit himself, he has a tendency toward megalomania.

分析

主句是 There are several reasons,后接 why 引导的定语从句,从句中的 magician 接另一定语从句 which the world press,an illusion 是同位语从句,说明其前的定语从句及其先行词 magician,其后接定语从句 which he failed,里面包含一个由 because 引起的状语从句,中间再插入一个由 as 引导的从句。

首先可以采用逆序翻译法进行分析和翻译:基辛格现在不再是魔术师一般

的人物;基辛格是魔术师一般的人物是报界宣扬的结果;基辛格对报界的宣扬没有阻止是因为他承认自己有一种自大狂的倾向;产生这些现象有原因。

译文

全世界报纸曾把他(基辛格)渲染成魔术师一般的人物,他也没阻止人们塑造这种错误的形象,因为他也承认自己有一种自大狂的倾向。现在他不再像是这样一种人物了,这里有几个原因。

◀ 原文 ▶

(3) The medical waste that has fouled beaches in the New York region at the peak of summer season has taken its toll on business all along the shore, driving vacationers away both from beaches that have been closed and from those that have remained open.

分析

主句是 The medical waste…has taken its toll on business all along the shore。主语是 The medical waste,后接定语从句 that has fouled beaches,句末使分词短语 driving vacationers away,里面又包含两个定语从句 beaches that have been closed 和 those that have。

全句有三层意思:①医疗用品生产厂家的废弃物污染了海滨;②这种污染严重影响了海滨浴场的生意;③污染严重给海滨商业区带来了巨大损失。

译成汉语时可先讲原因,后讲结果,既有顺译,也有逆译。

译文

医疗用品生产厂家的废弃物污染了纽约地区的海滩。时值盛夏,一些海滨浴场已经关闭,并赶走了大批的度假者,而那些尚未关闭的滨海浴场也是门可罗雀。污染使得整个海滨浴区的商业蒙受了巨大损失。

◀ 原文 ▶

(4) The Democratic-controlled House came up short Tuesday in an effort to override President Trump's veto of a measure aimed at rolling back

his declaration of a national emergency.

分析

本句中 in an effort...veto 承接上文表示众议院的动作状态;另外 aim at...national emergency 做定语修饰 a measure。因此全句包括 3 部分:①众议院目前处境艰难无计可施;②众议院此前想要推翻总统对一项措施的否决;③措施旨在撤销先前的政令。

译文

民主党控制的众议院在周二已无计可施,其想要推翻特朗普对一项措施的否决,该措施旨在撤销此前特朗普所宣布的全国进入紧急状态。

◀ 原文 ▶

(5) I must say that his statement was laudable for its frankness and quite plausible on the basis of premises which, I'm afraid, are invalid in the context of the United Nations Charter.

分析

宾语从句 that his statement was laudable 又包含一个定语从句 which are invalid in the context,定语从句中又包含一个插入语 I'm afraid,全句解读的重点是宾语从句,包含 2 层意思:①他的发言坦率是值得称赞的,听起来也颇有道理;②按照《联合国宪章》的精神,这些话所依据的前提是站不住脚的。

译文

应当说,他的坦率发言是值得称赞的,听起来也颇有道理,然而按照《联合国宪章》的精神,他的言论所依据的前提恐怕是站不住脚的。

(二)汉译英

在由若干小句组成的长句中,常常在中间变换主语。汉译英时,可以把由不同主语组成的句子译成不同的英语从句或小句。

◀ 原文 ▶

(1) 雪可以反射太阳光,融冰的表层发黑,吸收的太阳热量是雪的四倍。

分析

首先确定主体部分即"融冰的表层发黑",而"吸收的太阳热量是雪的四倍"作为附属成分,用现在分词表示主从之间的关系。"雪可以反射太阳光"是辅助说明它的吸热能量较差,最后用定语从句来解释其辅助说明。

译文

The melting surface darkens, absorbing up to four times as much energy from the sun as snow, which reflects sunlight.

◀ 原文 ▶

(2) 中国是一个地域辽阔,有着数千年悠久历史的多民族国家,它秀丽的自然风光、众多的名胜古迹和丰富多彩的灿烂文化,都是丰富的旅游资源。

分析

根据原文意思,采用切分法,将原文切分为两部分,一部分是整体介绍,一部分是细节描述。两部分采用不同的主语。在第一部分中,"中国是一个多民族国家"是原文的主体,"地域辽阔,有着数千年悠久历史"是对主体内容的修饰性描述,可以内嵌到译文中。

译文

China is a multi-ethnic country with a vast land and thousands of years of history. Its beautiful natural landscape, numerous scenic spots and historical sites and colorful, splendid civilization make up rich tourism resources.

◀ 原文 ▶

(3) 延安虽然还没有战争,但军队天天在前方打仗,后方也唤工作忙,文章太长,有谁来看呢?

分析

虽然原文有5个小短句,但实际上可以归纳为两层意思:军队和人民都很忙;作为文艺工作者,应该考虑到这种情况,写文章不要写得太长。第二层意思以一个反诘句结尾,意思清楚明了,具有很强的说服力。考虑英语的表达习惯,翻译时用两个完整的句子再现了原文的意思。

译文

Although there is as yet no fighting here in Yan'an, our troops at the front are daily engaged in battle, and the people in the rear are busy at work. If articles are too long, who will read them?

原文

(4)识字是男人和女人更好地了解世界的工具,识字是个人尊严的源泉也是社会健康发展的动力。

分析

原文实际上在谈论两个问题,因此,采用切分法,将原文切分为两部分来翻译,清晰明了。第一部分的核心词是"工具","男人和女人更好地了解世界"为内嵌部分;第二部分的核心词有两个,"源泉"和"动力","个人尊严"和"社会健康发展"分别为内嵌部分。

译文

Literacy provides tools for men and women to better understand the world. And it is a source of individual dignity and a motor for the healthy development of society.

原文

(5)古来一切有成就的人,都很严肃地对待自己的生命,当他活着一天,总要尽量工作,多学习,不肯虚度年华,不让时间白白地浪费掉。

分析

原文有7个小部分,前2个小部分为总括,可以作为第一部分;后5个小部分为细节描述，可以作为第二个部分。第一部分的主体为"人"，内嵌部分为"古来一切有成就的"；第二部分中的"不肯虚度年华，不让时间白白地浪费掉"作为"尽量工作，多学习"这一主体的附属补充，采用形容词短语的形式。

译文

People with great achievements since ancient times have been treating their lives solemnly. As long as they live, they would always make the most of their life time working and studying, unwilling to idle away life and waste time.

原文

(6)上海大剧院是由法国一家著名的建筑设计公司设计，总建筑面积为62 803平方米，总高度为40米，分为地下2层，地面6层，顶部2层，共计10层。

分析

该句子有5个主谓结构，即5个分句。主语各不相同，无法用一个英语句子表达。翻译时，应根据各分句之间的关系，从新组合，译成2个英语句子。第一个以大剧院为主语，说出其总面积和总高度，把汉语的第一个分句处理成英语的状语，形成英语的形合结构。第二个句子仍以大剧院(用形式主语It)作主语，表明该剧院共有10层，而后用同位语形式——说明。

译文

Designed by a well-known French architectural designing company, the Shanghai Grand Theater is 62 803 square metres in floor space and 40 metres in height. It has ten storeys, two under the ground, six on the ground, and another two on top.

原文

(7)灾难深重的中华民族，一百年来，其优秀人物奋斗牺牲，前赴后继，摸索救国救民的真理，是可歌可泣的。

分析

原文先分述,后总说,对前面的内容做一概括或评论。译文在原文句子的结尾部分断句,前半部分为单独一句,最后的判断部分单独译成了一个独立句。

译文

For a hundred years, the finest sons and daughters of the disaster-ridden Chinese nation fought and sacrificed their lives, one stepping into the breach as another fell, in quest of the truth that would save the country and the people. This moved us to songs and tears.

◀ **原文** ▶

(8)总之,微波只能以直线的方式传播,没有一系列的转播塔,它们就不能越过漫长的距离,把消息传递到遥远的地方。

分析

原文是一个长句,分为5个小部分,"总之,微波只能以直线的方式传播"实际上是一个概括句,总领了整句话的意思,译文将此句单独译出。后3部分进一步解释描述,属于分说部分,译文另单独起一句。

译文

In short, microwaves can only travel in straight line. Without a series of relay towers, it is impossible for them to send messages over long distances to remote places.

◀ **原文** ▶

(9)以农民为例,他们现在更乐于使用科学种田法,由于种植杂交水稻的面积增加,单位面积的产量也增加了。

分析

这是一个典型的比方句①。若原文的长句内含有比方句,英译时一般可以

---

① 汉语句子中经常可以看到"比如:……""拿……作比方""以……为例""拿……来说"之类的表达法,具有这类表达法的句子叫作比方句。

在句子的前半部分断句,将比方句单独译成一句①。这样,根据原文意义,可以将其解构为三个部分,译文也以三个独立句呈现。

译文

Take the peasants for example. They are now more eager to use scientific methods for farming. The amount of land devoted to hybrid rice has risen so that the per-mu yield has gone up considerably.

原文

(10)本世纪上半叶的上海曾经是中国工业、贸易、金融和商业的中心,有着远东大都会浪漫而传奇的历史,吸引过不少外来资本,因而一度成为"冒险家的乐园"。

分析

根据原文想要表达的意思,将原文切分为两部分:第一部分说明本世纪上半叶的上海在中国的地位;第二部分说明上海对外资的吸引力。译文将原文分译为两个整句,意思清晰明了。

译文

In the first half of this century Shanghai served as the industrial, trade, financial and commercial center of the country. It attracted many foreign investors as a mysterious oriental city and an adventurers' paradise.

三、翻译赏析

原文

1."得道多助,失道寡助"。美方不惜损害美国广大用户和公司的权益,将

---

① 汉语里的比方句与其后面的内容往往用逗号隔开,而在英语里,类似的表达要用祈使句式,祈使句式须有一个中心谓语动词。而根据英语的表达习惯,具有了中心谓语动词之后,整个句子就独立成句,不能再与另一个含有中心谓语动词的句子连成一句,否则就成为累叠句(run-on sentence),是一种语法错误的句子。因此,在进行英汉双语转换时,要进行结构上的调整。例如,我们将"拿我们这些人来说,很多人每年都有一些进步。"这句汉语译成英语,一般会译为2个独立的句子"Take for example those of us present here. Many of us make some progress each year."。

一己私利凌驾于市场原则和国际规则之上,肆意进行政治操弄和政治打压,换来的只能是自身道德滑坡、国家形象受损和国际信任赤字,最终也将自食其果。

译文

1. Chinese saying goes, "a just cause rallies abundant support while an unjust one finds little." The US side has put selfish interests above market principle and international rules to the detriment of US users and companies, and willfully resorted to political manipulation and oppression, which will only end up with its demoralization, eroded national image and trust deficit. All this will boomerang.

注:Boomerang 是澳大利亚土著人的传统狩猎工具,译为"回旋镖"或"飞去来器"。Boomerang 作为动词用在此处,指美国的这一举动不但起不到作用,还会搬起石头砸自己的脚,被自己扔出的回旋镖击中,即"自作自受,咎由自取"。

◀ 原文 ▶

2. 脱贫攻坚的重大胜利,为实现第一个百年奋斗目标打下坚实基础,极大增强了人民群众获得感、幸福感、安全感,彻底改变了贫困地区的面貌,改善了生产生活条件,提高了群众生活质量,"两不愁三保障"全面实现。

译文

The great victory in poverty reduction has laid solid foundations for the fulfillment of the first centenary goal-to finish building a moderately prosperous society in all respects by the time the CPC celebrates its centenary in 2021-and has boosted the people's feeling of gain, happiness and security. The livelihood of the people in poverty-stricken areas has been greatly improved, and the people have sufficient food and clothing, as well as access to compulsory education, basic medical services and safe housing.

 习题十三

英译汉

1. People's perception of the Great Wall changed at a critical moment of unprecedented crisis facing the Chinese nation in modern history of China when the Great Wall revealed how laborious and intelligent the ancient Chinese were and how powerful ancient Chinese was.

2. Soil erosion, desertification and degeneration of grasslands are worsening with each passing day, which weakens the ecological functions of wind break, sand fixing, water storage, soil preservation, and the protection of biodiversity.

3. The only meals regularly taken together in Britain these days are at the weekend, among rich families struggling to retain something of the old symbol of togetherness.

4. All members, in order to ensure to all of them the rights and benefits resulting from membership, shall fulfill in good faith the obligations assumed by them in accordance with present Charter.

5. Very wonderful changes in matter take place before our eyes to which we pay little attention.

实践篇

第十四章

再现与审美

一千个读者眼中就有一千个哈姆雷特(There are a thousand Hamlets in a thousand people's eyes.)。作为译者,首先是读者,不同的译者对源语文本会有不同的理解,在此基础之上,进而在译入语中呈现不同的表达。在理解与表达的过程中,有两个关键的要素,即原文的可再现性和译者的情商,特别是翻译具有美学价值的作品中,更是如此。

一、理解与再现

下面这段话,描写婚姻前后的生活,真情实感,扑面而来。但译者的感情丰富度、具有的敏感度以及是否有过类似经历,是决定译文质量的重要影响因素。

◀ 原文 ▶

When my husband, Bill and I were courting, just a phone call could send us quivering with excitement. We went on impromptu picnics, called each other Sweet Patootie and left mash notes in strange places. Cheeks flushed, hearts raced, palms sweated.

And then we got married.

Mortgage payment rolled in. A son, housekeeping, jobs and just plain old familiarity forced romance out. Faced with the choice of watching TV or sharing a passionate moment, I am embarrassed at how often we cast our vote for Jerry Seinfeld.

译文

(1) 曾经,我与爱人比尔尚在恋爱;曾经,一通电话意味着多少心潮澎湃;曾经的曾经,爱于我们它无处不在。回忆中,是一次次灵犀相通的野餐,一声声柔情蜜意的呼唤,是游览各色风物时留下的山盟海誓与便签。且不论我们时时羞涩的红脸,狠狠震颤的心尖,还有那愈渐湿润的手心。

然后,我们结婚了。

随之而来的便是房贷的压力,带孩子艰辛,理家务烦劳,彼此间新鲜感早已难再。那份浪漫与爱情就淡出了我们的生活空间。当我们终于得到了空闲,还能否重温激情的往昔?现实却用肥皂剧将两人尴尬藏起。

(2) 想当初在热恋期,我丈夫比尔和我只消通上一回电话就能让彼此兴奋颤栗,什么随时来一场说走就走的野餐,互称亲爱的,脸红、心跳、手出汗都是常事,那时简直恨不得到处留下彼此间的情话。

但后来我们结婚了。

房贷压得我们喘不过气来,孩子,房子,票子和那些平淡琐碎的事儿把生活填得满满当当,浪漫什么的,不存在的。而且说来惭愧的是,在看电视还是过二人世界的抉择中,我们夫妻大多是选择了前者。

(3) 当我和我的丈夫比尔处在恋爱期时,仅仅是对方的一通电话就可以让我们兴奋、激动得浑身颤栗。我们有时会突然兴起去野餐,兴起时甜蜜地称呼对方为"甜心、小可爱",并在一些陌生的地方留下互表爱意的纸条。我们在一起时脸颊会染上红晕,心脏会加速跳动,手心会潮湿冒汗。

我们结婚之后。

像雪花一样纷至沓来的按揭还款银行账单,一个开销巨大、需要长期投资的儿子,枯燥的工作以及一成不变、循规蹈矩的生活,这所有的一切致使恋爱时期的浪漫一去不复返。我每天都会面临因电视节目而产生的争吵或和他们抱怨一天中遇到的烦闷之事:我不知道什么时候把我们的选票投给杰瑞·宋飞(美国著名的脱口秀演员)。

(4) 那时我和我家先生比尔还在热恋中,旁人看来微不足道的一次通话便足以让我们心花乱颤。我们会出去野餐,一口一个小甜心地互相叫着,还喜把写着肉麻情话的小纸条随便塞到一个什么地方、等对方发现。我们也脸红害羞啊,心里的小鹿乱撞啊,手心甚至会因为对方的存在而紧张得有些发潮。

可在那之后,我们结婚了。

按揭贷款进入了我们的生活。一天到晚不仅要带儿子、做家务、忙自己的工作,还要处理生活里各种杂七杂八的琐碎事情,生生磨没了昔日那些甜蜜的浪漫。到现在,我们若是得在电视节目和夫妇间的小情趣里选一个……真的很抱歉,我们一般都会选择前者,我们宁可看杰瑞·宋飞说的脱口秀来放松一下。

(5)当我和我的丈夫比尔刚开始谈情说爱时,对方的一个电话就能让彼此激动不已。尽管是一场毫无准备的野餐,我们都会全心投入、尽情享受,彼此亲昵地呼唤着对方的爱称以示甜蜜。天涯海角,无论何地,只要是我们所到之处,都会留下我们爱情的印记。脸颊发烫、心跳加速、掌心冒汗,这便是两人"来电显示"的心动讯号啊!随后,我们步入了婚姻的殿堂。然而,未来所迎接我们的并不是爱情的甜甜蜜蜜,而是各种生活的烦心琐事,比如房贷的压力、育儿的辛苦、家务的劳累、工作的重负,再加上彼此之间的审美疲劳,婚前那种浪漫的感觉早已不复存在。每当夜幕降临,是面对电视为一个当红明星投票,还是和身边的眷侣卿卿我我、共度良宵?我们每每会选择前者,这使我内心很不是滋味。

注:以下内容为上文译者的翻译过程分析:该片段将夫妻二人之间婚前的如胶似漆和婚后的平淡如水进行了对比,通过 excitement、Sweet Patootie、mortgage payment、embarrassed 等词语将两人婚前和婚后的感情变化生动描绘,刻画出主人公心理情绪的转变。

在经过翻译和对比译文后,我发现译文的情感氛围比较浓厚,尤其是在刻画婚前生活时,二人初恋时的如胶似漆、如痴如醉都伴随着语言的细节刻画彰显得愈加浓烈。在翻译 left mash notes in strange places 这句话时,添加了"天涯海角,无论何地"的夸张描写。我认为,这样的描写既能体现出男女热恋之时依依不舍、你追我赶的情趣,又能营造出一种传统琼瑶剧的粉红爱情氛围——共同起誓、互许终身。此外,在"Cheeks flushed, hearts raced, palms sweated."这句话的描写中,引入了现代流行词语"来电显示"来描绘男女之间相互吸引的心动。传统与现代结合,使得细节描写更加生动、自然、形象。

译文中所描绘的婚后生活,译者将原本华丽的词藻换成了简单普通的文字,失去了激情、文采和美感,就好像夫妻二人的感情随着时间的流逝而逐渐变得如同白开水一般平静无华。在论述婚后生活的细节时,选用"不是……而是……"的手法,将婚前和婚后的生活进行了直接对比,再添加上细节就能使脉络更加清晰具体。但是,译文在细节前以一句"然而结婚之后呢?"的反问强调了夫妻二人感情生活的前后对比,则更能吸引读者的注意,且将主人公对于婚后平淡如水的生活的无奈与抱怨表达得淋漓尽致。

片段中的 Jerry Seinfeld 是当代美国肥皂剧的一个著名笑星,提到他的真实意义并不是为了描写主人公在看电视时喜欢看谁,而是为了强调夫妻二人之间宁愿花时间浪费在一个不认识的人身上,也不愿意在像初恋时那样互相关注对方。

(6) 当我和我的丈夫 Bill 处于热恋时期时,一个甜蜜的来电提醒都会使我们高兴半天,惊喜不已。我们想去野餐就去野餐,叫对方甜心啦,宝贝啦,这些肉麻的话,我们四处留"情",这是热恋时的火辣,伴随着羞红的脸蛋,握太久而出汗的手心,和一颗怦怦跳的、随时准备为爱奔赴的心。

然而婚姻是爱情的坟墓。

恋人间的甜蜜消失殆尽,取而代之的是各种账单。生活中的琐事使浪漫褪去,露出了生活原本的面目。现在的我们纠结于看电视还是分享激情时刻,我为我们为 Jerry Seindeld 投票的频率感到尴尬。

翻译总体感受与译文分析

(1) 理解与表达是翻译的两个核心要素。不同的译者主体,基于个人的情商、智商以及生活经历和体验,对于同一原文,必然存在不同的理解,也就会导致不同的表达再现,进而形成不同的译文。从以上译文中可以看出,对于同一个词,同一个场景,同一种情感,6 份译文,体现了 6 种不同的理解与表达。至于哪种表达更好,除了个别地方理解错误之外,很难有高低上下的区分,应该是各有千秋,各有可取之处。

(2) 当然,若从学术研究的角度来看,还有很多地方值得探讨,如性别与文体的相关性、译者性别与作者性别的相关性。此段是对一位女子个人的生活经历和心路历程的真实情感的描述和写照,从 6 份译文来看,女性译者的译文更丰富多彩,语言表达也更为细腻。

参考译文

对方的一个电话,就能让彼此激动不已。不经意的一个提议,双方都会欣然同意。他会柔情地叫我"小甜心",我也会亲昵的叫他"乖宝贝"。我们所到之处,都会留下爱情的写意。总之,只要两人在一起,都会有那种甜蜜的感觉:脸颊发烫,心跳加速,掌心冒汗。然而结婚之后呢?房贷的压力,育儿的辛苦,家务的劳累,工作的重负,再加上彼此之间的审美疲劳,使得婚前那种浪漫的感觉早已不复存在。夜幕降临,是面对电视对一个自己并没见过的当红明星投票,还是和那熟悉得不能再熟悉的爱人卿卿我我共度良宵?我们每每会选择前者,这使我内心真不是滋味。

翻译分析

原文本身就是精美的散文片段,作者对初恋如痴如醉、婚后生活平淡无奈的描述,皆为真情告白。文中应用了各种修辞手法,如"… just a phone call could send us quivering with excitement(impersonal subject sentence)"、"Cheeks flushed, hearts raced, palms sweated.(parallelism)"、"A son, housekeeping, jobs and just plain old familiarity forced romance out.(parallelism)"和"Faced with the choice of watching TV…vote for Jerry Seinfeld.(metonymy)"等。译文处理的非常到位,将原文的非人称主语句仍然译为非人称主语句,"对方的一个电话,就能让彼此激动不已";保留原文的排比句式,并译为汉语的四字结构"脸颊发烫,心跳加速,掌心冒汗";根据上下文,采用了增词、语序调整的翻译技巧,"房贷的压力,育儿的辛苦,家务的劳累,工作的重负",不仅译出了原文的内涵,译文表述也更符合中国的文化背景和社会现实,应该说是采用了归化的翻译策略。译者对于 just plain old familiarity forced romance out, passionate moment 和 embarrassed 的理解更是入木三分,"审美疲劳""和那熟悉得不能再熟悉的爱人卿卿我我共度良宵""内心真不是滋味"等不仅是原文深层信息的完美再现,更是译者深厚的中文功底和文化领悟力的真实体现。

二、审美与评析

对于具有双语能力的读者来讲,如何评价原文与译文,或者说译文在多大程度上再现了原文的基本信息和美学价值,不同的读者亦有不同的判断。

下面是一段非常美妙的中文散文,语言简练,对仗工整,修辞应用较多,内涵丰富,具有不同赏析能力的读者,针对同一译文,给出了不同的评价。

◆ 原文 ◆

江南的意境

那么江南到底独在何处,特在哪里呢?在我看来,江南的特色是小和慢。江南文化从不以大和快为衡量的规矩。以雄伟为标准,江南的山只能敬陪末座,望之压顶的泰山,横断南北的秦岭,都不会把江南的山放在眼里。用浩瀚为尺度,江南的水只能屈居后位,奔腾千里的黄河,浩瀚无涯的长江,也不会把江南的水当成对手。可是江南的青山绿水从不妄自菲薄,江南的山不与绝顶争风吃醋,却扬长避短,在蒙蒙细雨中酿造翠绿与生机。江南的水不把奔腾作为己任,却悠闲自得,在舟楫小桥间流出韵味与生活。这种温和的自然环境最容易孕育一种缓慢的生活节奏。正是在这种环境的熏陶中,江南人才能吟出了"却借乌篷舟一叶,飘然卧听水流声"的句子;也正是因为自然环境并不恶劣,因此江南人即使在争吵打斗时,也显得那么温文尔雅,让东北大汉见了都觉得太窝囊。不要希望在江南找到几个"路见不平一声吼,该出手时就出手"的英雄豪杰,他们大都在大漠孤烟之处,白山黑水之间。江南文化以小慢阴柔为特征,比较适合在细处品尝,却不宜从大处观赏。这样的文化从根本上看,是一种阴性文化,任何具有大快阳刚特质的人和物在江南文化里都显得格格不入,可能破坏江南的意境。

参考译文

Land of Charm: South of the Yangtze River

What's special about the land south of the Yangtze River? This is what comes to my mind: Things there seem to present themselves in a small scale and move at a leisurely pace. Worship of soaring grandiosity and warp speed is never part of southern culture. True, mountains in the south are dwarfed by the towering leviathan of Mount Tai or the vast Qinling mountain range. And judging by the power to inspire awe, rivers in the south pale in comparison with the raging Yellow River or the massive Yangtze. But the south doesn't need to feel inferior, for what it has to offer is never meant to be gauged by size or raw ferocity. There, mountains add a lively touch to a green landscape amid drizzle. Rivers flow at their own measured pace, winding their way under foot bridges, gently caressing boats that travel on them at an equally measured pace. Life's tempo is thus set amid a natural environment averse to rush. Such an environment, no doubt, shapes people's dispositions also. Little wonder folks there prize a lifestyle that they'd like compare to a leisurely ride on a boat with a black canopy—a typical sight on southern waterways—while listening to the sound of water splashing against the boat. Absence of hostile natural forces, which erases the need to be in a constant combative mood, seems to infuse a degree of gentleness into how local folks act, which often dampens an outburst of anger, even in a verbal brawl. That's not manly in the eyes of those who are used to roughing it in the Northeast. Indeed, few, if any, would be ready to jump into a fist fight the moment they perceive indignities being inflicted upon a friend. Those heroes usually roam a sparsely populated faraway land where they have to fight daily battles navigating a vast and tough terrain. Southern culture is, on the contrary, characterized by smallness, slowness, and gentleness. It's not there to overwhelm you with its breathtaking immensity; rather it's to be savored for its hidden details. It's on the Yin side of the Yin-Yang continuum, and as such ill-disposed to anybody or anything that exhibits too much yang. A surplus of Yang, after all, eclipse southern charm.

译文的分析与鉴赏

赏析一

1. 题目分析之增与减

译者在翻译题目时将题目进行了归化处理。"江南"一词从地理角度观之,是为长江之南。然其在此文中的含义不止于此。从题目"江南的意境"与其整体偏艺术性描写的文风可知,"江南"在此文中突显的是其文学与美学内涵,而题目也正应有所体现。"江南"之于国人,是一方充斥着诗情画意、所到处是小桥流水的鱼米之乡、富饶之地,更是一处文化圣地。那么译文中仅以地理位置来指代"江南"便缺失了对其文化内蕴的传递。

"意境"一词,是指一种情景交融,能够激发读者共鸣的艺术境界。而charm所表示的"魅力"仅仅能够体现出江南对于人们的吸引力,实则并不具体,而是将题目泛化了。因此,译者虽然增加了land of charm 三词,但在语义传递中仍然有所缺失。但从文化交流角度看,land of charm 属于英语语境中对于旅游胜地的常用描述,可以无误地传达"江南"对于游客的吸引力。若此文为旅游宣传类文本,则译文从语用角度看是够用的。但显然,此文是文学性文本,译文对于艺术性的表现远远不够。

2. 对特殊句法的把握

作者以两个问题开篇,这是常用的布局方法。但作者的巧思在于使用了互文的技巧。而互文这种特殊句法很难在英语中实现对等,因此译者便退而求其次,仅对句意进行了翻译,并着力实现了符合英语语境的文学效果。

3. 对句子主语的选择

全文第二句,原文简洁而凝练,用带有文学色彩的"小"和"慢"点出江南特色。译者在此也有奇思,将主句主语的"我"换为指代这件事的this,将从句主语的"江南"换为江南中的 things。这样一来就改变了作者的文风,从原文诗意而凝练的色彩转化为译文生动而活泼的展现。虽然并未体现出原文文风,但转化成了更符合英语母语者习惯的目标语文风,为读者呈现出另一种艺术性,是为另一种文字美。

4. 词语的对应

译者对原文中很多含蓄隐晦的词语进行了诠释,同时注意了对文章诗意的凸显。这种对于原文的诠释性译法,并不能完全传达语境,但能够让读者把握词义的正确方向。例如:"江南文化从不以大和快作为衡量的规矩",其中"大"是一种近似于大道至简的指代,体现了以一字而包罗万象的美感。而译文中的 soaring grandiosity 则是将"大"简化了,具象化了,虽然语义无误,但意境上有所缺失。反观译者对于"快"的翻译,以 warp speed 与上文 Worship 相呼应,构成头韵,为原文中本无意境的"快"字添了一分诗意,弥补了对"大"字翻译中诗意的欠缺。

译文也将原文中很多词语进行了词性转化,但在转化的过程中,原文中词语的结构美与文学美也随之被转化成了英语中普通的话语。这些词或句有的生动,如"望之压顶"与 the towering leviathan;有的简洁明了,如 "敬陪末座"与 are dwarfed by。

5. 对文风的把握

原文的文风其实有两种体现,一是极具内涵美与文采的辞藻堆砌,二则是拟人化的亲和笔锋。对于前者,译文囿于中英差别,无法实现对等。但译者抓住了后者的精髓,为整体译文的各主语赋予了"灵",增添了主语的主动性与译文的生动性。

6. 对历史典故及诗句的翻译

译者放弃了原文中的引用形式,而是将所引用的句意进行了解释补充。原文意境流失但句义得到了保留,信息传递功能基本实现。

赏析二

翻译存在可译性和不可译性。文化背景差异、词意不对等、语言使用习惯等因素都会造成翻译的不可译性。之前的课程中有提到,译者应该发挥自身

"主观能动性"来尽量弥补语言转换过程中被"客观制约性"扼杀的美感,也就是尽力而为地去减少这种不可译。而美文翻译中的得,可以看作一种巧妙的转换方式,让目的语接受者在某种程度上能够和原语读者一样感受到美文的妙处;美文翻译中的失,顾名思义,就是翻译过程中丢失的东西。丢失的可能是遣词造句的方法、方言的运用、文化典故、成语俗语等。

从标题来看,美文翻译的得失已经初现端倪。意境在我看来,是一种玄而又玄的东西。领悟"意境"更多像是一种心领神会:只要一写出来一个词、一句话就能够自动领会里头的未尽之意。对于中国人来说,江南的意义不仅是地理上的长江以南、不同时期的行政区划,更重要的是它背后的文化底蕴——小桥流水、温声软语、文人骚客、烟雨朦胧、鱼米之乡、富饶之地……而译文将之译为 South of the Yangtze River,则丧失了这种约定俗成般的文化印象。标题中的 Land of Charm,意思上与后文内容相关联,charm 也是一种带有氛围感的词汇,与"意境"相比虽然有一定出入,但是也存在异曲同工之妙。我认为这便体现了美文翻译中的"得"。类似地,后文的"东北大汉"也有其奇特的形象特点,但是翻译成 people in the Northeast 显然非常单薄无力,而译文译为 those who are used to roughing it in the Northeast,rough 与前文 gentleness 相对应,虽然并不准确且偏负面,却更能支撑"大汉"的形象。

选文第一句"那么江南到底独在何处,特在哪里呢?"中,"独"和"特","何处"与"哪里"都是近义词。将独特一词拆作两字,用在两句之中,读起来更具节奏韵律,有娓娓道来之感;同时,后文多用平行结构,整体行文的风格一致。但在译成英文时,这种用法便成了冗余。我觉得此处如果采用类似 safe and sound,这样具有韵律的近义词组合可能效果更接近原文。

语言的不对等容易造成翻译的"失"。文中的"英雄豪杰""大漠孤烟"带有侠客的概念,"白山黑水"本意泛指我国东北地区,文中指"东北大汉"。这些在英文中没有对应的词汇来表达,因此译文注定有偏差。但是在翻译"阴性文化"时,译文将其与八卦阴阳相联系,译为"It's on the Yin side of the Yin-Yang continuum",这种译法虽然与原意有出入,但是比起"阴性文化",八卦阴阳更具象,更为人所知,也更易于联想与理解。

简而言之,美文翻译要根据原文的特点,在信于原文的基础上实现"达",而后再兼顾译文的"美"。从这篇文本来看,译文虽然在句子结构方面有遵循原文之处,也有跳脱的发挥,一些用词也很出色,但是对一些中国特有的文化理解还不够到位,情感把握不够准确。由此,译文的得失也很清楚了。

赏析三

原文:"那么江南到底独在何处……的规矩。"

赏析:在翻译中国地名"江南"时,要把具体方位写出来,便于外国读者理解。"小""慢""大""快",关于这四个字的翻译,译者根据自身对江南的认识,赋予了更加丰富的含义,而不是简单的 small, slow, big, fast。"慢"译成 move at a leisurely pace 也生动再现了原文的意境美。但是前面的小和慢,与后面的大和快,很明显是一一对应的反义,在翻译时应一一对应,所以我认为 warp speed 运用不当,和前面的 move at a leisurely pace 意境相差较大。

原文:"以雄伟为标准……当成对手。"

赏析:译者擅长将中文里的四字词语用简单的英文词汇表达出来,又不失原文含义。例如,敬陪末座只用一个 dwarf(使相形见绌)的被动;屈居后位用一个 pale(失色)。此外,译者在充分理解原文的基础上做了适当的省译。"不会把江南的水当成对手"和前面"只能屈居后位"表达的是同一个意思,所以在译文中只出现了一次。"以雄伟的标准"也无需再译,因为后文"望之压顶""横断南北"就是该句的"雄伟"的具体体现。但是 leviathan 不够准确,这个词突出的是庞大,而原文望之压顶突出的是"高"这一特点。

原文:"可是江南的青山绿水……韵味与生活。"

赏析:在这段话里,译者适当的调整了语序,或者说"合并了同类意象"。第一句的"青山绿水"就包含了后面的"水","不把奔腾作为己任"和"不与绝顶争风吃醋"句式类似,所以这两小句合并成一句话,行文更流畅。"舟楫小桥间流出韵味与生活"这句中文过于抽象,很难用英文表达出实际含义。在这里译者应该是根据自己的理解适当进行了增译。caress 也运用了拟人手法。但是我认为 raw ferocity 不太恰当,带了贬义,而原文将江南的山水和其他巍峨高山奔腾流水做对比并没有一褒一贬的意思。而且 raw ferocity 和前面的 size 也不能并列。size 其实是从绝顶的巍峨和江南的山的秀美总结出来的一个中心词,所以我觉得这里也可以从流水的快慢总结出一个词 speed 来代替 raw ferocity。这也刚好和 size 并列。

原文:"这种温和的自然环境……都觉得太窝囊。"

赏析:这里的 averse to rush 运用了反译法。缓慢的生活节奏即 averse to rush,averse 一词也给自然环境赋予了生命。但是这里生活节奏译成 tempo,我觉得不太恰当,这里的节奏指的就是生活运行速度的快慢,或许用 pace 会更好。canopy 也不恰当。原文蓬舟其实就是轻快的小船,而不是篷子。brawl 用词过重。

原文:"不要希望在江南找到几个……白山黑水之间。"

赏析:白山黑水是指长白山和黑龙江,这里白山黑水和大漠孤烟指的就是中国北部,与前面的江南形成对比。所以我认为后面 a sparsely populated faraway land where they have to fight daily battles navigating a vast and tough terrain 有点多余。不用把所有具体意象都写出来,只要把作者的意思表达出来即可。

原文:"江南文化以小慢阴柔为特征……破坏江南的意境。"

赏析:the Yin side of the Yin-Yang continuum 是基于译者在对阴性文化的了解上译出来的,即强调群体内相合的文化是阴性文化,中国文化就是阴性文化的典型代表。强调个体间相反的文化是阳性文化,所以这里用 ill-disposed 修饰具有大块刚阳特质的人和物,很是恰当,也体现了原文感情色彩。

赏析四

"What's special about the land south of the Yangtze River?"在这句话中,原文将原本汉语中的"独特"一词拆解成了"独"和"特",前者表示独一无二之处,而后者则表示特别之处,虽然两者的意思相同,但是原文中两个字的使用却有一种强调其独特之感,并且符合汉语的语言节奏。译文直接用 special 代替了"独"和"特",简洁明了,但同时也丢了些节奏上的美感。"This is what comes to my mind…"在这句话中,译者采用了意译的方法,把小和慢所表示的内涵解释清楚,让读者也能够明白江南的特色。与之相对应的两个反义词——大和快在此处我认为是含有轻微贬义意味的,原作者这么做是为了与江南的小和慢做对比,从而突出江南的一种柔情意境之美。因此,译者选用 grandiosity 和 warp 这两个词都非常贴切。既表现出对大和快的不屑,也通过 culture 一词隐晦地表达了江南人的一种价值取向。"True, mountains in the south are dwarfed…"首先这两句话是有相对应的结构的,中文将三个及以上连续相同的句式结构称为排比句。虽然这句话严格意义上说构不成排比句,可是让人读起来很舒服。比如"以……为标准,山只能……""用……为尺度,水只能……"。除此之外,连续的四字词语也让句子读起来充满了韵律感。敬陪末座和屈居后位意义相近,原本用来形容人的词语用在此处恰到好处。包括接下来拟人的使用也给人一种泰山秦岭、长江黄河的霸气和狂妄之感,更让人对江南山水的娇小可人印象深刻,形成强烈的对比。而对翻译者来讲,就很难把这些修辞、结构和意境一一对应地翻译出来,只能是尽力而为。所以译文选择了用 leviathan 来写泰山之高,用 awe 来抒发一种敬畏之感。形式上虽然不及中文整齐有力,但是两者表达的情感是一致的。"But the south doesn't need…"这句话中译者处理得非常好。"不与绝顶争风吃醋""不把奔腾作为己任"这些都暗含汉语的韵味,直译也不是不可以,但是就会显得有些多余。所以译者选择将其前移至"妄自菲薄"之后起到解释作用。这样就既简单明了,又呼应了前文江南山水对大和快的不屑,形成一种志不在此的悠然之态。与上一句相似,这句话也采用了拟人的修辞手法,通过自然环境来体现出江南慢节奏生活的舒适和惬意。"Life's tempo is thus set amid…"感觉英译汉的过程中很多时候都会把主语和宾语的位置调换。比如这句话中,中文结构是"环境孕育节奏",而英文则变成了"节奏建立在环境之中"。虽然意思一样,但是仔细思考会发现英文是有侧重点的。就像英文习惯于把主要内容放在主语部分,先讲,而中文则习惯于铺垫很长,把重点放在句末,后讲。此外,这句话里 averse 的运用很巧妙,让句子同整段文字的内容有一个很好的融合。averse 本身具有反对的、不愿意的意思,用在此处呼应前文对快节奏生活的轻微蔑视,还间接突出了江南自然环境的温和柔美。同时也无须再刻意的直译"缓慢的"生活节奏。"Such an environment, no doubt, shapes…"首先这段话里的诗句是汉语所特有的一种表现形式,简洁凝练,是英文所无法替代的。内容方面译文梳理得似乎比原文更为清晰,并且译者对乌篷舟的景象做了解释,称其是江南水乡独特的风景线。我认为这在翻译中就很有必要,因为不以汉语为母语的人,或者不熟悉汉语的人在理解这句话的时候可能并不会产生我们心中江南水乡隽永秀美的景象。对于 roam 这个词,我印象比较深,它给人一种漫无目的的云游四方的感觉,用在这里去形容英雄豪杰特别贴切,带有一种侠的义气和风范。大漠孤烟和白山黑水表示的就是广阔孤寂而又危机四伏的地方,为了同水乡的地形特点做了一个对比,译者采用了直截了当的译法,用 vast and tough terrain 与 water 形成反差。"Southern culture is..." ill-disposed 这个词用得比较委婉,对于英语国家中直线思维的人来说理解起来更为合适。对于"破坏"一词,译者没有用 break 或者 ruin,反而用 eclipse,这就显得译文多了一种延续性和过程感。

第十五章 翻译错误分析

由于英汉语言之间的差异,在进行翻译的过程中,语意难免会存在一些错误,下面对一些常见错误进行分析与总结。

一、望文生义型错误

(1) Fight shy of the theoretical of approach to the learning of English.

从理论上讲,学英文的方法,就是要战胜害羞。(错误)

学英语要避免只学理论(而不去实践)。(正确)

解析

shy 的字面意思"害羞的"。根据大多数中国人学习英语的经历,不敢张口讲英语的原因之一就是不好意思,怕犯错误,在这个背景下,很容易将 fight shy 翻译成"战胜害羞"。但实际上 fight shy of 是一个短语,意思是"be unwilling to undertake (a task) or confront sb; avoid sth / sb 不愿承担(某任务)或面对(某人);避开(某事物/某人)"(Oxford Advanced Learner's Dictionary of Current English, fourth edition, 540)。短语是由单词构成的,但词无定义,有些单词在构成一个新的短语后,原有的意思往往会发生改变,不能再将该单词作为一个独立成分割裂开来理解。

(2) They made an example of the boy.

他们以这个男孩为榜样。(错误)

他们惩罚这个男孩以儆他人。(正确)

> **解析**

example 的确有"榜样"的意思,但一旦搭配不同的动词,便会形成不同的语境,可能就会产生不同的含义。make an example of 是一个短语,意思是"punish (sb) as a warning to others 惩戒(某人)以警戒他人"(Oxford Advanced Learner's Dictionary of Current English, fourth edition, 497)。"树立榜样/充当反面教员"所对应的英语表达是 set (sb) an example/ set a good, bad, etc example to sb。不能一看到 example 就武断地认为是"榜样"的意思,要结合具体短语/语境具体分析。

(3) He allowed the father to be overruled by the judge, and declared his own son guilty.

他设法让这位法官战胜了父子情并让他宣布儿子有罪。(错误)

他以法官的职责战胜了父子间的情分,他最终宣布儿子有罪。(正确)

> **解析**

the 是一个定冠词,对后面跟续的名词具有界定或限定的语法功能,进而使其产生更具体或更明确的意义。根据上下文所形成的语境,the father 和 the judge 被赋予了不同于 father 和 judge 的一般含义。当然,读者需要借助语境和常规逻辑才能明白其具体的含义。

(4) What's more, factory workers did not have enough money to send their children on country holidays away from home.

此外,工人们没有足够的钱,在全国性的假日里让孩子们离家外出度假。(错误)

此外,工人们没有足够的钱,所以在假日里不能让他们的孩子离家去乡村度假。(正确)

> **解析**

country 包含"国家"和"乡村"这两层含义,如何确定其含义,仍然取决于具体的语境和读者的逻辑判断能力。作为"国家"这层含义,主要指"地域范围或政治性(area of land that form a politically independent unit)"。而"全国性假期"无论是一种政府行为还是民间习俗,在英语中一般会使用 national holiday 这一表达。

(5) Hitler was the Fate of German people.

希特勒是德国人民的命运。(错误)

希特勒是德国人民的灾难。(正确)

解析

fate 的确有"命运"这层含义,但同时也具有"死亡,毁灭(death, destruction)"的意思。根据历史事实,这里将其理解为第二层意思更为准确和符合历史真相,也才能传递该词的真实意义。英语作为一种形态语言,单词的首字母大写本身也使得该词汇具有了一种特定的含义。

(6) 脸不改色,心不跳。

without one's face changing color or one's heart beating.(错误)

behave without one's face turning white or one's heart beating any faster, not show the slightest fear.(正确)

解析

英语的形合特征较明显,而汉语则具有意合特征。对于具有中国文化背景的读者而言,自然理解"色"和"跳"这两个词的真实含义。"改色"即为"因恐惧或紧张脸色发白","不跳"并不是指"心脏停止跳动",而是"心脏跳动的速度并没有加快",这句话的真实含义是要表达"临危不惧,坦然处之"的情态。翻译一定要"信"于原文的真实含义,只注重语言形式而不深入分析和领会其内涵,会导致传递信息不准确,甚至错误。

二、语法关系混乱型错误

(1) He (Einstein) had little concern for money, though he could have been extremely rich.

尽管他(爱因斯坦)可以成为富翁,但他却不在乎金钱。(错误)

他(爱因斯坦)很少关心金钱,尽管这样,他本来也还是可以成为富翁的。(正确)

> **解析**

这里首先要注意英语中虚拟语气所表达的语法功能。could have been 这一虚拟形态表示过去本来可以做某事但实际上并未实现。此外,本句表达中还存在一个逻辑问题。第一部分陈述事实,第二部分为虚拟假设,是对第一部分的强化,并非解释原因。

(2) He likes Mary better than I.

他喜欢玛丽胜过喜欢我。(错误)

他比我更喜欢玛丽。(正确)

> **解析**

这句话为省略句,完整的句子结构为"He likes Mary better than I like Mary."。其关键在主格 I,实际为从句的主语。如果将主格 I 变为宾格 me,就是译文"他喜欢玛丽胜过喜欢我"。"格"这一语法现象并不存在于汉语表达中,在进行英汉语言转换时需要特别注意。

(3) A man parked his car on a little bridge overlooking a picturesque, arid gully and took out his camera.

一名男子把轿车停在一座小桥上,俯视着桥下那美丽干涸的山谷,并拿出照相机准备拍照。(错误)

一名男子把轿车停在一座小桥上,小桥下面是一条美丽干涸的峡谷,这个人拿出相机准备拍照。(正确)

> **解析**

理解原文表达的关键在于确定 overlooking 这一现在分词的逻辑主语。作为一种非谓语动词形式,当主句主语与非谓语动词逻辑主语一致时,非谓语动词的逻辑主语往往被省略。读者或译者需要具有辨别出非谓语动词的逻辑主语的能力。将现在分词转换为定语从句,根据主语就近原则,不难发现 overlooking 的逻辑主语为 a little bridge,而非主句的主语 a man。

(4) Within the past two decades, four technological developments have produced profound changes in our way of life.

在我们的生活方式中,四种技术在二十年中发生了深刻的变化。(错误)

在过去二十年内,有四种技术发展使我们的生活方式发生了深刻变化。(正确)

解析

介词在英语表达中发挥着重要作用。在这句话中,介词 in 限定或补充说明了 changes 的范围,即"生活方式"的变化,不宜将介词短语部分与整体表达分割开来,这样会改变原文意义。

(5) I knew by July he would have been working there for 30 years.

我知道截止到七月,他就在那里工作整整 30 年了。(错误)

我七月才知道他在那里工作整整 30 年了。(正确)

解析

介词短语 by July 在句子中的位置,说明它限定的是主句主体动作发生的时间,而非从句主体动作发生的时间。将一个句法成分放置在不同的位置,会影响其所修饰的主体或内容。

(6) The Chinese Revolution produced a substantial quantitative change and soon led to a qualitative change in the world relationship of forces.

中国革命产生了巨大力量,不久对世界力量的对比引起了质变。(错误)

中国革命对世界力量的对比关系产生了巨大影响,不久引起了质变。(正确)

解析

连词 and 连接并列或顺接发生的两个动作,构成句子的谓语部分。介词短语 in the world relationship of forces 修饰整个句子,而非句子谓语的第二部分 soon led to a qualitative change。

(7) It did not rain all the month.

整个月都没下雨。(错误)

并不是整个月都在下雨。(正确)

解析

这句话需要明晰部分否定与全部否定两个不同概念。not all the month 为部分否定"并不是整个月都"。正如"并不是两者都"这一部分否定的英语表达式 not both/both not,但"两者都不"这一全部否定的表达为 neither。

(8) 许多人不但不植树,反而砍树。

Many people not only don't plant trees but also cut trees. (错误)

Many people don't plant trees, instead, they cut trees. (正确)

▎解析

中文习惯于将"不但……而且……"表达为英语的 not only...but also...,但这里的"反而"并不是"而且"的意思,而是表明相反的方面,因此用 instead 才更符合原文的真实意义。

(9) 把一个人的情感完全隐藏起来几乎是不可能的。

Entirely to conceal one's feelings is almost impossible. (错误)

To entirely conceal one's feelings is almost impossible. (正确)

▎解析

副词直接修饰或限定动词,而错误的翻译将其放在了不定式 to 所引导的非谓语动词所构成的主语部分前,不符合英语表达习惯。

(10) 你不去,我也不去。

You don't go there, I won't either. (错误)

If you don't go there, I won't either. (正确)

▎解析

汉语具有较强的意合特征。这句话前后两部分的关系并非并列关系(即便是并列关系,英语也需要使用 and 这个并列连词,将前后两句连接起来),而是假设关系或者条件关系。英语注重形合,需要借助一定的关系词,特别是连词,表明不同句子成分或者上下文之间的逻辑关系。

三、逻辑型错误

(一) 常识逻辑错误

(1) "I've served in nine presidential appointed offices, but nothing has

as tough and complex as this," said Elliot Richardson.

"我曾担任过九个总统任命的职务,没有哪一次像这样棘手和复杂。"埃利奥特·理查森说。(错误)

"总统任命的职务我曾担任过九个,没有哪一次像这样棘手和复杂。"埃利奥特·理查森说。(正确)

解析

无论是英语还是汉语,都存在几个限定词修饰同一主体的现象。原文的核心词是offices,前面几个限定词都是说明offices的情况,所以不应将nine视为对presidential的限定。此外,根据一般常识,"九个总统任命的职务"的状况,在现实中不太可能出现。

(2) Albert Einstein, who developed the theory of relativity, arrived at this theory through mathematics.

阿尔伯特·爱因斯坦发展了相对论,他是通过数学得出这一结论的。(错误)

阿尔伯特·爱因斯坦创立了相对论,他是通过数学得出这一结论的。(正确)

解析

develop确有"发展(make or cause sth more mature)"的意思,但也有(to grow gradually)逐步形成、创立的意思。客观事实是阿尔伯特·爱因斯坦创立了相对论,而非发展了相对论。

(3) No one is so foolish as to believe that anything happens by chance.

谁也不会笨到相信世界上有什么偶然发生的事。(错误)

谁也不会笨到相信世界上一切的事情都是偶然发生的。(正确)

解析

很显然,anything指"一切事情,任何事情",而并非"某种事情"。常识来看,"偶然发生的事"是存在的,但"一切的事情都是偶然发生的"是不符合客观事实的。

(4) Intense light and heat in the open contrasted with the coolness of shaded avenues and the interior of building.

强烈的光线和露天场所的炎热与林荫道上的凉爽和建筑物内部形成了对比。(错误)

露天场所的强烈的光线和酷热与林荫道上及建筑物内部的凉爽形成了对比。(正确)

解析

比较的对象应该处于同一层次,或者具有类同性。原文很显然将 intense light and heat 与 the coolness 进行对比,而非与 the interior of building 进行对比。前者弄错了对比的对象,混淆了对比逻辑关系,导致了错误的翻译。

(5) Slowly he put his suppliant hat on his head.

慢吞吞地,他把那求情的帽子戴在了头上。(错误)

他慢慢地把刚才为了表示谦虚而摘下的帽子又重新带上了。(正确)

解析

在原文中,suppliant hat 是采用了一种移就的修辞手法,suppliant 一般指人,这里用来修饰 hat,是将表达人的某种情感转移到了物上。汉语虽然也有移就这一修辞手法,但这里如果简单直接地进行翻译的话,译文不符合汉语表达习惯,也不能给读者呈现出原文的内在含义。正如在 "It's a busy day." 这句表达中,繁忙的不是 day,而是人在这一天繁忙。

(二) 时间逻辑错误

(1) 有人刚把灯关了。

Someone has just turned off the light. (错误)

Someone turned off the light. (正确)

解析

严格来讲,这句话的翻译很难说是正确与错误,因为可能存在具体的语境,但并没有提供给译者。一般过去时强调已经发生的客观事实,现在完成时强调过去发生的事情对现在造成的结果或影响。就本句话而言,仅表示"关灯"这一动作已经完成,事情已经发生。如果想表达对现在的影响,现在完成时态更合适些。

(2) 从图书馆借来的那本书已经找到。

The book which was borrowed from the library had been found. （错误）

The book which had been borrowed from the library was found. （正确）

解析

原文存在两个时间点，"借书"和"找到书"。就时间顺序而言，自然"借书"在前，"找到书"在后，因此，"借书"用过去完成时，"找到书"用过去时，才符合实践逻辑关系。

（三）不定式的逻辑主语错误

(1) 为了在搞科研中取得成功，需要坚持不懈。

To succeed in a scientific research project, persistence is needed. （错误）

To succeed in a scientific research project, one needs to be persistent. （正确）

解析

不定式 to 引导的非谓语动词的逻辑主语，与句子的主语一致时，可以省略。succeed 的主语显然是"人"。

(2) 这本书需要翻译成英语。

The book is required to put into English. （错误）

The book is required to be put into English. （正确）

解析

依据不定式谓语动词逻辑主语与主句主语相一致时可以省略的语法规则，翻译的主体是人，书是翻译的对象，当书作为句子的主语时，不定式需使用被动语态。

（四）分词的逻辑主语错误

(1) 老虎在笼子里，因而我不怕。

Being in a cage, I was not afraid of the tiger. （错误）

The tiger being in a cage, I was not afraid of it. （正确）

解析

分词亦是非谓语动词一种形式,有其自身的逻辑主语,当其自身的逻辑主语与主句主语不一致时,需要在表达中明确其自身的逻辑主语。

(2)由于时间很少,汤姆不能按时完成作业。

Having so little time, Tom's homework is faild to be finished on time. (错误)

Having so little time, Tom fails to finish his homework on time. (正确)

解析

首先是现在分词的逻辑主语与主句主语不一致的问题,分词的逻辑主语应该是 Tom;其次,在此语境中,fail 一般用作主动语态。

(五)动名词的逻辑主语错误

(1)他迟到使老师生气了。

He coming late made the teacher angry. (错误)

His coming late made the teacher angry. (正确)

解析

动名词的逻辑主语应该为形容词性物主代词 his,而非名词性主格代词 he。

(2)麻烦的是他们自己不能取得一致的意见。

The trouble was not being able to agree among themselves. (错误)

The trouble was their not being able to agree among themselves. (正确)

解析

当句子主语与动名词逻辑主语不一致时,应在表达中明确动名词的逻辑主语。

(六)主句与从句的逻辑主语错误

(1)众所周知,中国是一个发展中国家。

As we all know, China is a developing country. (错误)

As is well known, China is a developing country. (正确)

解析

"众所周知"在英语中一般表达为 as is well known,因为该语境下主语不需要特别明确指出,除非需要强调或有特殊含义。当然,known 的逻辑主语也暗含在这一英语表达中。

(2)我们都清楚,如果不谨慎处理,情况会更糟。

We all know that, if we do not deal with carefully, the situation will get worse.(错误)

We all know that, if not dealt with carefully, the situation will get worse.(正确)

解析

在主从复合句中,当从句的主语与主句的主语不一致时,需要在表达中明确从句主语;如果两者一致时,可以省略从句的主语。显然,if not dealt with carefully 更好地呈现了原文"如果不谨慎处理"所包含的信息。

(七)不合逻辑的比较错误

(1)加拿大的绿化面积比美国的绿化面积还大。

The green area in Canada is even larger than the United States.(错误)

The green area of Canada is even larger than that of the United States.(正确)

解析

原文进行对比的是两国的"绿化面积",错误的译文将 the green area in Canada 与一个国家 the United States 进行对比,一来没有正确反映原文信息,二来不符合比较逻辑。

(2)他的脸圆圆的,跟孩子的一样。

Her face is as round as a child.(错误)

Her face is as round as a child's.(正确)

解析

根据原文信息,对比的对象是"脸";而错误的译文将 her face 与 a child 进行对比,对比对象不一致,不符合比较逻辑。

四、缺乏背景知识型错误

(1) The sun sets regularly on the Union Jack these days, but never on the English Language.

现在太阳从英国国旗上有规律地落下,但是英语却不是这种情况。(错误)

现在,英国已不再是"日不落"帝国了,但是,英语却依然广泛使用着。(正确)

解析

Union Jack(the national flag of United Kingdom)英国国旗,这里实际上意指英国国家。英国曾经因拥有众多的殖民地,被称为"日不落"帝国。"太阳从英国国旗上有规律地落下",暗指英国原有的大部分殖民地都已经独立,英国也开始走向衰败。但随着全球化的发展,英语作为一种国际语言,没有像英国国家一样衰败,反而越发重要。

(2) After the dinner, we got out our checkbook and went Dutch.

晚餐后,我们拿出了我们的支票簿,然后去了荷兰。(错误)

晚餐后,我们拿出了支票簿,各付了各自的账。(正确)

解析

go Dutch 指各付各的账,平摊费用,AA 制的意思。16~17 世纪时的荷兰和威尼斯,是海上商品贸易和早期资本主义的发迹之地。因为商人的流动性很强,一个人请别人的客,被请的人说不定这辈子再也碰不到了,为了大家不吃亏,各付各的便是最好的选择了。而荷兰人因其精明算计、凡事都要分清楚的形象,逐渐形成了 let's go Dutch(让我们做荷兰人)的俗语。后英国人将这句话引申成"AA 制"。

(3) Television has changed the importance of issues. It can be argued that since the 1960 presidential debates we have elected people, not platforms.

电视台已经改变了政治见解的重要性。可以证明,自从1960年以来的总统选举中,我们选择的是人,不是政治平台。(错误)

电视台已经改变了政治见解的重要性。可以证明,自从1960年以来的总统选举中,我们选举的是人,不是政治纲领。(正确)

解析

platform 一词的原意是"讲台,讲坛",但经常被引申用来指美国各党的"竞选纲领",这是因为在美国总统大选期间,代表美国两大党派竞选的候选人都要在讲坛上阐述各党的竞选纲领。如果将 platform 简单翻译成"讲台或讲坛",则不能让读者明白其真实的含义。

(4) Individualism is the core of social values in the United States.

个人主义是美国社会文化准则的核心。(错误)

个人的价值是美国社会文化准则的核心。(正确)

解析

individualism(the belief that the rights and freedom of individual people are the most important right in society)意指个人主义价值观,与(collectivism)集体主义价值观相对,是一种不同文化背景下的行为规范和社会价值取向,是一个具有中性感情色彩的文化术语。

五、生搬硬套型错误

(1) 欢迎你来参加英语角活动。

Welcome you to join our English corner activities. (错误)

You are welcome to join our English Corner. (正确)

解析

英汉表达并非总是一一对应,其实很多情况下并不对应,不能完全将中文的思维和表达习惯套用到英语表达上。"You are welcome to do sth." 是一种较为固定的英语表达方式。

(2) 我们改革开放的步子要迈得更大一些。

Our steps of economic reform and open policy should be bigger. (错误)

Take a broader approach to economic reform and opening up. (正确)

> **解析**
>
> 这句话的内涵意思是"进行更大程度的改革开放",错误的翻译只是实现了形式上的转换,却不符合目的语(英语)表达方式。

(3)有空就到我们家来聊天吧。

If you are free, please come to our family to have a talk. (错误)

Drop in on us for a chat at any odd moment. (正确)

> **解析**
>
> drop in on 的含义是"偶然访问,顺便拜访"(pay a casual visit to a person or place),与原文意义正好吻合。chat 也恰恰是(friendly informal conversation)聊天的意思。错误的翻译给人机械地对应中式英语表达的感觉。

(4)我们的事业从一个胜利走向另一个胜利。

Our cause has won victories one after another. (错误)

We have won one victory after another for our cause. (正确)

A series of victories have been won for our cause. (正确)

> **解析**
>
> Our cause has won victories 不是一种地道的英语表达,主谓搭配不当。使用主动语态,"我们在事业上赢得了胜利",或者使用被动语态,"事业方面的胜利被赢得",更符合英语逻辑思维和表达习惯。

(5)风里来,雨里去。

Come in the wind, go in the rain. (错误)

brave the weather；go through wind and rain(正确)

> **解析**
>
> 原文借用事物的形象,用以表达形象背后的真实含义。错误的译文仅仅翻译了原文的表层形象,没有传达内在的真实含义。

(6)这条裙子的价格便宜,我买了一条。

The price of the skirt was so cheap that I bought one. (错误)

The price of the skirt was so low that I bought one. (正确)

The skirt was so cheap that I bought one. (正确)

解析

主谓搭配问题。cheap 本身就是指"价格低(low in price)",已经含有了 price 的意义,主语与谓语部分出现了意义重合。修正为"The price was so low",或者"The skirt was cheap",都是一种正确的表达。

六、语义结构型错误

(1)我能看出你的心事。

I can see your mind. (错误)

I can read your mind. (正确)

解析

"看出你的心事"中的"看出"是辨别、理解的意思,并非真正的看到,所以不宜用 see。read 具有"领会、解释(learn the significance of, interpret)"的意思,与原文意义相符,能够准确反映原文信息。

(2)从他的话音里,我能听出东西来。

I can hear something from the tone of his voice. (错误)

I can tell something from the tone of his voice. (正确)

解析

hear 意思是"听见,听到(perceive the sound with ears)",而原文中的"听出东西来"应该指"辨别出来",与 tell(distinguish)的意义比较接近。

(3)时间是一只永远在飞翔的鸟。

Time just like a bird and fly forever. (错误)

Time is a bird forever on the wing. (正确)

解析

翻译应该坚持"信"的原则,不仅"信"于原文的内容信息,也要"信"于原文的修辞。错误的译文不仅改变了原文的修辞手法,还存在一些语法错误和意义表达不准确的地方。相对来讲,on the wing 更能转表达原文"时间一刻不停运行"的状态。

(4)弘扬体育精神,促进国际往来。

Spreading over the physical spirits and promoting international communication.(错误)

Promote sportsmanship and international exchanges.(正确)

解析

无论是 physical spirits 还是 international communication,在英语读者眼中,都有些晦涩难懂或者过于宽泛。sportsmanship 才是"体育精神"的准确表达,international exchanges 强调双方互动,与原文中"往来"的意义相匹配。

(5)我们的当务之急是深化改革。

To deepen reform is the most urgent task.(错误)

To deepen our commitment to reform is the top priority.(正确)

解析

urgent 强调时间紧迫性(needing immediate attention, action or decision),而 top priority 强调重要性、层次性和先后顺序。显然,top priority 更符合原文语境。

(6)这个故事发生在上海。

The story takes place in Shanghai.(错误)

The story is set in Shanghai.(正确)

解析

take place in Shanghai 本身也并无太大问题,但具体到 story 而言,将上海视为"故事发生的背景或环境",更为符合原文情境。

七、英汉翻译中的标点符号错误

(1)我去过北京、上海、广州和其他一些城市。

I have been to Beijing、Shanghai、Guangzhou and some other cities.(错误)

I have been to Beijing, Shanghai, Guangzhou and some other cities. （正确）

> 解析

英文的标点符号体系中不存在"、"顿号这种符号，在进行英汉标点符号转换时，可以用英文中的","符号对应中文的"、"顿号。

(2) 她9岁时就阅读了《红楼梦》这部小说。

She read the novel《Dream of Red Mansion》at the age of 9. （错误）

She read the novel *Dream of Red Mansion* at the age of 9. （正确）

> 解析

英文表达中没有"《》"书名号这种标点符号，涉及"《》"转换时，可以用英文斜体对应中文的"《》"书名号。

(3) 他又回到了家乡，那是五年后的事情了……

He returned to his home town, that was five years late……（错误）

He returned to his home town, that was five years later...（正确）

> 解析

中英文都有表达省略的标点符号，但两者并不一致，中文表达省略的符号为"……"，英文为"..."。

第十六章

经典翻译赏析

一、汉译英翻译赏析

(一)汉译英领导讲话

◀ 原文 ▶

经济工作要适应经济发展新常态

科学认识当前形势,准确研判未来走势,是做好经济工作的基本前提。最近,国内外都有一些议论,说中国经济增速持续下降,是不是出了什么问题?也有一些人认为,中国经济增速已经降至7.5%以下,为什么不采取强刺激措施?等等。我想,分析和看待这个问题,必须历史地、辩证地认识我国经济发展的阶段性特征。

去年,中央作出一个判断,即我国经济发展正处于增长速度换挡期、结构调整阵痛期、前期刺激政策消化期"三期叠加"阶段。今年年中,在中央政治局会议上,我对"三期叠加"进一步作了分析,强调经济工作要适应经济发展新常态。不久前,在北京亚太经合组织工商领导人峰会上,我概要分析了我国经济发展新常态下速度变化、结构优化、动力转换三大特点。这里,我想用对比的方法,谈谈我国经济发展新常态带来的几个趋势性变化。

译文

Economic Work Should Be Adapted to New Normal

To improve our economic work, first of all, we should have a rational understanding of the current situation and a sound assessment of future trend. Recently, there have been comments both in and outside China: As China's economic growth slows down, is there anything wrong? The growth rate has dropped to below 7.5 percent—why not take stimulus measures? I think that to look at and analyze this question, we must understand China's various economic development stages from historical and dialectical viewpoint.

Last year, the central government decided that China's economic development is a stage of shifting the growth rate, restructuring the economy and addressing the impact of previous stimulus policies. In the middle of this year, at a meeting of the Political Bureau of the CPC Central Committee, I further analyzed this complex economic stage, emphasizing that our economic work should be adapted to the new normal. Not long ago, at the 2014 APEC CEO Summit in Beijing, I briefly analyzed the characteristics of the new normal in China's economic development—a slowdown in the rate of growth, optimization of economic structure, and shift of growth engines. Here, through comparison, I would like to talk about several trends brought by the new normal.

分析

在这部分的翻译中，涉及了以下一些翻译技巧和策略应用问题：

(1) 增词。将"科学认识当前形势,准确研判未来走势,是做好经济工作的基本前提。"译为"To improve our economic work, first of all, we should have a rational understanding of the current situation and a sound assessment of future

trends."增加了主语 we；将"说中国经济增速持续下降，是不是出了什么问题？"译为"As China's economic growth slows down, is there anything wrong?"增加了连词 as。

(2)减词。将"我国经济发展正处于增长速度换挡期、结构调整阵痛期、前期刺激政策消化期'三期叠加'阶段。"译为"China's economic development is at a stage of shifting the growth, restructuring the economy and addressing the impact of previous stimulus policies.",省略了已经包含的"三期叠加"意义。

(3)语序调整。将"科学认识当前形势，准确研判未来走势，是做好经济工作的基本前提。"译为"To improve our economic work, first of all, we should have a rational understanding of the current situation and a sound assessment of future trends.",将表示目的的状语 To improve our economic work 放至句首。

(4)择词。译文并没有将"科学认识"中的"科学"简单地译为 scientific，而是结合上下文译为 rational；也没有将"准确研判"中的"研判"简单地译为 judgment，而是译成了 assessment，这样处理都更为符合原文的实际意义。再如，将"中央作出一个判断"译为 the central government decided that 也是一个比较成功的处理。

(5)附属结构。将原文中的"我对'三期叠加'进一步作了分析，强调经济工作要适应经济发展新常态。"译为"I further analyzed this complex economic stage, emphasizing that our economic work should be adapted to the new normal",采用现在分词作为附属结构。

(二)汉译英领导讲话

◀ 原文 ▶

建设世界科技强国

纵观人类发展历史，创新始终是一个国家、一个民族发展的重要力量，也始终是推动人类社会进步的重要力量。不创新不行，创新慢了也不行。如果我们不识变、不应变、不求变，就可能陷入战略被动，错失发展机遇，甚至错过整整一个时代。实施创新驱动发展战略,是应对发展环境变化、把握发展自主权、提高核心竞争力的必然选择,是加快转变经济发展方式、破解经济发展深层次矛盾和问题的必然选择,是更好引领我国经济发展新常态、保持我国经济持续健康发展的必然选择。

科技是国之利器,国家赖之以强,企业赖之以赢,人民生活赖之以好。中国要强,中国人民生活要好,必须有强大科技。新时期、新形势、新任务,要求我们在科技创新方面有新理念、新设计、新战略。我们要深入贯彻新发展理念,深入实施科教兴国战略和人才强国战略,深入实施创新驱动发展战略,统筹谋划,加强组织,优化我国科技事业发展总体布局。

译文

Build China into a World Leader in Science and Technology

The history of human development proves that innovation has always been important for promoting the development of a country and its people as well as human society. One will fall behind without innovation, and just as much if one is too slow in innovation. We will face strategic passiveness and miss opportunities for development—or miss an entire era—if we fail to seek, recognize and respond to change. Seeking innovation-driven development is a natural choice if we are to adapt to changing developmental conditions, hold the decision-making power for our development, and improve our core competitiveness; if we are too speed up the transformation of our growth model and solve deep-rooted conflicts and problems; if we are to better steer the new normal in economic development and sustain sound growth.

Science and technology are the bedrock upon which a country relies for its strengths, enterprises for success, and people for a better life. Great scientific and technological capacity is a must if we are to make China strong and improve lives.

New missions and tasks of the new era require us to develop new concepts, designs and strategies regarding technological innovation. We should implement new development concepts, and invigorate our country through science and technology and fostering people of high caliber. We should further implement the innovation-driven development strategy, and promote the development of science and technology through overall planning and coordination.

分析

对该部分所应用的翻译策略和技巧分析如下：

(1)增词：增加表面无、实际有，或者根据上下文意义和目的语语法结构、表达需要补充的词汇，如：将"建设世界科技强国"译为 Build China into a World Leader in Science and Technology，原文省略了"建设"的客体，译文添加补充了 China，以便使译文更符合英语的语言逻辑关系。

(2)减词：减去原文出于语言表达习惯、但并无实际意义的范畴词，或出于强调而重复表达的内容，如："纵观人类发展历史，创新始终是一个国家、一个民族发展的重要力量，也始终是推动人类社会进步的重要力量。"译为"The history of human development proves that innovation has always been important for promoting the development of a country and its people as well as human society."，既省略了范畴词"力量"、近义词"发展"与"进步"，也省略了重复的部分。

(3)语法功能调整及词性转换。根据汉英不同的语言特征，进行必要的语法功能调整及词性转换，以符合目的语的表达习惯。将原语中的状语转化为目的语中的主语，将原语中的名词"发展"转换为目的语中的动词。当然，还应用了增词的翻译技巧，增加了谓语动词 prove。

(4)择词。根据上下文，确定一个词的具体含义及在目的语中对应的词汇。如：对原文中的"民族"，翻译成 nation, ethics, 还是 people 呢？译文最终选择了 people；如：对原文中"强国"，翻译成 country, state, power, 还是其他哪个词呢？译文将其译成了 world leader。

(5)词序、语序的调整。根据目的语的文化特色和表达习惯，对原语信息的表达顺序进行必要的调整。如,"如果我们不识变、不应变、不求变"译为"if we fail to seek, recognize and respond to change",将"识、应、求"调整为"求、识、应"。

(6)平行结构的处理。平行结构是英汉都有的一种句法结构,但汉语中更为多见。在翻译过程中,可以将汉语中的平行句翻译为英语的平行句,也可以根据实际情况进行处理。如,译文为"Science and technology are the bedrock upon which a country relies for its strength, enterprises for success, and people for a better life.",就是按照对等的原则进行翻译的。

(三)汉译英风景描写

◀ 原文 ▶

漫步山间时,听得四处竹林间的淙淙泉声,众多的细泉汇成一条狭长而深邃的小溪,顺山势而下,及至悬崖处,猛然跌落二三丈,形成一瀑布,水珠飞溅,凉透肌肤。

译文

Strolling along the path you can hear springs singing everywhere in the bamboo forest. Several little springs assemble into a narrow but deep little river, running along the mountainside. Meeting a small cliff, it falls down two or three feet with drops splashing, forming a thin water curtain which gently covers your skin.

分析

原文是由一系列意义紧密相连的分句组成的一个长句,描写山间小溪由远及近、最后形成瀑布的情景。一气呵成,读来似流水,极为顺畅。而译文则层次分明,先从声觉(听到的是声音),再到视觉(看到的是小溪、以及小溪形成的瀑布),最后到感觉(感到水珠的清凉),译文采用独立句依次译出,读来富有很强的节奏感。

(四)汉译英诗歌

◀ 原文 ▶

敕勒川

敕勒川,阴山下。
天似穹庐,笼盖四野。
天苍苍,野茫茫,
风吹草低见牛羊。

译文1

Chilege Song

By the side of the rill,

At the foot of the hill,

The grass land stretches neath the firmament tranquil.

The boundless grassland lies,

Beneath the boundless skies.

When the winds blow,

And grass bends low,

My sheep and cattle will emerge before your eyes.

译文2

Chilege Song

At the foot of the hill,

By the side of the rill,

The grass land stretches neath the firmament tranquil.

The boundless grassland lies,

Beneath the boundless skies.

When the winds blow,

And grass bends low,

My sheep and cattle will emerge before your eyes.

分析

两个译文均为许渊冲的杰作。两个译文的不同之处在于,第一、二两行句序的不同。英语在顺序方面的表达习惯一般为:从小到大,从微观到宏观,因此,译文一与原诗保持了一致。但是在这首具有画面美感的民歌中,作为审美主体的读者的视野,则正如电影镜头一样,从 hill 到 rill 渐退为背景,一望无际的 grassland 进入镜头,随着视野的扩大,出现悠然的 firmament 以及远景中的 sheep and cattle。前后顺序,层次井然(张智中,2006)。可见,许渊冲调整的不仅是句序,而是读者审美视野的自然顺序。

(五)汉译英小说

原文

跑了一程,辕马遍身冒汗,喷着鼻子,走得慢一些,赶车的就咕噜起来:"才跑上几步,就累着你了?要吃,你尽拣好的,谷草、稗草还不乐意吃,要吃豆饼、高粱。干活你就不行了?瞅着吧,不给你一顿好揍,我也不算赶好车的老孙啦。"

译文

After covering a few steps, the perspiring team snorted and began to slow down. "So you're tired after a few steps," grumbled the carter. "When you eat, you must have the best of food – soya bean cake and kaoliang, not satisfied with hay or weeds. But when it comes to work, you jib. I'll give you a good hiding(体罚,痛打), sure as I'm a good carter."

分析

老孙头的几句唠叨,把这个人物描写得栩栩如生,呼之欲出。译文也体现了同样的功能。"你尽拣好的"如按字面译为"You must have good food"就不如

"You must have the best of food"生动醒豁。"干活你就不行了"如按字面译为"When you work, you're no good"就不如"When it comes to work, you jib"可取,不仅因为 When it comes to 是符合习惯用法的地道英语,而且因为 jib 是马车夫用语,指马"停止不肯前进"。最能表达老孙头身份的是最后一句粗鲁的话:"不给你一顿好揍,我也不算赶好车的老孙头。"译文"I'll give you a good hiding, sure as I'm a good carter"也充分体现了这一功能,其中 sure as 是习惯用语,作"和……同样无疑的"解。

(六)汉译英新闻

▶ **原文** ◀

世界上一些国家发生问题,从根本上说,都是因为经济上不去,没有饭吃,没有衣穿,工资增长被通货膨胀抵消,生活水平下降,长期过紧日子。如果经济发展老是停留在低速度,生活水平就很难提高。人民现在为什么拥护我们?就是这十年有发展,而且发展很明显。假如我们有五年不发展,或低速发展例如百分之四、百分之五,甚至百分之二三的经济增速会产生什么影响?这不只是经济问题,实际上是个政治问题。

译文

(1) Fundamentally speaking, the root cause of all problems that arise in some countries lies in their failure to boost the economy. They lack adequate food and clothing, and since wage increases are offset by inflation, living standards decline and consequently severe hardship must be endured for long periods. A prolonged low rate of economic development makes it very difficult to raise living standards. Why do our people support us? Because we have achieved progress, indeed remarkable progress, over the past 10 years. Let us suppose that we remain at a standstill for five years, or progress slowly, at, for example, an annual rate of 4-5 or even 2-3 percent, what would be the effect? This is actually a political issue.

(2) Most problems in some countries are in nature economic. With wage increase offset by inflation, people there lack adequate food and clothing. With their living standard decreasing, they will have to suffer a lasting hardship. It goes without saying that slow development of economy at a low rate would not much improve people's life. Why do people in our country lend full support to us? Because over the past 10 years we have brought about remarkable economic development and kept improving people's life. What would have happened if we had failed to boost the economy or developed it at a low annual rate of 4-5 or even 2-3 percent? Economic problems may well give rise to political ones.

分析

以上两个译文在译入语词汇选择、断句、语序调整、句子结构、句子成分的摆放位置、内涵意义的表达以及翻译技巧的应用等方面,均存在很大的差别,以至于对再现原文的信息方面存在了一定的偏差。

(七) 汉译英人物简介

原文

艾芜(1904—1992)四川新都人。原名汤道耕。早年曾在昆明及缅甸、马来西亚、新加坡等地流浪,做过报馆校对、小学教员等,是"左联"成员。艾芜写边野地方的风情,擅于描写那些被生活挤出正常轨道的人们,擅于将抒情、叙事、写人结合起来。以表现手法别致,内容的新鲜和风格的优美,为人们所赞誉。他的小说在粗犷的浪漫主义氛围中,呈现出不屈的生命力量。《石青嫂子》是其短篇代表作之一。

译文

Ai Wu(1904—1992), originally named Tang Daogeng, was from Xindu, Sichuan. In his early life, he spent times in Kunming of China, Malaysia and Singapore, working as a newspaper proofreader and a primary school teacher. He was a member of the League of Leftist writers. He wrote about customs, habits and ways of life in border and remote regions and portrayed people pushed out of the normal rails of life. He was good at combining emotion expression, story telling and portrayal of men. He was praised by readers for his uniquely original method, fresh content and beautiful style. His writings demonstrated an unrelenting strength of life through the portrayal of uninhabited romantic atmosphere. *Mrs. Shi Qing* is a representative short story of his.

分析

在人称代词第三人称单数形式衔接功能方面,英汉两种语言之间的差异值得关注。尽管现代汉语中人称代词第三人称的三分是代词形式欧化的结果,但现代汉语中人称代词"他(们),她(们),它(们)"同音,在口语中降低了它们之间的明细程度。出于这一原因,尽管汉语第三人称单复数形式比英语多(英语只有一个复数形式 they),在性别(gender)或单复数(number)上的区分也更细,但使用频率却远远低于英语,而更多地采用省略和原词复现等形式。英语中许多使用代词的地方在汉语中则不是必要的,甚至尽量避免使用。

(八)汉译英新闻

原文

党的新闻舆论工作的职责和使命是:高举旗帜、引领导向,围绕中心、服务大局,团结人民、鼓舞士气,成风化人、凝心聚力,澄清谬误、明辨是非,连接中外、沟通世界。要承担起这个职责和使命,必须把政治方向摆在第一位,牢牢坚持正确舆论导向。

译文

The mission of the Party's media work is to hold high the banner(标点符号改变,顿号改为逗号), provide guidance for the public(增加对象所指), focus on the core issues, serve the country's overall interests(对"大局"的解读), unite the general public, instill confidence and pool strength(两句合为一句), tell right from wrong and connect China to the world. To do so(避

免重复), they should put political direction first and stick to guiding public opinion on the correct path in every aspect and stage of their work(增加具体的界定).

(九)汉译英散文

◀ 原文 ▶

好多人说自己孤独,说自己孤独的人其实并不孤独。孤独不是受到了冷落和遗弃,而是无知己,不被理解。真正的孤独者不言孤独,偶尔做些长啸,如我们看到的野兽。

弱者都是群居者,所以有芸芸众生。弱者的奋斗目标是转化为强者,像蛹向蛾的转化,但一旦转化成功了,就失去了根本满足和享受欲望的要求。国王是这样,名人是这样,巨富们赚钱是一种职业,种猪们的配种更不是为了爱情。

我见过相当多的郁郁寡欢者,也见过一些把皮肤和毛发弄得古怪的人,似乎要显示孤独,这不是孤独,是孤僻。

译文

Some people claim(主观认为,这个词好) that they are lonely. Actually those who say this out loud(这个短语应用地也恰如其分,"大声说出来",表达出了原文的内涵) are not(采用了省略的翻译技巧). (译者原文的一句话,切分成两个完整的英语句子进行翻译)Loneliness is not a matter of (增加表达状态的词汇) feeling the cold shoulder(具体化、形象化,在英语里,用 give the cold shoulder 直译"给冷肩膀",这个短语来形容一个人对其他人十分冷漠,爱搭不理的态度) or being abandoned. Rather it comes about when you have no bosom friends and are misunderstood by others. (同上,根据意义,将原文的一句话调整为两句话,明确了情况发生的条件背景)Someone who is genuinely lonely will not mention this(用代词 this 替代原文名词). Instead they will just heave(吃力、缓慢地发出某种声音) long sighs like a beast(与原文的暗喻修辞手法保持一致).

The weak always congregate together(名词转化为动词). So many

ordinary folks do just that.(这句话翻译地非常好,将"所以有芸芸众生"理解为"很多人都是以以上描述的方式这样生活",改变了原文句型结构,很准确,很到位)The weak struggle on in life with purpose of becoming strong. Just as a pupa metamorphosising into a moth, once the change is complete, they promptly lose their original drive to satisfy and fulfill a desire. Monarchs, as well as celebrities, have been through this process too.(将"是这样",结合上文语境,进行具体化为"经历这个转变过程")For the superrich, making money is a profession, just like(这里采用了增词技巧,体现了前后两句的类比关系)breeding boars who spread their seed without needing love(将原文单句转化为复合句).

I have met lots of melancholy and sullen people. I have also met some who have tattoos and dyed their hairs(通过增译,对皮肤和头发古怪的真实状况进行了内容上的外显)in a very weird way. They try to put on an air of(这里的增词应用也特别到位,站在了译入语读者角度考虑、进行了基于译入语表达需要的真实情况的添加)being lonely. This is not true loneliness but eccentricity.

◀ 原文 ▶

一年后这位作家又出版了新作,在书中的某一页上我读到了"圣贤庸行,大人小心"八个字,我终于明白了,尘世并不会轻易让一个人孤独的,群居需要一种平衡,嫉妒而引发的诽谤、扼杀、打击和迫害,你若不再脱颖,你将平凡,你若继续走,走,终于使众生无法赶超了,众生就会向你欢呼和崇拜,尊你是神圣。神圣是真正的孤独。

走向孤独的人难以接受怜悯和同情。

译文

A year later, this writer published another(省略了 new 这个词,another 已经包含了 new 的内容。类似的例子还很多,如彻底粉碎,不要用 completely smash,因为 smash 已经包含了 completely 的意思)book. On one of its pages I found（不必机械地将"读到"翻译成 read，译成 find 很好）eight words "Great saints behave vulgarly, great people act cautiously（存在一个正确理解原文的问题）." I finally understood:（标点符号的改变）the world is never quick to make somebody feel lonely（将"尘世"解读为 the world，将"不会轻易"解读为 be never quick to，都是比较准确的）. Communal living requires a kind of balance. Jealousy triggers off slander, homicide, humiliation, attacks and persecution（将原中文以逗号隔开的几个分句部分译为独立的句子，各表达一个完整的意思）. If you do not stand out of the crowd（补充"脱颖"的介词宾语）, you will remain common. If you toil on and on, the others can no longer catch up with or surpass you. They are（根据上文的语境，这里采用被动语态翻译，是完全符合逻辑的）then（时间副词起到了承上启下的衔接作用）compelled to worship and applaud you, exalting you as some divine being. Those who are divine are truly lonely（Those who...地道英语表达句型的使用）.

It is very hard for a man walking towards loneliness to accept the pity and sympathy of others（这里采用了增词的翻译技巧，增加了句子中隐含的 of others 的外在表达）.

◀ 原文 ▶

每个行当里都有着孤独的人，在文学界我遇到一位。他的名声流布全国，对他的诽谤也铺天盖地，他总是默默无闻，宠辱不惊，过着日子，进行着写作。

译文

There are lonely people in every walk of life（行当）I met one such person in the literary field（对相同或相近概念，用不同的词汇或短语进行表述，符合英语表达习惯）. He was famous all over China（将"国"具体化）, and the slander spouted（滔滔不绝地说）about him could blot out（遮住）the sky and cover up the earth（将"铺天盖地"直译为 blot out the sky and cover up the earth，传达了原文的形象性。当然，这里也可以采用意译的方法来表达原

文的内在含义)。However(增加了表达转折意义的连词 however), he remained silent. Regardless of whether he was being flattered or trampled upon(将"宠辱"翻译为 being flattered or trampled upon,既传达了原文的含义,也呈现了"宠辱"的具象,让译入语读者获得了美感情趣),he carries on his daily life and writing.

(十)汉译英新闻

◀ 原文 ▶

今年粮食丰收已成定局。国家粮食和物资储备局10月27日表示,2020年我国粮食产量稳定,丰收已成定局。近日秋粮收购已全面启动。据国家粮食和物资储备局粮食储备司司长秦玉云介绍,当前秋粮收获接近尾声,我国粮食供应充裕,丰收已成定局。我国总粮食产量来自早稻、夏粮和秋粮。秋粮产量占全年粮食总产的四分之三。秋粮主要包括玉米、中稻和晚稻。国家粮食和物资储备局表示,当前我国粮食库存可满足市场一年以上消费需求。截至上周,已通过国家粮食交易平台累计销售政策性粮食9000万吨左右。

译文

China(增加主语) will see(无灵主语搭配有灵动词) a bumper harvest this year with stable cereal grains output, and large-scale cereal purchases have kicked off recently, the National Food and Strategic Reserves Administration revealed on Tuesday(在中文报道中,时间往往被表达为具体的日期,而英文中则相应地以星期几来表示). "With the autumn harvest ending soon, we've already seen(这里注意择词技巧,对于 see 这个词的意思和用法的把握) an abundant cereal supply that can ensure a bumper harvest for the whole year," said Qin Yuyun, head of the administration's food reserves department. China's total cereal output consists of three parts(根据具体的意思,先总述,再分述) —early rice, summer grain and autumn production(为了避免重复,对于"夏粮"和"秋粮"中"粮"所对应的不同英文的表述). Autumn grain crops, which include corn, middle- and late-season rice, account for three quarters of a whole year's grain production(根据逻辑关系,将原文中的两句话合并为一句话)。According to the administration, China's current cereal storage can meet the country's total consumption for a whole year. As of last week, a total of 90 million tons of grain crops have been traded on the State-owned platform.

(十一)汉译英新闻

◀原文▶

北京时间11月24日4时30分,我国在海南文昌航天发射场,用长征五号遥五运载火箭成功发射嫦娥五号探测器,开启我国首次地外天体采样返回之旅。

译文

China Tuesday launched a spacecraft to collect and return samples from the moon, the country's first attempt(增词) to retrieve samples from an extraterrestrial body. A Long March-5 rocket, carrying the Chang'e-5 spacecraft, blasted off from the Wenchang Spacecraft Launch Site on the coast of southern island(增加方位) province of Hainan at 4:30 am(省略北京时间)。

(十二)汉译英新闻

◀原文▶

脱贫摘帽不是终点,而是新生活、新奋斗的起点。要接续推进全面脱贫与乡村振兴有效衔接。

译文

Being lifted out of poverty is not an end in itself(增加表示内涵的词) but the starting point of a new life and a new pursuit. We need to synchronize poverty alleviation with rural vitalization.

二、英译汉翻译赏析

(一) 英译汉新闻

◀ 原文 ▶

How to Recognize and Prevent Cyber-attacks

Cyber-attacks may sound like something that happens only in Hollywood movies. You picture a team of talented hackers gathered around computer monitors trying to break into a secure bank or government server. In reality, cyber-attacks are much less exciting but no less dangerous.

A typical attack involves a cyber-criminal sending out thousands or even millions of links and files. They assumethat someone will eventually fall for their trap and open an infected file or page. Somebody always does. The best way to protect yourself is to learn how to recognize cyber-attacks as well as how to prevent them from happening in the first place.

Cyber-attack can happen to anybody

It doesn't matter who you are; cyber-criminals can target you. While many often think of hacking victims as clueless about digital security best practices, this isn't always the case. Hackers are smart. True, there are plenty of apparent scams like the "Nigerian Prince" emails. But there are as many attacks that can fool even the savviest computer users.

Nowadays, cyber-criminals create fake websites and email addresses. You may think you're clicking a link to Dropbox only to download malware onto your computer. And you may never know when you have visited the wrong site and download an infected file. So, it's up to you to be vigilant and protect yourself.

How to recognize the signs of cyber-attack

You need to recognize suspicious activity on your accounts or devices.

While some things may be obvious such as account passwords changes, other aren't so easy to spot. Usually, hackers insert pieces of code into legitimate files and programs. And then, you might receive a file from a trusted sender whose email has been compromised. Sometimes, the data are even real, but the hacker may have inserted a few lines of code that can also infect your computer.

You may take the time to check your "Task Manager" to get a sense of what program are running. Check anything suspicious that's running in the background. That's often the sign of malware.

译文

网络攻击的识别与防范

听起来,网络攻击也许只会出现在好莱坞大片里。想象一下,一帮神通广大的黑客围在电脑显示器旁,试图入侵银行或政府的安全服务器。在现实世界里,网络攻击没那么令人兴奋,却同样危险。

在典型的网络攻击中,网络犯罪发送数千甚至数百万个链接和文件。他们认为终会有人落入陷阱,打开感染病毒的文件或页面。总有人这么做。保护自己的最佳方法是学习如何识别网络攻击并防患于未然。

任何人都可能遭受网络攻击

无论你是谁,网络犯罪都可能攻击你。很多人往往以为黑客受害者对保护数字安全的最佳做法一无所知,但事实并非总是如此。黑客非常聪明。诚然,有很多类似"尼日利亚王子"邮件这样明显的骗局,但也有很多攻击能让最精明的计算机用户上当受骗。

如今,网络犯罪创建虚假网站、伪造邮箱地址。你以为你点击的只是多宝箱的链接,结果却下载了恶意软件到电脑上。你可能永远都不知道自己什么时候访问了错误的网站,还下载了被感染的文件。所以,你必须提高警惕,保护自己。

如何识别网络攻击的迹象

你需要识别账号或设备上的可疑行为。有些情况或许很明显,比如篡改账号或密码,但其他情况就不那么容易被发现。通常,黑客会在合法的文件和程序插入一些代码。然后,你可能会收到可信发件人的文件,而其他电子邮件已被盗取。有时,数据甚至是真实的,但黑客可能插入了几行代码,它们也可能感染你的电脑。

你应该花点时间检查"任务管理器",搞清楚哪些程序在运行。检查后台任何可疑的运行程序,那通常是恶意软件的迹象。

分析

译者通过采用一些翻译策略,使得译文符合汉语表达习惯,比如将具有句子结构特征的题目"How to Recognize and Prevent Cyber-attacks",通过改变词性、调整词序等方法,译成了汉语的名字性短语"网络攻击的识别与防范",简洁明了,信息呈现清晰。虽然原文是一篇科普性新闻报道,但译文读起来颇具生活气息,在词汇应用和语言表达上很有特色。如第一句"Cyber-attacks may sound like…",译者首先调整了语序,将谓语动词 sound 译成独立成分并置于居首,似乎作者在对网络攻击的事情娓娓道来。此外,将 Hollywood movies 译为"好莱坞大片"、a team of 译为"一帮"、talented 译为"神通广大",都非常符合汉语语境和表达习惯,拉近了读者和作者之间的距离,读起来自然而亲切。增词和减词是译者经常使用的翻译策略。译者通过在译文中增加"在……中",将 A typical attack 这一名词短语主语改变为情景状语;将"While some things…"中连词 While 省略翻译,令译文更显汉语意合特征。译者使用了一些中文读者熟悉的汉语成语和四字结构,如"神通广大""一无所知""上当受骗""防患于未然"等,使得译文更加顺畅。当然,译文中也有值得商榷或需进一步打磨的地方,如原文"much less exciting but no less dangerous."表达形式对称,意义相对,具有美感功能。但译文"没那么令人兴奋,却同样危险"无论形式还是意义,离原文都存在一定的差距。

(二)英译汉小说

◀ 原文 ▶

There a no such a thing as a good hangover. They're all bad.

But some are worse than others, and this one's a killer. I feel as though only every fourth or fifth brain cell is working, the rest mired in the slush left over from last night's parting.

I had a good time at Pete and Sue's. At least, I think I had a good time. I recall arriving at seven, earlier than most of invited guests. Pete poured me a tall scotch and water, but it seemed to evaporate quickly. Being the good host, he continued to refresh the glass for me until, until… The last thing I remember was talking to Vivian, the new computer genius at work. I can't remember what happened after that, but there's no sign of her here, so I guess I struck out. I'll call Pete later and asked him. Maybe he'll remember.

My hands are shaking so badly I can't drink my coffee like a civilized human. I have to put the cup down and lower my mouth to the brim, sucking up the hot liquid like a vacuum cleaner. It looks like I'll spend the day relaxing, recuperating, regurgitating. Of course, they say the best and fastest cure for a hangover is a drink. The way my insides feel now, I think I'll stick to coffee for the time being.

I sit, collapse is more like it, in my favorite chair an turn on the TV. Maybe I'll be lucky enough to find some mindless sitcom that'll help divert attention from my churning, grumbling stomach. Even my name hurts.

译文

(1)世上没有好的宿醉。它们都是有害的，但其中一些比别的更糟。而这一次的宿醉是致命的。我感觉好像只有四分之一或五分之一的脑细胞在工作，其余的则陷在昨晚聚会留下的困境之中。

我在皮特和休那里度过了一段美好的时光。至少，我认为我玩得很高兴。我回想自己是七点左右到那里的，比他们邀请的大部分客人要早。皮特用一个高脚杯给我倒了一杯苏格兰威士忌加水，但它似乎蒸发的很快。作为一个好主人,他不断为我添杯,直到,直到……我记得的最后一件事是在和维维安交谈,她是个在工作中崭露头角的电脑天才。在那之后我不记得发生了什么事,但这儿没有她来过的迹象,因此我猜我失掉记忆了。过一会我给皮特打个电话,问问他。也许他会记得当时的情景。

我的双手颤抖得非常厉害,使我不能像一个有教养的人那样喝我的咖啡。我不得不把杯子放下,把我的嘴凑下去,去凑杯子的边,像一个真空吸尘器那样吸着那杯热饮。看起来我将在放松、恢复、反胃中度过这一天了。当然,他们说对于宿醉来说,最好和最快的方法是喝点什么。从我现在肠胃的感觉看,我想我将暂时坚持喝咖啡。

我坐在我喜欢的椅子里,并打开电视机,几乎处于虚脱状态。也许我够幸运,会发现一些不用费脑子思考的情景喜剧,那将帮助我把注意力从我剧烈搅动和咕哝作响的胃部转移开来。即使我的名誉受到损害。

(2)宿醉有害,无一例外。不仅害己,而且害人。昨晚这一醉,真是害了人了。到现在我感觉只剩四分之一的脑细胞在工作,其余的怕还没(从昨晚的烂醉中)苏醒过来。

昨晚我在皮特家玩得很开心。反正,我觉得挺高兴的。我大概是七点左右到的皮特家,比其他客人都早。皮特用高脚杯给我倒了一杯苏格兰威士忌加水。那酒像是会蒸发似的,走的特别快。皮特是个好主人,不停地为我添酒,一杯,又一杯……我能记得的最后一杯是在跟那个叫维维安的电脑界高手聊天,后来的事我就记不得了。不过,我这儿没有她来过的痕迹,这么说昨晚我跟她没有聊出什么"成效"。过会儿我得给皮特打个电话问问,或许他会记得怎么回事。

我得手抖得厉害,端不稳咖啡,只能放下杯子,把嘴凑上去,吸杯里的咖啡,就像吸尘器似的。恐怕这一天我就只能放松放松,恢复恢复,同时还得忍受反胃的痛苦。有人说,喝醉了酒,最好是醒了再喝。不过,以我现在肠胃的状况来看,还是喝点咖啡好了。

我坐在平常最喜欢的椅子上,其实差不多是全身陷在椅子里。我打开电视,说不定能碰上一幕情景喜剧什么的,不用动脑筋,又能转移视线,省得我老觉得胃里咕噜咕噜的难受。这会儿我可顾不上别人说看情景喜剧品位低下了。

分析

该段讲述的是:"我"昨晚在朋友家喝醉了酒,第二天酒醒了看新闻才知道自己酒后开车回家途中撞死了一个10岁的男孩,从而悔恨交加,认识到宿醉有百害而无一利。原文语句简短,语义警醒,但是译文(1)却拖泥带水,语意不清,没有把握原文的精神。其原因是没有把握英汉两种语言的语句特点,没有在译文时对句子进行调整。原文第一句是"存现句",一般情况可翻译为"有……",甚至在没有地点状语的情况下,可以宽泛地译成"世上有……"。就该句而言,其实际主语是 such a thing as a good hangover。而且从第二句 They're all bad 来看,They 无疑是指 hangover,因此不妨直译为"宿醉"。值得注意的是,在英语中,hangover 是可数名词,可以用数量词来修饰;在汉语中,"宿醉"是不可数名词,不可以用数量词来修饰。换言之,"一些宿醉"有悖于汉语的表达习惯。正常的说法是"宿醉有时会……有时会……"将 But some are worse than others 译为"但其中一些比别的更糟"理解不准确。该句原文可作两种理解,既可以理解为"宿醉没有对人有益的,只有对人有害的,有时特别有害,"也可以理解为"宿醉没有对人有益的,只有对人有害的,有时甚至对'别人'有害。"从紧接下来的 this one's a killer. 来看,似乎第二种理解为宜,因为我因醉酒撞死了人。

原文第二段的第一句 I had a good time at Pete and Sue's. 承接第一段最后一句,指的是我受到皮特夫妇的邀请,去参加昨晚的聚会。但是译文(1)就事论事,将之直接译为"那里度过了一段美好的时光"有欠考虑。虽然短短的几个小时也是一段时光,但译文(1)读起来给人的感觉是我在皮特家住了一阵子,容易使人产生误解。"so I guess I struck out"中的 struck out 应该理解为 to be unsuccessful in trying to do something 意思是说我一边喝酒,一边聊天,本想通过聊天来取悦维维安,结果因为喝醉了,没有聊出什么成效——"跟我一起回家"。将 drink my coffee like a civilized human 译成"像一个有教养的人那样喝我的咖啡"值得推敲。

(三) 英译汉座右铭

原文

My motto is: Contented with little, yet wishing for more. (Charles Lamb, English essayist, 1775—1834)

译文

我的座右铭是:满足于涓滴,却向往海洋。(查尔斯·兰姆,英国散文家,1775—1834)

分析

该句翻译的难点在于 little 和 more,这两个词很抽象,需要进行具象化翻译,但具象化到何种程度、落脚于哪个点,取决于译者个人的理解。

(四) 英译汉学术研究

原文

(1) Racism refers to a variety of practices, belief, social relations, and phenomena that work to produce a racial hierarchy and social structure that yield superiority, power, and privilege for some, and discrimination and oppression for others.

译文

种族主义指的是各种行为、观念、社会关系及现象(标点符号的改变)(先完成主句翻译),在它的作用下(解构谓语部分,动词转化为名词),重构出一种种族等级制度和社会结构(下面的定语翻译成目的状语)让一些人从中得到优势、权力和特权,却(and 一词的择词)让另一些人(比"其他人"更符合汉语表达)遭受(增加搭配名词的动词,或为名词转化为动词)歧视或压迫。

原文

(2) Racism exists when ideas and assumptions about racial categories are used to justify and reproduce a racial hierarchy and racially

structured society that unjustly limits access to resources, rights, and privileges on the basis of race. Racism also occurs when this kind of unjust social structure is produced by the failure to account for race and its historical and contemporary roles in society.

译文

有关种族有别(这个表达用得好,假如将 categories 简单地译成分类,似乎不如"有别"更能强调高低的差异性,也就不能凸显种族主义的内涵)的观念及假设被用来重构某种社会(这里采用了奈达的核心句理论,将主体的"重构某种社会"首先摘选出来,然后再处理副词状语或定语部分)——这种社会按种族设立等级及架构,基于种族不公地限制资源、权益与特权的分配——并将其合理化时(这里应用了语序调整,这个调整也非常有必要,将 unjust 和 justify 两个相对的表达恰如其分地连接在一起,非常符合逻辑,表达也较为顺畅),种族主义便产生了(中英思维差异的体现:英语思维,一般讲主体或结论先提出,后面叙述细节;而汉语思维相反,首先摆明各种细节内容,然后再进行总结或归纳)。

(五)英译汉新闻

原文

(1) The real battle is not with China but with America's own giant companies, many of which are raking in fortunes while failing to pay their own workers decent wages. America's business leaders and the mega-rich push for tax cuts, more monopoly power and offshoring—anything to make a bigger profit—while rejecting any policies to make American society fairer.

译文

美国真正的敌人不是中国,而是自己本国的大公司(将 battle 这一抽象的事件转化为具体的对象——敌人,明确了所指)。其中很多大公司没有给员工支付体面的工资,反而在攫取财富(调整了语序)。美国商界领袖和超级富豪们都在敦促减税、扩大(变换进行搭配的动词)垄断、增加离岸外包(专业术语的翻译)等任何能获取更多利润的措施,同时拒绝任何使美国社会更加公平的政策。

◀ 原文 ▶

(2) Trump is lashing out against China, ostensibly believing that it will once again bow to a Western power. It is willfully trying to crush successful companies like Huawei by changing the rules of international trade abruptly and unilaterally. China has been playing by Western rules from the past 40 years, gradually catching up the way that America's Asian allies did in the past. Now the United States is trying to pull the rug from under China by launching a new Cold War.

译文

特朗普正在猛烈攻击中国,从表面上看(将副词状语拿出来单独翻译,将前后分开,后面单独成句),他认为中国会再次向一个西方大国低头。美国通过突然单边地改变国际贸易规则,蓄意(这个词比较准确地道)打压华为这样的成功企业。过去四十年,中国一直(将现在完成时时态表达的时间概念译了出来)按照西方的规则行事(将 play 译为行事,也非常符合文体和语境),像美国亚洲盟友一样赶了上来。现在,美国试图通过发动一场新的冷战,突然给中国制造麻烦(pull the rug from under 本意指"停止帮助"的意思,但鉴于作者是站在美国角度进行的论述,并不符合实际情况,所以这里译为"制造麻烦"是可以接受的)。

(六)英译汉散文

◀ 原文 ▶

Keep your dreams alive. Understand to achieve anything requires faith and belief in yourself, vision, hard work, determination, and dedication. Remember all things are possible for those who believe. (Gail Devers, American athlete, 3-time Olympic champion in track and field, b. 1966)

译文

让梦想之树长青(译文采用了意译的翻译方法,赋予了原文抽象概念和信息以形象性和生命力)。要懂得(将动词部分拿出来单独翻译,传递了原文语言的祈使功能或呼唤功能),若使美梦成真,需要信念、自信、远见、苦干、百折不挠和倾心以赴(四字句的使用,更显汉语的优势和特色,能够使译入语读者获得美感享受)。请记住(同上,将动词部分拿出来翻译,传递了原文语言的祈使功能呼唤功能,能够使译入语读者获得美感享受),有梦的人无所不能(将从句译为主句,调整语序,使之更符合汉语表达习惯)。(盖尔·德弗斯,美国田径运动员,三届奥运田径金牌得主,生于 1966 年)

(七)英译汉小说

◀原文▶

(1) Julie's Wolf Pack: With all his sense alert now, Kapu tuned in on yet another threat to his leadership of Avaliks. On a wind rode an aggressive scent from the Nuka River Pack. They held the territory to the west and south. Their scent signal was followed by howl. They had closed in on Avalik territory and were only a night's trot away. Kapu rotated his ears to fine-tune the sounds to the center of his eardrum, where he could hear best. The Nukas were nine strong. The Avaliks were six.

译文

朱莉的狼群:卡普如今调动起全身的器官(增词,将卡普提前作为句子的主语),来对付另一只威胁(将 threat 转换词性)他阿瓦里克河头狼地位的事件(增加核心词"事件",让中文句子顺畅)。风中飘来纽卡河狼群颇具侵略性的气味。他们的地盘(将主语 they 转化为"地盘")在西边和南边。接着又有伴随气味而来的嚎叫。他们正在靠近阿瓦里克河区域,相隔不过一夜小跑的距离。卡普转动着耳朵,让耳鼓的中心对准远处的声音,以便听得更清楚。纽卡河狼群至少有九只狼。而(增词)阿瓦里克河狼群只有六只。

◀原文▶

(2) When the Nuka howled again that night, they were closer. Kapu arose. The guard hairs stood erect on his back. He beat his tail, twisting it

toward them like a saber, threw back his head, and howled. His pack howled, sliding up to their harmonizing notes, sliding down, and fading out. Then all was silent.

译文

夜里,纽卡河狼群再一次嚎叫,他们离得更近了(译文句式发生改变,时间状语从句被改为联动句式,避免了翻译腔"当……的时候")。卡普站起身。他后背的针毛(guard hairs 术语)直立起来。卡普先(表达主句在时间上的先行性)是拍打尾巴,然后(表达现在分词附属结构在时间上的后续性)尾巴像军刀一样弯曲着指向纽卡河狼群(将代词指代具体化。英语惯用代词,汉语惯用名词,这也是两种语言表达的区别之一),仰起头(省略代词 his),嚎叫起来。卡普的狼群跟着嚎叫,调子(增词)越升越高,形成和声,然后又(添加表达时间顺序的连接词和动作反复的词)降低,逐渐消逝。接下来一片寂静(这一段原文简练生动,译文也尽量模仿)。

(八)英译汉新闻

◀ **原文** ▶

(1) The football legend Diego Maradona died on Wednesday after suffering a cardiac arrest. He was 60.

译文

传奇球星迭戈·马拉多纳 11 月 25 日(省略 after)突(增词)发心梗去世,(省略主语)享年 60 岁。

◀ **原文** ▶

(2) The news sparked an outpouring of emotion as the Argentine government declared three days of mourning.

译文

马拉多纳的去世(增词)引发了人们的(增词)悲痛之情(具体化,增词)。(减词 as)阿根廷总统府(本地化翻译)宣布,全国进入(增词)为期三天的哀悼期(增词)。

◀ 原文 ▶

（3）The body of Diego Maradona will lie in state at the presidential palace in Buenos Aires during three days of national mourning.

译文

在此期间(减词)，马拉多纳的灵柩(虚化)将在布宜诺斯艾利斯的总统府停放，供民众前往悼念[举行国葬(注：殡殓后任人凭吊，葬前供公众瞻仰)]。

◀ 原文 ▶

（4）Maradona also had a glittering club career, playing for clubs such as Barcelona and Napoli.

译文

马拉多纳的俱乐部生涯也很辉煌，曾效力(专业术语)于巴塞罗那和那不勒斯等足球俱乐部(增词)。

(九) 英译汉新闻

◀ 原文 ▶

China has achieved the feat of removing all 832 counties from the country's poverty list. The last nine impoverished counties, all in southwest China's Guizhou province, have eliminated absolute poverty, the provincial government announced on Monday.

译文

11月23日，贵州省宣布剩余的9个贫困县消除绝对贫困。至此(增加表示时态的词)，我国832个贫困县全部脱贫。(语序调整)

(十) 英译汉新闻

◀ 原文 ▶

Graduates of universities on the Chinese mainland have been enjoying a rise in their job prospects over the past decade, with it now listed as the fifth-most competitive country or region in a higher education report.

译文

过去十年,中国大陆高校的毕业生的就业形势持续改善,在近日的一份国家高等教育就业竞争力榜单中,中国大陆排名升("升"字为画龙点睛之笔,翻译出了 have been enjoying a rise 的动态性)至第五。

参考文献

[1] EUGENE A. NIDA. Language and Culture: Contexts in Translation[M]. Shanghai: Shanghai Foreign Language Education Press, 2001.

[2] EUGENE A. NIDA, CHARLES R. TABER. The Theory and Practice of Translation[M]. Leiden: Brill, 1969/1982.

[3] HALLIDAY, M.A.K, et al. An Introduction to Functional Grammar[M]. 2nd ed. Beijing: Foreign Language Teaching and Research Press, 2000.

[4] HALLIDAY, M.A.K, HASAN, R. Cohesion in English[M]. London: Longman, 1976.

[5] PETER NEWMARK. A Textbook of Translation[M]. London: Prentice Hall, 1987.

[6] WOLFRAM WILSS. The Science of Translation: Problems and Methods[M]. Shanghai: Shanghai Foreign Language Education Press, 2001.

[7] 陈德彰. 翻译腔[J]. 英语世界, 2020(4).

[8] 陈宏薇. 汉英翻译基础[M]. 上海: 上海外语教育出版社, 2000.

[9] 陈荣东. 一篇不该忽视的译论: 从《论翻译》一文看林语堂的翻译思想[J]. 中国翻译, 1997(4): 27-31.

[10] 方梦之. 译学词典[M]. 上海: 上海外语教育出版社, 2004.

[11] 傅勇林, 唐跃勤. 科技翻译[M]. 北京: 外语教学与研究出版社, 2012: 191.

[12] 辜正坤. 翻译标准多元互补论[J]. 中国翻译, 1989(1).

[13] 黄振定. "艺术"和"科学"的辨义与辩证[J]. 中国翻译, 1999(4).

[14] 刘宓庆. 新编当代翻译理论[M]. 北京: 中国对外翻译出版公司, 2005.

[15] 刘重德. 文学翻译十讲[M]. 北京:中国对外翻译出版公司,1991.

[16] 罗选民. 话语层翻译标准初探[J]. 中国翻译,1990(2).

[17] 倪建华. 清凉世界:莫干山[J]. 今日中国,1995(11).

[18] 彭宣维. 英汉语篇对比研究[M]. 上海:上海外语教育出版社,2000.

[19] 秦洪武,王克非. 英汉比较与翻译[M]. 北京:外语教学与研究出版社,2010:12.

[20] 申雨平. 西方翻译理论精选[M]. 北京:外语教学与研究出版社,2002.

[21] 司显柱. 论功能语言学视角的翻译质量评估模式研究[J]. 外语教学,2004:45-50.

[22] 宋红波,朱明炬. 实用文体翻译教程[M]. 北京:清华大学出版社,2016:159.

[23] 索绪尔. 普通语言学教程[M]. 北京:商务印书馆,1980.

[24] 孙致礼. 翻译:理论与实践探索[M]. 南京:译林出版社,1999.

[25] 谭载喜. 翻译学[M]. 武汉:湖北教育出版社,2005.

[26] 谭载喜. 新编奈达论翻译[M]. 北京:中国对外翻译出版公司,1999.

[27] 王天明. 谈谈文学翻译中的等值[J]. 现代外语,1989(4):20-27.

[28] 张经浩. 翻译不是科学[J]. 中国翻译,1993(3).

[29] 张培基. 英汉翻译教程[M]. 上海:上海外语教育出版社,2006.

[30] 张泽乾. 翻译经纬[M]. 武汉:武汉大学出版社,1994.

[31] 张智中. 许渊冲与翻译艺术[M]. 武汉:湖北教育出版社,2006.

[32] 庄绎传. 英汉翻译教程[M]. 北京:外语教学与研究出版社,2009.

参考答案

习题一答案

一、简答题

1. 翻译是科学,翻译也是艺术。前者认为翻译应该通过语言对等的转换来再现原文的信息。它注重对翻译过程的描写、语言的结构和形式等方面的研究,揭示翻译的客观规律。后者认为翻译是用另一种语言对原作进行重新表达与创作。它强调翻译效果及影响。

2. 文化层次,专业层次,情境层次,语言层次。

3. 理解,表达或再现,检查或校对

二、翻译词组与句子

1. 山寨产品

2. 生态村

3. the carefree excursion

4. On you is placed the hope of China and mankind

5. CPC delegates urged to faithfully perform duties

6. 火一上来她就是个母夜叉

7. What can you expect from a dog but a bark? / A filthy mouth can't utter decent language.

8. 某些固体物质有一种保持原状的特性,在外力的作用下其形状发生变化,一旦外力消失,就立即恢复原状,这种特性被称为弹性。

习题二答案

简答题

1. 中西翻译发展史。中国的翻译始于两千多年前汉代的佛经翻译,至今主要经历了四次高潮。第一次翻译高潮是东汉至唐宋时期的佛经翻译,第二次高潮是明末清初的科技翻译,第三次高潮是鸦片战争至"五四"时期,第四次翻译高潮起源于20世纪70年代至今。西方的翻译理论发展及研究主要经历了五次高潮:第一次翻译高潮起始于公元前3世纪中期;第二次翻译高潮发生在公元4世纪至6世纪;第三次高潮是在11至12世纪之间;第四次高潮发生在14至16世纪的文艺复兴时期;第二次世界大战结束以后迎来了第五次翻译高潮。

2. 社会符号学理论、交际翻译理论。社会符号学理论的代表人物是奈达、韩礼德。奈达是当代西方重要的翻译理论家、交际理论学派的代表人物,他所提出的"等效论"在翻译理论界具有广泛而深刻的影响,他的理论核心为"功能对等或动态对等",提倡翻译要努力实现原文和译文在语言交际功能上对等,而不是刻意追求在语言表层形式上的对应。该理论重点关注读者或目的语信息接受者的作用,强调如何将原文信息最大限度地传递给目的语读者,目的语读者被视为交际(翻译)的终极目标,译文与原文的等效程度和译文的可接受程度被视为翻译的最高标准。

交际翻译理论的代表人物是英国翻译教育家和理论家彼得·纽马克(Peter Newmark)。彼得·纽马克认为,译者应根据文本的不同功能采取相应的翻译方法,而不能仅仅强调目的语读者的反应,这点不同于奈达提出的翻译"等效论"。纽马克认为不分原作语篇类型,一律采用等效翻译法不可取。他创立了一个多元的翻译模式,包括逐字翻译、直译、忠实翻译、语义翻译、改写、意译、交流翻译等多种翻译模式和方法,而最常用的两种翻译模式为语义翻译和交流翻译。语义翻译要求译文要忠实于原文的语篇,最大限度地实现与原文在形式上的对等;交流翻译要求译者要重组语言结构,翻译要忠实于目的语读者,译文要追求通顺、地道,易于读者理解。

习题三答案

简答题

1.（1）客体型思维与本体型思维

西方文化以物本为主体，以自然为本位，比较偏重于对自然客体的观察和研究，逐渐形成了客体型的思维方式，即把客观自然世界作为观察、分析、推理和研究的中心。与之相对，中国文化以人本为主体，以人生为本位，富有人文意识和人文精神，本质上是一种人本文化。

语言是思维表达的载体，不同的思维方式必然会反应在不同的语言上。客体型和本体型两种不同的思维方式反映在语言形态上，其标志之一，就是在描述事物和阐述事理的过程中，特别是当涉及行为主体时，英语习惯于用表示非生物的名词（inanimate）作主语，而汉语则习惯于用表示人或生物的词（animate）作主语。

（2）分析型思维与综合型思维

一般可以将人类的思维方式分为两种基本类型：分析型思维和综合型思维。分析型思维，顾名思义，是把事物的整体分解为许多部分，其优点是能比较深入地观察事物的本质，其缺点是导致过于关注细节，忽略整体。综合型思维是把事物的各部分关联起来，使之成为一个不可分割的整体。综合型思维强调事物的普遍联系，既关注部分，更强调整体。分析型思维和综合型思维并不是完全分割的，是东西方民族共有思维方式。但由于受到传统文化的长期影响，最终形成了"西方重分析，东方重综合"的思维习惯。

西方哲学的分析型思维表现为，将自然作为人类的认知对象，将认识宇宙、征服自然视为人类的根本任务；人和自然永远处于一种矛盾对立关系。当然，在近代科学的发展过程中，也有综合性思维和综合法的融入，但主体是分析法。医学上的解剖学、神经学、文化学中的个人主义等就是典型分析型思维和分析法的产物。

中国哲学的综合型思维表现为人与人、人与自然的和谐统一，将"人与天地万物为一体""天人合一"作为最高境界，倾向于从总体上观察事物的特征，对事物从整体观点进行综合研究。传统中医的望、闻、问、切、文化学中的集体主义、和谐社会就是综合型思维和综合法的产物。

分析型与综合型是两种不同的思维方式,对英汉两种语言的结构形态造成了一定的影响:以分析型思维方式为典型代表语言的英语为例,有明显的词形变化,多样的语法形式,灵活的语序结构;再看作为综合型思维方式的典型代表语言的汉语,无词形的变化,语法形式主要依靠词汇手段表达,主要依据语义逻辑和动作发生的时间先后决定词语和分句的排列顺序。

英汉两种语言在表达形式上具体体现为:焦点式与散点式、树型与线性句子结构。

2. 英汉语言的主要特点

(1)英汉两种语言属于不同语系

英语属于印欧语系(Indo-European Family),是拼音(alphabetic)文字;形态变化丰富,词形上的变化同时也表示意义的变化。有通过词的派生表示词性或词义的变化,有通过名词的单复数形式表示数量及人称的变化,还有通过动词的不同时态表示时间的变化,通过语态表示动作主体和客体的变化,以及不同的人称代词表示不同格的变化等。所以,英语是一种形合的语言。

汉语属汉藏语系(Sino-Tibetan Family),汉语文字是表意文字(ideographic),用非语音化的词序手段表达意义,这是与形态变化相对立的另一种方式。汉语在表示动作和事物关系上完全依赖意念和感觉。所以,汉语是一种意合的语言。

英语是综合性(synthetic)的语言,汉语是黏着性(agglutinative)语言。

综合性语言的主要特征是名词、代词、形容词、冠词和动词有性、数、格的变化(此外,动词还有时态的变化);黏着性语言的特点是词的组合主要依靠词素的黏着。汉字虽然形态匮乏,但文字本身意义丰富,一字多义、同音异义,使用起来灵活方便,词的次序、位置稍有变化,就产生新的含义,包括语法意义。例如,胡子(beard)一词,通过黏着其他一些词汇,便可形成具有新的意义的一些词汇,"络腮胡子"(whisker)、"山羊胡"(chin tuft)、"八字胡"(moustache/handle bars)等。

(2)英汉两种语言在词法、句法结构上的主要区别

基本上来讲,英语是注重逻辑分析的一种形合(hypotaxis)语言(英语以形态表意),而汉语则是注重综合整体的一种意合(parataxis)语言(汉语以词汇表意)。区别表现在以下词法方面名词的数、名词的格、动词的时态、动词的语态;句法方面主要表现为形合和意合。

习题四答案

简答题

1. 中西两种思维方式和汉英两种语言既有相似之处,也有相异之点,关注不同,重点有别。因此,译者在翻译过程中,应注意处理好因不同思维方式和语言表达差异而造成的英汉两种语言转换时产生的问题和困难,主要表现在以下几个方面,即:动态表达法与静态表达、概略化表达法与具体化表达法、有生命主语句与无生命主语句、形合法与意合法。

2. (1)动态表达法与静态表达:Mary is a lover of popular music. 玛莉喜欢流行音乐。英语中的名词转化为汉语中的动词。(2)概略化表达法与具体化的转换:For decades those fuels such as coal and oil have been regarded as the chief energy sources used to transport men from place to place. 几十年来,煤和石油等燃料一直被认为是交通运输的重要能源。将 transport…place 的字面意义是"将人从一个地方运输到另一个地方"概略化为"交通运输"。(3)有生命主语句与无生命主语句的转化:Bitterness fed on the gentleman who devoted his whole life to the welfare of the disabled. 这位一心致力于残疾人事业的绅士自己却饱尝辛酸。表示生理、心理状态的名词和表示某种遭遇的名词做主语搭配有灵主语。(4)形合与意合之间的转换:You tend to be forgetful when you get old. 人老了,就容易健忘。省略复合句中表示时间状语引导词。

习题五答案

汉译英

1. He began to realize that he was talking to the ghost of a drowned man.

2. I did not want to miss the chance to take a snapshot of the enchanting seascape.

3. Health is precious to everybody.

4. Ignoring the colder weather, they gazed intensively at the TV screen.

5. With the passing of years our enthusiasm waned.

6. No doubt he had been walking in the rain, but he was so completely drenched that rain alone could not account for it.

7. I never felt so keenly how superficial my knowledge was.

8. Her disheveled hair glistered with raindrops.

9. My aunt lives a simple and uneventful life in the country.

10. More rain came, this time accompanied by a cold wind.

习题六答案

一、英译汉

1. 原来我以为这不过是一种亲热的表示,但是现在看来,这是为了闻一闻羊羔的味道,来断定是不是自己生的。

2. 在观看足球比赛之后,他有一个重要的会议去参加。

3. 他没有致闭幕词就宣布结束会议。

4. 就基本内容而言,这一学说提出的论点包括:光速是宇宙中最快的速度……

5. 最理想的情况是,有朝一日研究人员能够对地震的成因及其集体断层的性质有足够的了解,从而能够准确预测地震。

二、汉译英

1. He likes to point out other people's shortcomings, but he means well.

2. The more you elaborate on empty theories, the more people disgust them.

3. This little boy always washes his hands before meals and then dry them with napkins.

4. It is only during the night when she lies in bed that she feels she has a clear

mind.

5. There are also others whom we should not recruit into leading bodies or place in important posts. They include those persons whose revolutionary will has waned and who are content to eat three square meals a day and do nothing.

习题七答案

一、英译汉

1. 我要是学摩托车的话,就一定去买一辆新车。

2. 说得好,不如做得好。

3. 那个不诚实的孩子根本没病,他在游泳池里还活蹦乱跳的,我们都看见了。

4. (如果)你明天不去,他们会生气的。

二、汉译英

1. The Premier had a lot of work to do before (attending) the concert.

2. She has been talking in French for two hours without (making) any mistake.

3. Poor ruffians, their lives vanished like a dream (in Nanke).

4. We have a few people now who act like overlords (as they have become officials), and some of their behavior is truly shocking.

5. The mastery of language is not easy and requires painstaking effort.

6. From the Zhou and Chin dynasties onwards, Chinese society was feudal, as were its polities and its economy.

习题八答案

一、英译汉

1. 政府号召建立更多的技术学校。

2. 我非常感激父亲,因为在我小时候他总是不断地鼓励我。

3. 官方宣布,巴黎应邀出席会议。

4. 他既有藏书癖，又爱好书法。

5. 他的大吼吓走了他的敌人。

二、汉译英

1. He has long been used to last-minute decisions.

2. He was between sheets by eleven.

3. He is indiscriminate in reading.

4. She is a real beauty.

5. Don't you think he's an idiot?

习题九答案

汉译英

1. He went to the front door, his companions following him.

2. Two men rushed into my room, one fat and the other thin.

3. He wrote many poems, some of them sonnets.

4. After lunch, both Xiao Zhang and Xiao Li left school in a hurry, the former to catch train, the latter to go to the station to meet his friend.

5. A warm smile on his face, she came out to greet me, her big eyes flashing.

6. He gave a penetrating analysis of some of the questions, clarifying much of confusion.

7. Known for its beautiful landscape, Guilin has been attracting an ever growing number of tourists.

8. He fell plop into the river, never to rise again.

9. Now here, now there, on the hills and in the meadows appeared villages.

10. Everywhere, to the left, to the right, in the front and at the back, he saw coffins, large and small, black and white, finished and unfinished, gold or silver.

习题十答案

一、英译汉

1. 能不做的事情,她是绝对不做的。

2. 你把这些书给她还不如烧毁了好。

3. 请不要把这个消息说出去。

4. 各种材料在力的作用下,多少都会有些变形。

5. 这个公园美得无法形容。

二、汉译英

1. You can't be too careful in doing experiments.

2. Don't tell him more than you can help.

3. I have yet to learn the new skill.

4. The wood bridge is anything but safe.

5. What appeared to me wonderful was that none of the ants came home without bringing something.

习题十一答案

一、汉译英

1. At first only a few sentence patterns can be learnt. Consequently a teacher will find it difficult to make the work interesting and natural.

2. Something was said here just now which should not have said.

3. Although the road of life is long, its most important sections are often covered in only a few steps, especially when a person is young.

4. The avenue was lined with neatly-spaced plane trees.

5. Interest has been generally reduced in Anhua, and there have been reduction in other counties, too.

二、英译汉

1. 许多人要求建立一个阿拉伯共同市场。

2. 在举行个别交谈之前,我已将所有要讨论的问题预先拟好了备忘录。

3. 一个横穿马路的男孩子被汽车压死了。

4. 新的司令部成立后,我在那的任务就完了,于是我就回国向下议院作汇报。

5. 这位客人受宠若惊,深为感动。

习题十二答案

一、英译汉

1. 因为距离遥远,又缺乏交通工具,农村社会与外界是隔绝的。这种隔绝状态,由于通信工具不足,就变得更加严重了。

2. 如果要从智力方面进行任何比较的话,那么对所有被比较者来说,前两个因素必须是一定的。

3. 班纳特一直想去拜访宾利先生,所以他是最早去拜访他的人之一,但他对太太说自己并不想去,而且直到拜访后的那天晚上太太才知道。

4. 我说它掩映山林之中,坐临溪流之畔,不是把它描写成了一个可爱的住所了么?

5. 随后,我把玩偶放在膝头上枯坐,还不时东张西望,看看有没有什么比我更坏的东西光顾这昏暗的房间,这样直坐到炉火暗淡。

二、汉译英

1. I put on my clothes by the light of a half-moon just setting, whose rays streamed through the narrow window near my crib.

2. At the sight of the land, the river, the marshes along the river and the green reeds in them, Yan Zhihe's heart was overflowing with great joy.

3. Even the wild animals of his homeland, it seemed to Kunta, had more dignity than these creatures.

4. We had been dismayed at home while reading of the natural calamities that followed one another for three years after we left China in 1959.

5. There will come a day when people the world over will live a happy life under

the sun of socialism.

习题十三答案

英译汉

1. 到了近现代,在中华民族面临空前危机的时刻,长城体现出我国劳动人民的心血和智慧,以及长城反映出的我国强大国力,使大家对长城的理解发生了转变。

2. 水土流失、荒漠化以及草地退化等现象日益加重,削弱了防风固沙、蓄水保土,保护生物多样性等生态功能。

3. 现如今在英国,习惯性聚餐仅出现在富裕家庭的周末里,他们竭尽全力想保持住某些古老并象征着团结的东西。

4. 为了确保全体会员国因加入本组织而享有之权益,各会员国应一秉诚意,履行依照本宪章规定所承担之义务。

5. 物质中那些奇异的变化常常就发生在我们眼前,尽管我们很少注意到这一点。

后　记

历经几年,书稿终于付梓。

我读研究生时学习翻译理论与实践,老师上课的情景仍历历在目,课上老师讲解的一些翻译实例,也深深印在了脑海;近两年我为研究生和本科生讲授翻译类的课程,还经常用到这些例子。虽然经过了二十余年,这些例子仍然具有很强的说服力。这应该就是经典的翻译例句吧。为了将这些例句保存下来,于是就产生了编写一部教材的想法。

经典理论固然好,但也要与时俱进,具有时代感,才能增加课程的活力,适应年轻人的品位。"从学生中来,到学生中去。"只有坚持这种理念,教材才能赢得学生的喜欢和被学生接受。为了编写此教材,我在学生中间进行了调研和访谈,并邀请部分研究生和毕业的本科生参与教材的编写。

理论与实践、知识与应用、素质与能力、教书与育人,终归是一体的。本教材所探讨的理论、技巧和实践,也终归是服务于翻译人才的全面培养。人才的培养,首先要回答"为谁培养人,培养什么人,怎么培养人"的问题。本教材除了常规性地进行经典翻译理论介绍、翻译技巧例证以及翻译实践赏析,还设计了翻译小贴士板块,帮助教师进行课程素材梳理,提升学生的翻译实践技能。

教学相长,本教材还存在一些不足之处,希望在今后的教学实践中完善和改进。

感谢参与本教材编写的所有老师和同学!感谢学校的大力支持!感谢出版社编辑的指点和帮助!